Margaret Barker is an independ
preacher and a former President of t!
She has developed 'Temple Theolc_.
studies, and was given a DD for her work on the temple and ori
gins of Christian liturgy. For many years, she has been a member
of the Ecumenical Patriarch's Symposium on Religion, Science and
the Environment, and has made Temple Theology the basis for her
work on the environment. This is her fourteenth book, reading the
Christmas stories as Temple Theology.

Her recent books include: *Temple Themes in Christian Worship*
(2008), *The Hidden Tradition of the Kingdom of God* (2007), *Temple
Theology* (2004), *An Extraordinary Gathering of Angels* (2004), *The Great
High Priest* (2003) and *The Revelation of Jesus Christ* (2000).

CHRISTMAS

The Original Story

MARGARET BARKER

First published in Great Britain in 2008

Society for Promoting Christian Knowledge
36 Causton Street
London SW1P 4ST

British Library Cataloguing-in-Publication Data
A catalogue record for this book is available from the British Library

ISBN 978–0–281–06050–4

1 3 5 7 9 10 8 6 4 2

Typeset by Graphicraft Ltd, Hong Kong
Printed in Great Britain by Ashford Colour Press

Produced on paper from sustainable forests

In memory of
David Melling
who died in September 2004

The people who walked in darkness have seen a great light;
those who dwelt in a land of deep darkness, on them has light shined.
Isaiah 9.2

Lighten our darkness, we beseech thee, O Lord; and by thy
great mercy defend us from all perils and dangers of this night;
for the love of thy only Son, our Saviour Jesus Christ.
Collect for Aid against all Perils
Book of Common Prayer

Contents

Contents

Preface

For many years I have been leading pre-Christmas study days: 'Exploring the Christmas Stories'. These looked at the well-known texts in the New Testament, and then at the less well-known, such as the *Infancy Gospel of James*, the *Arabic Infancy Gospel*, and the Qur'an. Eventually they became this book.

The great festivals of the Church have been almost taken over by supermarkets and sporting events. Easter is a time for bonnets and bunnies and chocolate eggs; Christmas, which starts at the end of October, is for reindeer and mistletoe and mince pies. Nativity plays have come a long way since St Francis first set up his crib. Either they are banned to satisfy the politically correct, or they are modern and have the birth in a bus shelter, or they are sentimental and have squirrels and even sea creatures at the crib.

The original story is so much better. It has suffered from over-familiarity, and the words are sometimes lost in a flurry of domestic distraction. Reread and repondered, the original story of the incarnation is one of the greatest treasures in the Bible.

I dedicate this book to the memory of a dear friend, who shared my love for the ancient traditions of the Church.

Margaret Barker
Easter 2008

Introduction

The Christmas stories are not only beautiful; their meaning is at the heart of the Christian faith, and they show how the first generations expressed their understanding of Jesus as both God and man. The creeds are later statements of Christian belief, summarizing the essentials. The first to be set out formally was the Apostles' Creed, the declaration made before baptism in the Western churches which was in use in Rome at the beginning of the third century.[1] It says nothing about the life of Jesus as depicted in the four Gospels, nothing about his parables and miracles, about debates with the Jews of his time, or about his disciples. It records his birth, and then his death and resurrection: Christmas and Easter. The events in Bethlehem and Jerusalem were recognized as the essentials of the faith. Of Christmas the Apostles' Creed says: 'Jesus Christ His only Son our Lord, who was conceived by the Holy Ghost, born of the Virgin Mary'.[2]

The other creed most familiar to Christians is the Nicene Creed, recited[3] at the Eucharist in churches of both Eastern and Western traditions. It was probably developed from a baptismal creed used in Palestine, was adopted by the Council of Nicaea in 325 CE, and expanded by the Council of Constantinople in 381 CE. The precise history of its development is complex. Like the Apostles' Creed, it lists as essentials of the faith only the teachings about the birth and death of Jesus. Of Christmas it says: 'One Lord Jesus Christ, the only-begotten Son of God, begotten of His Father before all worlds, God of God, Light of Light, Very God of very God, Begotten not made, Being of one substance with the Father, By whom all things were made: Who for us men and our salvation came down from heaven, And was incarnate by the Holy Ghost of the Virgin Mary, And was made man . . .'. This is the theology of the Christmas story, but it is in two stages. There is the only-begotten Son of God, begotten of

---

[1] Hippolytus, *Apostolic Tradition* 21.
[2] The Apostles' Creed and the Nicene Creed are quoted in the form in the Book of Common Prayer.
[3] The important difference in the statement about the Holy Spirit does not concern us here.

his Father before all worlds, and there is the Son of God who became incarnate of the Virgin Mary.

Christians have always been careful to remember and distinguish the 'two births'. The Orthodox Church calls Christmas 'the Nativity according to the flesh', a constant reminder of the 'other' birth. Augustine, who died in 430 CE, summarized this in a Christmas sermon:

> Our Lord Jesus Christ, the Son of Man as well as the Son of God, born of the Father without a Mother, created all days. By his birth from a Mother without a Father, he consecrated this day. In his divine birth he was invisible; in his human birth, visible; in both births, awe-inspiring.[4]

Both births are found in the New Testament: the Son of God was *born* in eternity, beyond our understanding, as John wrote in the prologue to his Gospel: 'In the beginning was the Word . . .' (John 1.1). The Son of God *became incarnate* with the Bethlehem birth – the Virgin birth, and of this birth John wrote: 'the Word became flesh and dwelt among us' (John 1.14). *The Christmas story does not describe the birth of the Son of God; it describes the incarnation of the Son of God who was 'born' in eternity.* Throughout any exploration of the Christmas story there is the problem of words with a special meaning that differs from their normal use. If this mystical element is not recognized, the result can be a literalism that, far from being faithful to the fundamentals of the story, in fact distorts it.

At the heart of Jerusalem today is the Muslim shrine of the Dome of the Rock, erected on what is popularly believed to be the site of the ancient temple of Solomon. The first Muslim structure there had been the simple wooden building erected when Omar conquered the city in 637 CE, but this was replaced in 691 CE by the magnificent shrine familiar today. Two domes then dominated Jerusalem: the dome of the great Church of the Resurrection, built by Constantine over the site of Jesus' tomb, and the Dome of the Rock. On the inner and outer faces of the octagonal arcade of the Muslim shrine there is a huge inscription, some 240 metres long: excerpts from the Qur'an are set amidst invocations and other pious words.

The first quotation on the outer face is an early Meccan surah: 'Say: He is Allah, the One and Only: Allah the Eternal, Absolute; He

---

[4] Augustine, *Sermon 13, Christmas Day*.

begetteth not, Nor is he begotten; And there is none like unto Him' (Surah 112, 'Purity of Faith'). An explanatory note adds here: 'This is to negative the Christian idea of the godhead, "the Father", "the only-begotten Son" etc.'[5] The inscription continues with: 'Praise to Allah who begets no son and has no partner in (His) dominion . . .' (Surah 17, 'The Night Journey', 111). The explanatory note says: 'A first step towards the understanding of Allah's nature is to clear our mind of superstitions, such as that Allah begot a son.' On the inner face of the arcade there is:

> O people of the Book!/ Commit no excesses/ In your religion: nor say/ Of Allah aught but the truth./ Christ Jesus the son of Mary/ Was (no more than)/ A Messenger of Allah,/ and His Word,/ Which He bestowed on Mary,/ And a Spirit proceeding/ From Him: so believe/ In Allah and His messengers.   (Surah 4, 'The Women', 171–2)

The explanatory note says: 'Here the Christian attitude is condemned, which raises Jesus to an equality with Allah; in some cases venerates Mary almost to idolatry; and attributes a physical son to Allah.' The next piece is a third-person form of words attributed to Jesus himself in Surah 19.33–5.

> Peace is on him, on the day of birth, on the day of death and on the day he is raised up again. This is Jesus son of Mary. It is a word of truth in which they doubt. It is not for God to take a son. Glory be to him when he decrees a thing. He only says 'be' and it is.[6]

Notes to this text explain:

> The disputations about the nature of Christ were vain, but also persistent and sanguinary. The modern Christian churches have thrown them into the background, but they would do well to abandon irrational dogmas altogether. Begetting a son is a physical act, depending on the needs of men's animal nature. Allah Most High is independent of all needs, and it is derogatory to Him to attribute such an act to Him. It is merely a relic of pagan and anthropomorphic materialist superstitions.[7]

Here is the heart of the matter – *the meaning of the Christmas stories*. The inscription with its extracts from the Qur'an makes clear

---

[5] All the translations and notes are from *The Holy Quran. Translation and Commentary* by 'Abdullah Yusuf 'Ali, Birmingham: IPCI, except the translation in n. 6.

[6] Translation in O. Grabar, *The Dome of the Rock*, Cambridge, MA: Harvard University Press, 2006, p. 92.

[7] *The Holy Quran* (see n. 5), p. 855.

that the point at issue is the meaning of Sonship. Was it a question of physical begetting, or was there another meaning of 'sonship'? In what sense was Jesus the Son of God, and how did the earliest Christian traditions record their beliefs? What was the original Christmas story?

1

The setting

Our images of Christmas have been shaped by familiar carols and above all by the paintings that appear on traditional Christmas cards. There is a winter scene with a wooden stable, a manger, shepherds, Mary wearing a halo, an ox and an ass sharing the stable, and then maybe the shepherds or the wise men. In the sky, or dancing on the roof of the stable, there may be angels. The emphasis, depending on the preaching needs of the time, may be on the status of Mary as a homeless woman, or as a humble girl who accepted the will of God. Investigating journalists will seek to establish the truth or otherwise of the stories by attempting to identify the Quirinius, governor of Syria mentioned in Luke's account of the birth of Jesus (Luke 2.2); or to amaze the public with the revelation that Luke's 'inn' was in fact a guest room,[1] and that there is nothing in Luke's story about Mary and Joseph knocking on many doors to find themselves a place to stay.

The real 'setting' for the Christmas stories, however, is the world in which they were first written. For the Jewish people of Palestine in the first century CE, the world was shaped by the temple. Their culture was shaped by its calendar and its taxes, its purity rules and its sacrifices, and especially by the holy books and prophecies that were preserved there. The temple had long been the focus of their politics, since the Romans controlled the country through the high priests. There were, however, many who thought the temple impure and longed to see it replaced – but this was as much a political aspiration as it was religious. The promised Messiah would destroy the temple and rebuild it, they said.

All this, and much more, was the setting for the Christmas stories as they were first told. The truth of the stories will elude us if we substitute our own sense of 'accuracy' and wrench the stories from their cultural, political and theological setting.

---

[1] Luke 2.7 uses the word *kataluma*, which appears also in Luke 22.1 as the 'guest room' where the Passover was eaten.

The world of the temple

The people who wrote the Christmas stories lived in a world filled with angels. They expected angels, and they expected the ancient prophets to reappear. When Jesus asked his disciples what people were saying about him, they said: 'Some say [you are] John the Baptist, others say Elijah, and others Jeremiah or one of the prophets' (Matt. 16.14). Mark records Herod's fear:

> Some said, 'John the baptizer has been raised from the dead; that is why these powers are at work in him [Jesus].' But others said, 'It is Elijah.' And others said, 'It is a prophet like one of the prophets of old.' But when Herod heard it he said: 'John, whom I beheaded, has been raised.'
> (Mark 6.14–15)

Judas Maccabeus, struggling to free his people from their Syrian over-lords,[2] had dreamed about Onias the high priest meeting Jeremiah in the temple. The prophet had given him a golden sword to strike down his enemies (2 Macc. 15.11–16). Angels came to defend the temple when Heliodorus tried to loot its treasures (2 Macc. 3.22–30); angel armies appeared in the sky over Jerusalem just before Antiochus attacked the city (2 Macc. 5.1–4) and before the Romans attacked and destroyed it in 70 CE (Rev. 14.1). John Hyrcanus the high priest, when he was offering incense, heard a voice in the temple saying that his sons had that day been victorious in battle (109 BCE). He emerged and announced this to the waiting people.[3] Angels and ancient prophets were woven through the realities of life. Nobody would have questioned that Zechariah conversed with an angel in the temple (Luke 1.11), nor that the shepherds of Bethlehem heard the heavenly host (Luke 2.8–14), nor that John had seen angels coming from heaven and heard their voices, as he recorded in the book of Revelation.

The world view of the first Christians was expressed in, and derived from, the shape and the liturgy of the temple in Jerusalem. Tradition attributes the original temple to Solomon, although the plan for it had been revealed to David (1 Chron. 28.11–19). It had been rebuilt by the exiles who returned from Babylon in the sixth century BCE – the 'second' temple – and by Herod the Great, whose temple Jesus knew. The rebuilding is mentioned in the Fourth Gospel, when the Jews disputed what Jesus meant when he said he would rebuild the temple. 'It has taken forty-six years to build this temple, and will

---

[2] They recaptured and purified the temple in 164 BCE.
[3] Josephus, *Antiquities* 13.282–3.

you raise it up in three days?' (John 2.20). There were other major restorations, most famously in the time of Josiah, 623 BCE, who purged the temple and the religion of his kingdom (2 Kings 22.1—23.25).

All the temples had the same plan and proportions, or rather, should have had the same plan and proportions; and they were built for one purpose: so that the LORD could dwell in the midst (Exod. 25.8). Any departure from this plan was a sign of disobedience; a distorted temple meant disobedience and distortion elsewhere in society too. In the sixth century BCE, Ezekiel had a vision of the glory of the LORD departing from the temple (Ezek. 10.1—11.25), and later, a vision of an angel instructing him exactly how the temple should be rebuilt after the exile, so that the glory of the LORD could return (Ezek. 43.1–5). The words of the angel show that errors in the temple meant errors in society. 'You, son of man, describe the temple to the house of Israel, so that they are ashamed of their iniquities/distortions, and measure the measurement/proportion' (Ezek. 43.10). In Hebrew, 'iniquity' and 'distortion' derive from the same word, and so wordplay was possible. Ezekiel ended his oration on temple measurements by condemning the rulers of the time: they had to turn away from violence and oppression, restore justice and righteousness, and have a just economic system (Ezek. 45.9–12). The Second Isaiah, his younger contemporary, said the same: if the restored community would amend their ways, 'then shall your light break forth like the dawn' (Isa. 58.8). The glory would return. This was the world view of the early Christians. Like so many others, they were longing for the glory to return, and so John described the coming of the Messiah as the return of the glory. 'We have beheld his glory' (John 1.14). Jesus drove from the temple the traders who were abusing the holy place (Matt. 21.12–13 and parallels), and the mighty angel commanded John to *measure the temple* just before the Romans destroyed it (Rev. 11.1–2).

The desert tabernacle described in Exodus 25—40 shows the basic structure of the temple: a rectangle divided into two areas by a curtain – the veil – which separated the holy place from the most holy place (Exod. 26.31–33). The tabernacle and the later temples represented the creation, the most holy place beyond the veil being the invisible creation, the glory of the LORD and the angels; and the outer area the visible, material world. The two areas were also two aspects of time: the visible creation was the state of time and change, and the invisible creation the unchanging state of eternity. 'Eternity' and 'hidden' in Hebrew are written in the same way. More wordplay. What the temple structure depicted was the hidden glory of God at the heart of the material world, the eternal within the temporal. Thus Paul, thinking in this temple framework, could write: 'God sent *forth* his Son . . .' (Gal. 4.4). The Son coming into the world was envisaged as One emerging from the glory into our material world, passing from eternity into time.

The division between the two parts of creation was marked by the veil, and there were detailed instructions as to how it should be woven: 'blue and purple and scarlet stuff and fine twined linen; in skilled [*hošeb*] work shall it be made, with cherubim' (Exod. 26.31–33). No explanations were given for the prescriptions for the tabernacle/temple and its furnishings – or rather, none was made public in the scriptures. The meanings were, apparently, the secrets of the high priesthood; 'all that concerns the altar and that is within the veil' were entrusted to the sons of Aaron (Num. 18.7). Even the porters who carried the tabernacle in the desert were not allowed to see the furnishings. The sons of Kohath had to wait until the high priests had wrapped the sacred items, before they could take them up (Num. 4.5–15).

Josephus, a member of the high priestly family and a younger contemporary of Jesus, did reveal the meaning of the temple furnishings. Nobody knows when the explanations he knew originated, but he said the veil represented matter. 'For the scarlet seemed to represent fire, the fine linen the earth, the blue the air and the purple the sea, the comparison in two cases being suggested by their colour, and in that of the linen and the purple by their origin, since one is produced by the earth and the other by the sea.'[4] Josephus' rationalizations about the white and the purple could well have been his own, but the veil as a symbol of matter was widely known. Philo, an older contemporary who lived in Egypt, explained the tabernacle veil in the same way: 'What is spoken about is the workmanship of the materials woven together, which are four in number and are symbols of the four elements: earth, water, air and fire . . .'[5]

Only the high priest was permitted to pass beyond the veil into the holy of holies, and this symbolized his going into the divine presence. He entered the world of the angels, and stood before the throne. There are many descriptions of Jewish mystics making this 'ascent', but it is not always possible to date them. Texts found among the Dead Sea Scrolls, however, can be dated, and these show

---

[4] Josephus, *War* 5.213.
[5] Philo, *Questions on Exodus* II.85.

that mystical experiences were known when the Christmas stories were written. One text describes an unnamed person who sits in the congregation of the heavenly beings (4Q 491.11); another prays that someone may stand with the angels of the presence (1QSb IV); in another, someone declares he has been cleansed of great sin in order to stand among the holy ones, the sons of heaven (1QH XI). John described his own ascent to stand among the angels. First he saw the risen Lord in the outer part of the temple – the man with the seven lamps (Rev. 1.12) – and then he was summoned: 'Come up hither' (Rev. 4.1) and he stood with the angels before the throne. The early Christians knew of the world beyond the veil.

The high priest's outer vestment was made of the same fabric as the veil: blue, purple, scarlet and linen, interwoven with gold (Exod. 28.5). It represented the created world: 'Upon his long robe the whole world was depicted' (Wisdom of Solomon 18.24), and he wore it only when he officiated outside the holy of holies. Within the veil he wore white linen robes like the angels, as he was deemed to be one of them. In other words, those who entered the state of glory became a part of it. The high priests and kings of ancient Jerusalem entered the holy of holies and then emerged as messengers, angels, of the Lord. They had been raised up, that is, resurrected; they were sons of God, that is, angels; and they were anointed ones, that is, messiahs. The robes of the high priest in these two parts of the temple symbolized his passing from the angel state into the material world. He came from the glory, and by putting on a vestment that symbolized matter, he veiled that glory when he was in the world. The first Christians used these images to describe the incarnation. The writer of Hebrews could say, without any explanation, that the curtain of the temple was the flesh of Jesus, the great high priest (Heb. 10.20), and the Gospels record that the temple veil tore when Jesus died (Matt. 27.51; Mark 15.38; Luke 23.45). 'Veiled in flesh the Godhead see' is one of Charles Wesley's best-known lines, familiar to anyone who has sung Christmas carols.

The secret rituals of the holy of holies can only be reconstructed from texts in the Old Testament that seem to describe them, but the problem here is the date of the texts. Many parts of the Old Testament were compiled and even edited in the sixth century BCE, and some much later, that is, in the exile or in the troubled years that followed resettlement in Judah. The Davidic monarchy disappeared from history, and the high priests became the rulers in Jerusalem. The history of the high priesthood is not easy to reconstruct, especially in the period of time of the kings, when the high priests descended from Aaron are hardly mentioned,[6] and the king himself seems to have been the high priest 'after the order of Melchizedek' (Ps. 110.4). It was Solomon who blessed the congregation and consecrated the temple (1 Kings 8.14, 22), presumably as the priest 'after the order of Melchizedek' – if that is what those words mean. When he became 'Melchizedek' he became the divine Son: 'Today I have begotten you' (Ps. 110.3) – if that is what those words mean.

This psalm is undoubtedly about someone becoming king, 'Melchizedek' and the divine Son, but when was it written? Some say it was 'late', composed about 100 BCE for the Hasmonean kings, but if a more traditional date is allowed, then it described temple rituals of the Davidic kings. Since this psalm and Isaiah 53 are quoted in the New Testament more than any other passages, and since this psalm describes the royal birth as high priest, it must be important for understanding how 'the great high priest' of the Christians was born (Heb. 4.14). He too was identified as one 'after the order of Melchizedek' (Heb. 7.15) and as Son of God (Luke 1.35). At the point where the psalm describes the 'birth' of the royal high priest, the Hebrew text is damaged, and English versions give, 'on the day you lead your host upon the holy mountains, From the womb of the morning, like dew your youth will come to you' (RSV); or 'in the day of thy power, in the beauties of holiness from the womb of the morning: thou hast the dew of thy youth' (AV). The Greek has: 'in the day of your power, in the glory of the holy ones, from the womb, before the dawn I begot you' (v. 3).[7] The gist of the Hebrew may once have been: 'On the day of your birth in the glory of the holy ones, from the womb I have begotten you as the Morning Star.' When Eusebius was writing a commentary on the Psalms early in the fourth century, he knew a version of Psalm 110.3 that had 'Mary' where the present Hebrew text has 'womb'. The Hebrew *mrhm*, 'from the womb', had been read as *mrym*, 'Miriam', that is, Mary.[8] This is not impossible: the letters *ḥ* and *y* look very similar in the ancient Hebrew script that was still used at the end of the second temple period, for example on coins. The Hebrew word *ḥyl* can mean either 'power' or 'birth pangs'.

---

[6] The places where they do appear are thought to be later additions to the text. The Aaronite priests were prominent in the period when the Moses tradition was most prominent in Jerusalem. 'Melchizedek' represented the earlier cult in the time of the kings.

[7] For detail of this complex text, see my book *The Great High Priest*, London: T&T Clark, 2003, pp. 218, 241.

[8] Patrologia Graeca-Latina, XXIII.1344. Epiphanius also knew this version, *Heresies* 65.

Perhaps in this psalm it meant both, since birth as the Son would have meant empowerment. And the dew, which later became a symbol for resurrection, was represented by the myrrh oil used for temple anointing.

This verse, whose Hebrew text is now unreadable, is the key to understanding what the Christians meant by the birth, divine Sonship, incarnation and resurrection of Jesus. Paul knew an early formula derived from this temple mystery. At the beginning of his letter to Rome, Paul linked birth and resurrection: 'the gospel concerning his Son, who was descended from David according to the flesh, and designated Son of God in power, according to the Spirit of holiness, by his resurrection from the dead' (Rom. 1.3–4). 'Descended from David according to the flesh' could mean that Jesus' human father was Joseph or that Mary had also been of the house of David. Later accounts, as we shall see, emphasized her Davidic descent and the Virgin birth. Ignatius, bishop of Antioch early in the second century, was also ambiguous: 'Under the Divine dispensation, Jesus Christ our God was conceived by Mary of the seed of David and of the Spirit of God.'[9] 'Designated Son of God in power, according to the Spirit of holiness' shows that this formula did not originate in Greek. 'Spirit of holiness' is a literal rendering of the Hebrew idiom; we should say, 'The Holy Spirit designated him son of God *in power/at his birth* when he was resurrected.' This is the temple mystery, the moment of birth/resurrection when the human was transformed by the sacrament of the myrrh oil in the holy of holies. Ignatius was aware of the philosophical problems this posed, because he prefaced his words about the divine conception by saying: 'Where is your wise man now, or your subtle debater? Where are the fine words of our so-called intellectuals?' Trying to express the mystery of the holy of holies in terms of Greek philosophy was to occupy the Church for centuries.

There is a curious passage in the *Gospel of Philip* which shows how the mystery of the holy of holies was described by some early Christians. This 'Gospel' is sometimes described as an anthology of writings in the manner of Valentinus, a mid-second-century teacher in Rome who had come from Alexandria. Irenaeus attacked him as a Gnostic, but his followers were serious students of the scriptures and could hold office in the Church. Whatever label we now give him, 'Valentinian' writings preserve some remarkable glimpses of what

---

[9] Ignatius, *To the Ephesians* 18.

can only be temple tradition. The sequence of baptism and chrism, Eucharist and redemption, and then the bridal chamber[10] seems to correspond to the laver in the outer court, the table of shewbread within the temple, and then the mystery of the holy of holies, 'the bridal chamber where only the high priest enters'.[11] One passage seems to describe the mystery of the holy of holies, and explain why it was called the bridal chamber: 'He who [was begotten] before every-thing was begotten anew. He [who was] once [anointed] was anointed anew . . . Is it permitted to utter a mystery? The Father of everything united with the virgin who came down, and a fire shone for him on that day. He appeared in the great bridal chamber. Therefore his body came into being on that day. It left the bridal chamber as one who came into being from the bridegroom and the bride . . .'[12]

Reconstructing beliefs about the ancient kings is not easy, but what can be gleaned from surviving material shows how important they were in shaping Christian belief, especially about the birth and resur-rection of Jesus. Jesus was described as the Morning Star (Rev. 22.16), one of the titles for the sons of God (Job 38.7). David was *raised up* and anointed and then spoke words from the LORD (2 Sam. 23.1–2). The word 'raised up' here also means 'resurrected'.[13] Psalm 89 describes the same temple scene: 'I have exalted[14] one chosen from the people . . . With my holy oil I have anointed him . . . He shall cry to me "Thou art my Father" . . . And I will make him the first-born . . .' (Ps. 89.19–20, 26–27). The resurrected one was anointed, spoke of God as his Father, and was given the status of the first-born. He became divine, and *his birth was described as his resurrection.* Another psalm has some words from the ritual: 'I will tell of the decree of the LORD: He said to me, "You are my son, today I have begotten you"' (Ps. 2.7), and Isaiah recorded the words of the angels in the holy of holies as the royal 'birth' took place: 'For to us a child is born, to us a son is given; and the government will be upon his shoulder, and his name will be called "Wonderful Counsellor, Mighty God, Everlasting Father, Prince of Peace." Of the increase of his govern-ment and of peace there will be no end, upon the throne of David, and over his kingdom, to establish it, and to uphold it with justice

---

[10] *The Gospel of Philip*, CG II.3.67.

[11] CG II.3.69.

[12] CG II.3.71.

[13] Compare Ps. 88.10: 'Dost thou work wonders for the dead? Do the shades *rise up* to praise thee?' And similarly Isa. 26.14, 19.

[14] A different word for raising up.

and with righteousness from this time forth and for evermore' (Isa. 9.6–7). This was the promise to the Davidic line: anointing and consecrating in the holy of holies transformed the human king, who had an earthly father, but also a heavenly Father. This is clear from Nathan's oracle to David about his son and heir: 'I will *raise up*[15] your offspring after you . . . I will be his father and he shall be my son' (2 Sam. 7.12, 14).

This was divine sonship in its temple setting. 'Son' and 'begotten' did not mean reproduction in the human sense. They were ways of describing a process beyond human comprehension. As with so many descriptions of the heavenly realm, the prophets and seers struggled to express what had been revealed to them. Ezekiel saw the throne, and his description is full of such words as 'as it were', 'likeness', 'in appearance', 'the likeness as it were of a human form' (all in Ezek. 1). John too struggled to describe his vision of heaven: the One on the throne appeared like jasper and carnelian, and the rainbow was like an emerald, and there was 'as it were' a sea of glass before the throne (all in Rev. 4). In the same way 'Son' or 'born from' distinguished the relationship from that of a Creator and his creation. There was a unity that could only be expressed in family terms, and so the Christians were later to describe the Son of God as 'begotten not created'. Furthermore, in the Hebrew idiom 'only' meant 'dearly loved' not 'unique'. Abraham was told: 'Take your son, your *only* son Isaac whom you love', but in the Greek it became 'Take your *beloved* son Isaac whom you love . . .' (Gen. 22.2).[16] Isaac was not Abraham's only son – there was Ishmael too. The 'only son' did not mean there were no other sons. The mighty angels were called the sons of God (Job 38.7).

There were two stages of sonship in temple tradition. The Unity of the Divine included the angels, who were known as the sons of God Most High. The oldest parts of the Old Testament distinguish God Most High (El Elyon) and the LORD (Yahweh). Yahweh was the first-born of the sons of God Most High, appointed as the Guardian Angel of Jacob, that is, of his descendants (Deut. 32.8, in the oldest known Hebrew text of that verse that was found among the Dead Sea Scrolls). *Yahweh the Son of God Most High, the God of Israel who*

---

[15] The same word as in 2 Sam. 23.1, so it could mean that David's heirs would also be 'raised up' in the holy of holies.

[16] This way of translating *yaḥid*, 'only', is true for all the instances in the Hebrew scriptures except Ps. 25.16.

appeared in the Old Testament theophanies, in turn had a son, who was the human being in whom he was present with his people. This way of thinking about God and the divine presence did not fracture the Unity of the Divine; it extended it. The Davidic king was known as Immanuel, which means 'God with us' (Isa. 8.8 and more famously, Isa. 7.14). The psalmist described a procession into the temple when he saw 'My God, my King' going into the holy place (Ps. 68.24). When Solomon was made king, he sat on the throne of the LORD as king (1 Chron. 29.23), and all the people 'bowed their heads and worshipped the LORD, the king' (1 Chron. 29.20, the literal translation of the Hebrew). The human king, in a way that they understood and we do not, was the LORD. He was the Son of God Most High with his people. This problem of the human nature and the divine nature was to perplex Christian thinkers for generations; it was one of the temple beliefs that was never explained, or rather, never put into the public domain.

What the temple tradition understood by the divine birth lay at the heart of the Christian understanding of Jesus, but this was obscured and confused when early Christian teachers tried to express the inherited Hebrew/temple culture in terms acceptable to Greek philosophy. This resulted in theological debates about the nature and origin of the Son of God and his incarnation, debates about how the human related to the divine, the 'natures' of the Second Person. Temple texts just describe the ritual that symbolized the human king and the LORD becoming one, and they use the language of sonship. 'You are my son; Today I have begotten you' was a decree of the LORD to the king (Ps. 2.7). 'I have found David my servant . . . He shall cry to me "Thou art my Father" . . . and I will make him the first-born' (Ps 89.20, 26, 27) was the LORD speaking about the king. The LORD declared the king a priest for ever like Melchizedek after his birth in the holy of holies (Ps. 110). 'Behold the Virgin shall conceive and bear a son and call his name Immanuel' (Isa. 7.14). All these texts describe what the Christians were to call incarnation, the LORD, the Son of God Most High making himself present with his people in the anointed Davidic king. The Christians saw all the temple ritual as foreshadowing the reality of the incarnation, but there were questions about the detail, the process as applied to Jesus. Was Jesus really born, or did he just appear as an adult man? Was Jesus a man who became God, or a divine being who only took a human form? Above all, what was meant by the Virgin birth? These were the questions about the 'second' birth.

There were also questions about the 'first' birth, the birth in eternity of the Son of God, and here there was no guidance in the Old Testament. The relationship of God Most High and Son of God had to be deduced from the titles. The most ancient description of God Most High was 'Begetter of heaven and earth' (Gen. 14.19, translating literally): this was how Melchizedek blessed his God. Later sensitivities modified the language, because in the sixth century BCE, there were massive developments in the religion of Israel, centred around the temple purges of Josiah. The distinction between Father and Son was lost in the attempt to impose literal monotheism, and the language of fatherhood was changed to that of creation; God Most High the Begetter became the LORD, the Maker. The idea of a Father God and his Son fell out of favour among those who equated the LORD and God Most High.[17] All this influenced the way the Old Testament texts were preserved and transmitted, and yet the first Christians clearly knew the older ways – God Most High and his Son – ways of thinking associated with Melchizedek, with Abraham, and with the Davidic kings, and these surfaced as discussion of the Trinity. When the early Christians read the Old Testament, they recognized that the LORD was the Son of God Most High, the One they were eventually to call the Second Person. It was the LORD who became incarnate, and the theophanies in the Old Testament were pre-incarnation appearances.

The 'first birth' of the Son of God raised many questions. Was there ever a time when God the Father was not the Father of the Son? The first fruit of these debates was identifying certain teachers and their positions as heretics, most famously Marcion, the teacher from Pontus, and Arius the teacher in Alexandria, 'the little spark from whom a great fire was kindled'.[18] The first version of the Nicene Creed in 325 CE had an emphatic statement appended that is not in the version we use today: 'The Holy Catholic and Apostolic Church anathematizes those who say that there was a time when the Son of God was not, and that he was not before he was begotten. And that he was made from that which did not exist, or who assert that he is of other substance or essence than the Father, or that he was created or is susceptible to change . . .'.[19] We still remember these disputes when we sing the second verse of 'O Come all ye faithful': 'God

---

[17] See my book *The Great Angel*, London: SPCK, 1992, pp. 18–21.
[18] Socrates, *Church History* 1.6.
[19] Socrates, *Church History* 1.8.

of God, Light of Light, Lo he abhors not the Virgin's womb. Very God, begotten not created . . .' He was really born in Bethlehem – the Virgin birth, but he had existed from all eternity – 'the eternal generation of the Son'.

Both the first and second sonships are found in the New Testament. Jesus, in a debate with the Jews and so presumably using arguments they would recognize and accept, said: 'Do you say of him whom the Father consecrated and sent into the world, "You are blaspheming," because I said, "I am the Son of God"?' (John 10.36). This is the imagery of the ancient monarchy and high priesthood; a human being is consecrated and then *sent out* into the world as the Son of God. Paul said something similar: that God had *sent forth* his Son (Gal. 4.4). Paul warned against contemporary polytheism – 'many gods and many Lords' – and declared that for Christians there was 'One God, the Father, from whom are all things and for whom we exist, and one LORD, Jesus Christ, through whom are all things and through whom we exist' (1 Cor. 8.6). One Father and One LORD, just as in the older versions of Deuteronomy, where Yahweh was described as one of the sons of El Elyon, God Most High.

Jesus, nevertheless, saw this relationship as a unity: 'I and the Father are one [thing]' (John 10.30). His prayer after the last supper showed this extended unity. His disciples were One in the same sense as Jesus and the Father were One. 'I in them and thou in me, that they may become perfectly one, so that the world may know that thou hast sent me . . .' (John 17.23). The disciples were 'in Christ' and so were the human presence of the LORD just as Jesus had been. Jesus knew he was returning to the presence of God, to 'the glory which I had with thee before the world was made' (John 17.5). The implication of this is that all people can become sons of God, exactly what John and Paul said: 'But to all who received him, who believed in his name, he gave power to become children of God; who were born, not of blood, nor of the will of the flesh, but of God' (John 1.13); 'For all who are led by the Spirit of God are sons of God' (Rom. 8.14), and these would share the image of the Son, so that he would be 'the first-born among many brethren' (Rom. 8.29) – the image of the first-born among sons of God from Deuteronomy 32.8.

Human beings could become angels, and then continue to live in the material world. This transformation did not just happen after physical death; it marked the passage from the life in the material world to the life of eternity. For Christians this happened at baptism, and so Paul could write to the church at Colossae: 'If *you have been raised* with Christ, seek those things that are above' (Col. 3.1). This resurrection is often described nowadays as being 'born again', as in the words of Jesus to Nicodemus: 'Unless one is born anew/born from above, he cannot see the kingdom of God' (John 3.3). Seeing the Kingdom meant seeing the heavenly throne, that is, seeing beyond the veil into the invisible world. When you saw the angels you joined them. When you glimpsed the glory, you became a part of it.

Origen, the great biblical scholar who died in 253 CE, quoted some lines from a text that has not survived, *The Prayer of Joseph*, which he described as one of the 'apocrypha presently in use among the Hebrews'. He was explaining how John the Baptist could have been both a man and an angel, one who 'took a body in order to bear witness to the light'.[20] In *The Prayer of Joseph*, Jacob the man was also 'Israel, an angel of God and a ruling spirit'. Nobody knows when *The Prayer of Joseph* was written, or how widely it was known. Nevertheless, it is proof that some people believed that key figures in the story of Israel were angels in human form. This means that some human beings became angels in the temple ritual, and some angels took human form. Temple beliefs ritualized this by passing through the veil from the visible to the invisible world.

Human history, then, was not just a drama in the material world; beings from eternity could and did enter that world to become a part of its story, and some human leaders had access to heaven. The *War Scroll* found at Qumran outlines in detail the plan for a great, final battle against the Romans, who were the current embodiment of the forces of evil. On 'the day appointed from ancient times for the battle of destruction of the sons of darkness', the heavenly and earthly assemblies joined forces – the sons of light against the sons of darkness (1QM I). The high priests in special war vestments would inaugurate the battle by sounding the sacred trumpets, and the human warriors had to be in a state of absolute ritual purity in order to mix with the angel hosts (1QM VII–VIII). The description of the battle plan is interspersed with four hymns: in other words, the battle was a religious ritual. The Christians had a similar text, the book of Revelation, which describes the Lamb and his heavenly host assembled on Mount Zion (Rev. 14.1) and then riding out to defeat the hordes of evil (Rev. 19.11–21). The setting for the whole of the book of Revelation is the temple, and the drama takes place

---

[20] Origen, *Commentary on John* II.31.

both in heaven and on earth. So too, as we shall see, with the drama of the Christmas stories: 'on earth as it is in heaven'.

Beyond the veil was the glory. This was described as 'the presence' or 'the face' of the LORD. Presence and face are the same word in Hebrew, a plural form, as is the usual word for God: *'elohim*. The words themselves, even though they are usually translated as a singular form – face, presence, God – imply that the divine, though a unity, was a manifold or compound unity. The Hebrew word for presence or face is *panim*, and when this was translated into Greek it became *prosopa*, another plural form that became familiar in Christian discourse as the 'persons' of the Trinity. The unity of God was perceived and described as manifold.

The glory came to the tabernacle when it was consecrated. The cloud covered the tent, 'the glory of the LORD filled the tabernacle' (Exod. 40.34), and Moses could not enter when the glory filled the tabernacle. When Solomon consecrated the temple, 'the glory of the LORD filled the house of the LORD' (1 Kings 8.11), and the priests could not stay in its presence. When the glory left the temple, Ezekiel saw it in Babylon as 'a great cloud with brightness round about it . . .' *in whose midst was a human form*, 'the appearance of the likeness of the glory of the LORD' (Ezek. 1.4, 28). In his vision of the future, he saw it return: 'The glory of the God of Israel came from the east, and the sound of his coming was like the sound of many waters, and the earth shone with his glory' (Ezek. 43.2).

To see the glory of the LORD's presence – to see beyond the veil – was the greatest blessing. The high priest used to bless Israel with the words: 'The LORD bless you and keep you: The LORD make his face to shine upon you, and be gracious to you: The LORD lift up his countenance upon you, and give you peace' (Num. 6.24–26). Isaiah saw the LORD in the temple, enthroned with the seraphim, and, according to the Greek version of the Old Testament, the temple was filled with his glory.[21] The seraphim called out that the whole earth was full of his glory (Isa. 6.1–3). The Psalmist called on the LORD to shine forth: 'Thou who art enthroned upon the cherubim, shine forth' (Ps. 80.1); 'O LORD . . . shine forth' (Ps. 94.1). 'God shines forth from Zion' (Ps. 50.2). When the LORD became king, he shone forth and came with his holy ones (Deut. 33.2–5). Here, perhaps, is a clue as to the temple setting of this shining forth; it was when the king or high priest emerged from the holy of holies as the presence of Yahweh with his

---

[21] The Hebrew says it was filled with his robe.

people. There is no text that describes the king's robes, but the high priest wore vestments that were 'for glory and for beauty' (Exod. 28.2). A poem describing Simon the high priest[22] said: 'When he put on his glorious robe, and clothed himself with superb perfection . . . he made the court of the sanctuary glorious' (Ben Sira 50.11). When he came out from the holy of holies, he was like 'the morning star among the clouds . . . like the sun shining upon the temple of the Most High' (Ben Sira 50.6–7). This was the glory in human form that Ezekiel saw in his vision. Isaiah recorded what was enacted in the temple ceremony: 'The people who walked in darkness, have seen a great light; those who dwelt in a land of deep darkness, on them has the light shined . . . For unto us a child is born . . .' (Isa. 9.2, 6).

Seeing the glory, however, became controversial. Nobody knows why. There is one strand in the Old Testament that is absolutely opposed to any idea of seeing the divine. Two accounts of the story of Moses on Sinai will illustrate the point. In one, he saw the God of Israel, with a sapphire pavement at his feet (Exod. 24.9–10); in the other, the people were reminded that they had seen no form when the LORD spoke from the midst of the fire on the mountain: there was only a voice (Deut. 4.12, 15). Moses spoke with the LORD face to face as a man speaks with a friend (Exod. 33.11), and yet when Moses asked to see the glory of the LORD, he was told he could not see the LORD: 'You cannot see my face; for man shall not see me and live . . . my face shall not be seen' (Exod. 33.20, 23). Isaiah saw the LORD, enthroned in the temple (Isa. 6.1), and Ezekiel saw the likeness of the glory of the LORD (Ezek. 1.28). Jesus said: 'Blessed are the pure in heart, for they shall see God' (Matt. 5.8); and John saw 'one seated on the throne' (Rev. 4.2). There can be no doubt where the early Christians stood on this matter. Peter, James and John saw beyond the veil when they saw Jesus transfigured. They saw into the state of glory that was outside time, since Moses and Elijah were with Jesus in their vision. When Peter told Cornelius the story of Jesus, he said that only a few people had seen the risen LORD, those who had been 'prepared beforehand as witnesses' (Acts 10.41, translating literally). Those who had seen the transfigured LORD were able to recognize the risen, heavenly LORD. John began his Gospel by saying, 'We have beheld his glory' (John 1.14), and Luke said that the glory of the LORD shone around the shepherds at Bethlehem (Luke 2.9). The veil between the two worlds had been opened.

---

[22] About 200 BCE.

Telling the stories

When Jesus joined the two disciples on the road to Emmaus, 'he interpreted to them in all the scriptures the things concerning himself' (Luke 24.27). Only Luke records this story, and in so doing, he tells us two things: that from the beginning, the Christians interpreted the death of Jesus in terms of prophecy and fulfilment; and that *this use of prophecy went back to Jesus himself.* Whether he told the story of his own birth and early years in the same way we can never know, but relating the stories of his life to prophecy was remembered as characteristic of his teaching. In the synagogue at Nazareth, at the start of his public ministry, Jesus claimed that the words he had just read from Isaiah were being fulfilled at that very moment (Luke 4.21). The high proportion of allusions to Isaiah in the Gospels and in the rest of the New Testament could indicate that Jesus had quoted Isaiah more than any other prophet, and that the fulfilment of Isaiah's prophecies was remembered by the New Testament writers as especially important in his life. It had 'unique prominence among the scriptural quotations in the Gospels, Paul and Acts . . .'.[23] If there had been an Isaiah scroll in his home community – and synagogues did not have many costly scrolls apart from the Law – then Jesus would have known well the words of that particular prophet.

Studying the scriptures and finding in them predictions of their own times was one of the ways that prophecy was read in the time of Jesus; some would say it was the most important way. The sufferings of Christ were predicted by the prophets, according to 1 Peter: 'The prophets who prophesied of the grace that was to be yours searched and inquired about this salvation; they inquired what person or time was indicated by the Spirit of Christ within them when predicting the sufferings of Christ and the subsequent glory' (1 Pet. 1.10–11). It was not only the Christians who read the prophecies in this way. Texts among the Dead Sea Scrolls interpreted the smallest detail in the prophets as indicating events of their own time. The *Habakkuk Commentary* warned the unfaithful generation that they would not believe the true interpretation of prophecies revealed by the Teacher of Righteousness, 'the priest [in whose heart] God set [understanding] that he might interpret all the words of his servants the prophets . . .'; 'the Teacher of Righteousness, to whom God made

---

[23] J. F. A. Sawyer, *The Fifth Gospel: Isaiah in the History of Christianity*, Cambridge: Cambridge University Press, 1996, p. 29; 27 of Paul's 37 quotations from the prophets are from Isaiah, pp. 21–2.

known all the mysteries of the words of his servants the prophets' (1QpHab II, VII). John saw the mighty angel who told him that when the seventh trumpet sounded, 'the mystery of God, as he announced to his servants the prophets, should be fulfilled' (Rev. 10.7).

Some events that fulfilled prophecies were brought about by the actions of others – the Roman occupation of Judaea, the wicked ways of the high priests in Jerusalem, the cruelty of Herod – and so these could be set within the revealed plan of history. Other events could be organized to show those who knew the prophecies what was happening. Jesus did not have to ride into Jerusalem on a donkey: 'This took place to fulfil what was spoken by the prophet, saying, "Tell the Daughter of Zion, Behold your king is coming to you, humble and mounted on an ass, and on a colt, the foal of an ass" ' (Matt. 21.4, quoting Zech. 9.9). Matthew interpreted the prophecy over-literally, in so far as he has two animals in his story, whereas the other accounts have only one (Matt. 21.7; cf. Mark 11.7; Luke 19.30; John 12.14). All four accounts agree that Jesus did ride a donkey into Jerusalem; it was only Matthew who added a second animal because he had not taken into account the parallelism of Zechariah's poetry, and characteristic way of using 'and' in Hebrew: 'Mounted on an ass/ and on a colt, the foal of an ass'. *Jesus chose to perform this significant act*, and his Gospel writers chose to record it.

John makes clear, however, that some of Jesus' actions and sayings were not understood at the time. Rebuilding the temple, for example, was not understood as a prophecy of the resurrection until after the event. 'His disciples remembered that he had said this' (John 2.22). Similarly, the entry into Jerusalem on Palm Sunday. John quoted the prophecy from Zechariah about the king entering the city on an ass, and added: 'His disciples did not understand this at first; but when Jesus was glorified, then they remembered that this had been written of him and had been done to him' (John 12.16). It was later reflection on Jesus' life, what happened to him and *what he chose to do* that enabled them to piece together what had been happening.

Paul said that seeking signs was characteristic of the Jews, they *demanded* signs (1 Cor. 11.22), and Jesus had said something similar: the Pharisees wanted a sign from heaven, but none would be given to that evil generation (Mark 8.11–12). Matthew and Luke have a longer version of the saying: no sign would be given except the sign of Jonah (Matt. 12.38–40; Luke 11.29–30). When the Pharisees and Sadducees asked for a sign from heaven, Jesus said that they could read the signs of bad weather coming, but they could not read the signs of the times (Matt. 16.1–4). Jesus was creating some of these signs. One saying in the *Gospel of Thomas* makes clear how the 'signs' were understood: 'They said to him, "Tell us who you are that we may believe in you." [Jesus] said to them, "You read the face of the sky and of the earth, but you have not recognized the one who [or: that which] is before you, and you do not know how to read this moment." '[24] We assume that John the Baptist could read the signs. When he sent disciples to ask Jesus 'Are you the one who is to come?' Jesus reminded him of the miracles he had performed (Luke 7.18–23). The blind could see again, the lame could walk and the deaf could hear, all signs of the glory of the LORD (Isa. 35.2, 5–6). The dead had been raised, and the poor had heard good news, signs of the presence of Adonai,[25] according to a fragment of text from Qumran (4Q 521). The answer to John's question was: 'Read the signs', 'Recall the scriptures'.

Recognizing when prophecy was being fulfilled was a way of reading the signs of the times. The signs could be miracles, as John said when explaining how he compiled his Gospel: 'Now Jesus did many other signs in the presence of his disciples, which are not written in this book; but these are written that you may believe that Jesus is the Christ, the Son of God . . .' (John 20.30–31). John selected from the material available to him, to make his point. It is not that he invented material – he simply selected. The same is true of the Christmas stories. A basic story was told, but not with the mundane detail that modern writers might choose to include. There was no mention of, for example, nappies or whatever was used at the time, although the infant Jesus doubtless needed them. But there was mention of the manger, and so we ask, Why was that detail included? Those elements in the story that could be linked to prophecy, and illuminated by it, were naturally the most emphasized. This is not to say that the story of Jesus' life was simply compiled from prophecies, as some have suggested. Rather, the incidents seen to be significant were emphasized, and the material of interest to modern biographers was not.

Fulfilment of prophecy was a very important element in the earliest Christian proclamation, so much so that some important texts 'disappeared' from the Hebrew scriptures. In *The Letter of Barnabas*, for example, attributed to Barnabas 'the Levite from Cyprus' (Acts

---

[24] *Gospel of Thomas* 91.
[25] Often used instead of Yahweh, to avoid using the sacred name.

4.36) and at one time included in the New Testament,[26] there are several quotations from Scripture which cannot be found in the Old Testament we have today. There is a prophecy about the day of atonement that is very important for understanding the Eucharist: 'And what does it say in the prophet? "Let them eat of the goat which is offered for their sins at the fast, and let all the priests, but nobody else, eat of its inward parts unwashed and with vinegar." '[27] The 'lost' prophecy explained why the Gospels emphasized that Jesus drank vinegar before he died (Matt. 27.48; Mark 15.36; Luke 23.36; John 19.29–30), thus preparing himself to be the sin offering. Had Barnabas not included this prophecy, we should never have known the significance of that detail recorded by all four Gospel writers. *The Letter of Barnabas* quoted five other 'lost' prophecies,[28] and also regarded 1 Enoch as 'scripture'.[29] The same may be true of the Christmas stories; there may be details in them that would have alerted the original readers to a prophecy being fulfilled, but that prophecy was so important that it 'disappeared' from later texts of the Hebrew scriptures.

This process of editing the scriptures was described by Justin, writing in the mid-second century. In his dialogue with the Jew Trypho, they debated the points at issue between Jews and Christians at that time. This dialogue may be a literary fiction, or it may have been drawn from life; that does not affect the content. Justin maintained that Jewish teachers had been removing texts from the scriptures: 'They have deleted entire passages . . .'[30] He gave several examples of texts that had been removed, texts which were known to other early Christian writers and quoted by them.[31] He also complained to Trypho that Jews had changed the old Greek translation of the scriptures, made in Alexandria by the seventy elders long before the time of Jesus, and accepted by the community at that time as an accurate translation. The word 'Virgin' had been removed from Isaiah 7.14, he said, and replaced with the word 'young woman'. This is clear evidence of a disputed prophecy relevant to the Christmas stories.

---

[26] For example in the Sinai Codex which was written in the fourth century and is the oldest complete New Testament.

[27] *Barnabas* 7.

[28] *Barnabas* 2, 6, 11, 15, 16.

[29] *Barnabas* 16.

[30] Justin, *Dialogue with Trypho* 71.

[31] See my book *The Great High Priest*, London: T&T Clark, 2003, pp. 295–8.

It used to be assumed that this was mere rhetoric, that the Christians were making these claims in order to strengthen their case. They had, in effect, added a few prophecies, because it was unthinkable that the Jews had changed the Hebrew scriptures. Fragments of Scripture found among the Dead Sea Scrolls, however, showed there had indeed been different wording in the Hebrew scriptures before the time of Jesus. One key Christian proof text, Deuteronomy 32.43, had existed in Hebrew in a longer form, and so the 'long' Greek version of it was not a Christian expansion after all. The 'long' version is the messianic proof text in Hebrews 1.6 – 'Let all God's angels worship him' – and is the prophecy as the early Christians knew it, but *it did not appear in the Hebrew text that was accepted and used by post-Christian Judaism.* Only a small fraction of the Hebrew scriptures has been found among the scrolls, and so a complete survey of the differences and a complete check of Justin's claims is not possible. The existence of just a few 'different' texts that are significant for Christian claims, however, shows that Justin's accusations were well-founded.

In addition, there was no fixed and recognized list of Hebrew scriptures in the time of Jesus. When he spoke of Moses, that is the Law, and the prophets (Luke 24.27), we do not know which prophets he included in that list. Enoch was accepted and quoted as a prophet, as at Jude 14, and Josephus mentioned ancient prophecies that are not in the Old Testament. When addressing the people besieged in Jerusalem during the war against Rome, he said: 'Who does not know the records of the ancient prophets, and the oracle which threatens this poor city, and is even now coming true? For they foretold that it would be taken whensoever one should begin to slaughter his own countrymen . . .'.[32] Jesus had given this same example as one of the signs that the temple was about to be destroyed: 'Brother will deliver up brother to death and the father his child, and children will rise against their parents and have them put to death' (Mark 13.12–13). If Josephus could describe this saying as an ancient oracle, what book of prophecy was Jesus quoting, or alluding to? Presumably one known to the early Church but not to us, *one that could have contained other prophecies relevant to the Christmas stories.*

The writings of the time were steeped in prophecies, but they were also sensitive to other patterns of symbolism. Perhaps the most familiar in the New Testament is the temple symbolism in Hebrews, which was not explained for the readers. They must have known what

---

[32] Josephus, *War* 6.110.

it meant. The outer part of the temple was symbolic of the present age, but the writer could not reveal the meaning of the inner parts. Presumably s/he knew the meaning (Heb. 9.9). Jesus was the great high priest, and presumably the readers also knew what this implied. The temple with its complex system of furnishings and festivals, rites and rituals was assumed by early Christians as their world view. The way opened 'through the curtain, that is through his flesh' (Heb. 10.20) is a meaningless statement outside the world of the temple. Paul's exhortation: 'Cleanse out the old leaven that you may be a new lump' (1 Cor. 5.7) assumes that his readers know the traditions associated with Passover. 'Christ . . . the first fruits of those who have fallen asleep' (1 Cor. 15.20) assumes a knowledge of offerings and their meaning. William Tyndale in 1526 could use this term 'fyrst frutes', and yet some modern versions of the New Testament avoid it. 'Christ has been raised from death, as the *guarantee* that those who sleep in death will also be raised' (1 Cor. 15.20, Good News Bible[33]). By losing the reference to first fruits – and 'guarantee' is hardly a good translation – the reader of the Good News Bible is deprived of all the theology implicit in the ritual of the first fruits: the initial offering that gives thanks for and consecrates the remainder of the harvest; and the fact that the first of the first fruits, the spring barley, was offered on the first day of the week after the Sabbath of Passover (Lev. 23.11). In other words, the day of the resurrection was the first day of the first fruits, and so the image is doubly apt. 'Christ . . . the first fruits of those who have fallen asleep'. Such subtlety was part of early Christian discourse, and raises the question: What are we not seeing in the Christmas stories?

Another great difference between the way the first Christians read the Old Testament and the way that many read it today, is the understanding of Yahweh 'the LORD'. For them, the One described in the Old Testament as the God of Israel, or the Holy One of Israel, the One who appeared to Abraham, was not God the Father, but God the Son – to use the later Christian distinction. The earliest Christian interpreters of the Old Testament are quite clear about this. Justin, the earliest writer whose work survives in any quantity, taught in Rome. He knew that the appearances of Yahweh or the angel of Yahweh were appearances of the pre-existent Christ.[34]

---

[33] GNB also avoids first fruits as at Jas. 1.18.
[34] See my book *The Great Angel: A Study of Israel's Second God*, London: SPCK, 1992, pp. 190–212.

> Neither Abraham nor Isaac nor Jacob nor any other man ever saw the Father and LORD beyond all description of all things and of Christ himself; but (they saw) him who, according to his will, is God his Son, and his angel because he serves him.[35]

Fifty years later, towards the end of the second century CE, Irenaeus, a man from Asia Minor who was bishop in southern Gaul, wrote a summary of Christian belief. He regarded himself as a guardian of true Christian teaching and wrote a huge work *Against Heresies*, so we can assume that what he said was widely accepted. 'Abraham was a prophet', he wrote, 'and saw what was to come to pass in the future, the Son of God in human form . . . and all visions of this kind signify the Son of God in his speaking with men and his being with them'.[36] Fifty years later, Novatian, the first theologian of the church in Rome, wrote an exposition *On the Trinity*. He explained that it was the Second Person who was the agent of creation, came down to Babel, appeared to Abraham and wrestled with Jacob: 'We are led to understand that it was not the Father, Who never has been seen, that was here seen, but the Son.'[37] John had attributed similar teaching to Jesus: 'His (the Father's) voice you have never heard, his form you have never seen . . . You search the Scriptures . . . and they bear witness to me' (John 5.37–38); and had explained that Isaiah had seen the preincarnate Christ enthroned in the temple (John 12.41), because 'No one has ever seen God' (John 1.18). *When the first Christians told the story of the birth of Jesus, they were describing how Yahweh the LORD, the Son of God Most High, became incarnate.*

Characteristic of texts written at about this time was the long established idea of history repeating itself. Events in the past were deemed a guide to the present. Isaiah had used the motif of the Exodus from Egypt to describe the return from Babylon; it was a second Exodus (Isa. 51.9–11). The Christians fleeing from Jerusalem also saw these events as their Exodus, followed by another forty years in the desert during which they had to keep the faith (Heb. 3.7—4.9). Those who wrote about, and reflected upon, the destruction of the temple in 70 CE, did so as though they were writing about the destruction of the first temple. 'Ezra' was adopted as a pseudonym by one of these writers, and his book, known as 2 Esdras, was set in Babylon thirty years after the destruction of Jerusalem (2 Esdr. 3.1). The description of

---

[35] Justin, *Trypho* 127.
[36] Irenaeus, *Proof of the Apostolic Preaching* 44, 45.
[37] Novatian, *On the Trinity* XVIII.

how 'Ezra' restored the scriptures after the disaster is in fact an account of how the scriptures were collected around 100 CE (2 Esdr. 14.1–48). Baruch, Jeremiah's scribe (Jer. 36.4), was another ancient figure to whom books were attributed at this time. He described how Jerusalem was surrounded by the Babylonians, and how angels came to destroy the city lest the enemies should boast that they had overthrown Zion (*2 Bar.* 7). Jeremiah and Baruch had watched all this. If history repeated itself in this way, there may well be motifs from the sixth century BCE woven into the Christmas stories, themes from the period immediately before the destruction of the first temple.

And last, but by no means least, there was *Haggadah*, that characteristically Jewish way of storytelling that drew upon all these elements and more. It is defined thus by the *Jewish Encyclopaedia*:[38] 'The interpretation, illustration or expansion in a moralising or edifying manner, of the non legal portions of the Bible. In a narrower sense, it denotes the exegetical amplification of a biblical passage and the development of a new thought based thereon.'

The politics

The political situation in Palestine had been unsettled for centuries, and the roots of the problem went back at least to the eighth century BCE.[39] People reading the Enoch texts – which the first Christians used as Scripture – would have found there an account of how the LORD handed over his people to foreign rulers long ago in the time of Isaiah. These Enochic histories were written as an animal fable, with no characters identified. We have to guess who they were, but it is clear that well before the destruction of the first temple in 597 BCE, certain 'sheep' had forsaken the temple and become blind, that is, lost their spiritual vision. The LORD gave them into the hands of lions and tigers, that is, the Assyrians and Babylonians (*1 En.* 89.54–55). Isaiah, writing of the situation in the sixth or early fifth century BCE, used the same imagery: 'All you beasts of the field, come to devour – all you beasts of the forest. His watchmen are blind, they are without knowledge . . . The shepherds also have no understanding; they have all turned to their own way, each to his own gain, one and all' (Isa. 56.9–11). These were the shepherds Jesus spoke about

---

[38] *The Jewish Encyclopaedia*, New York and London: Funk and Wagnells, 1904.
[39] One might compare the situation in Ireland, where the roots of the troubles in the twentieth century lay deep in the troubled history of Ireland and England.

when he said that he was the good shepherd: 'All who came before me are thieves and robbers' (John 10.8). He was contrasting himself with those who had ruled his people for centuries; in his time the wicked shepherds were the Romans and their agents, the high priests in Jerusalem. A contemporary writer described them thus: 'The last priests of Jerusalem, who shall amass money and wealth by plundering the peoples, but in the last days, their riches and booty shall be delivered into the hands of the army of the Kittim [the Romans].[40]

The Enochic histories also rejected everything that had developed in Jerusalem and Judaea since the return from Babylon in the sixth century BCE. The exiles who returned from Babylon were 'an apostate generation . . . and all its deeds (were) apostate' (*1 En.* 93.9). They had built an impure temple and table, 'but all the bread on it was polluted and not pure' (*1 En.* 89.73). The Dead Sea Scrolls have a similar view of the history of their people since the destruction of the first temple. According to the *Damascus Document* the period had been an age of divine wrath. After 390 years 'a group of blind men groping for the way' had established themselves, and after twenty more years, the Teacher of Righteousness (or perhaps the 'Righteous Teacher') was raised up to guide them.[41] As with the Enoch texts, no names are given; we have to guess.

Just as it is a mistake to read the New Testament texts with twenty-first-century eyes, so too it is unwise to read the *Damascus Document* with the dating system that has been established by modern scholars of ancient history, which dates the destructions of the first temple in 597 and 586 BCE. The people who wrote the *Damascus Document* are more likely to have used the system of jubilees used for the (later) Talmudic calculations, or something similar. A table of these calculations in the *Jewish Encyclopaedia* reveals some startling dates.[42] Giving the equivalent dates for the modern calendar (rather than the originals which dated from the year of creation), the temple was destroyed in 422 BCE, rebuilt after seventy years in 352 BCE and destroyed by the Romans in 68–9 CE. Reading the *Damascus Document* in the light of these dates, 390 years after the destruction of the temple gives 32 BCE for the founding of the 'blind men groping for the way'; and twenty years after that, 12 BCE for the appearance of the Teacher.

---

[40] *Commentary on Habakkuk* 2.7–8, 1QpHab IX.
[41] The *Damascus Document* CD I.
[42] The article 'Sabbatical Year and Jubilee'.

The people of the *Damascus Document* called themselves 'the members of the new covenant' defined as 'the covenant with the fore-fathers'.[43] This suggests they were the people of the *renewed*, rather than the *new* covenant. If they withdrew to the desert in 32 BCE, this was a significant date. It was the year when Herod killed all the priests who had been scrutinizing Daniel's prophecy of the 490 years (Dan. 9.24–27). They decided that Herod could not be the promised Holy One, and they were perplexed, because, in earlier times of trouble, under Nebuchadnezzar and under Antiochus, there had been pro-phets to guide the people and tell them how long the troubles would last.[44] Herod was informed of their deliberations, and killed them all. Then there was an earthquake. Was this when the 'blind men grop-ing for the way' withdrew?

Many people were watching the calendar for a significant event. The prophecy of the seventy weeks of years in Daniel is one of the most obscure in the Old Testament. After 490 years, said Gabriel to Daniel, prophecies about his people and their holy city Jerusalem would be fulfilled: 'to finish the transgression, to put an end to sin, to atone for iniquity, to bring in everlasting righteousness, to seal both vision and prophet [this probably means to fulfil both the vision and the prophecy] and to anoint a most holy one' (Dan. 9.24). The prophecy was describing the restoration at the end of the age of wrath, the great day of atonement which required the great high priest. Reckoning 490 years from 422 BCE gives the date 68 CE, when the Jews began the war against Rome.

The *Melchizedek Text*[45] from Qumran has the same scheme, but instead of describing 490 years as seventy weeks of years, it has ten jubilees, that is, ten periods of 49 years. Only the last part of this text has survived, and so we do not know when the first jubilee began. The *Damascus Document* suggests it could have been reckoned from the start of the age of wrath, and if so, then the tenth jubilee of the scheme began about 20 CE. The Qumran text says that Melchizedek was expected to reappear during the first seven years of that tenth jubilee, that is, between 20 and 27 CE, and, as the great high priest, would officiate at the final day of atonement at the end of the tenth jubilee. The *Melchizedek Text* is full of quotations from the Old Testament, implying that Melchizedek was not only divine but also

---

[43] CD VI.
[44] Josephus, *War* 1.364–70 in the Slavonic version.
[45] 11Q 13.

the 'anointed one' prophesied by Daniel (Dan. 9.24). Melchizedek was also the anointed one of Isaiah 61, who would proclaim liberty to captives (Isa. 61.1). This was the text Jesus read at Nazareth and claimed to fulfil (Luke 4.21). In addition, Luke says that Jesus was 'about thirty years of age' when he began his ministry (Luke 3.23), and Matthew says that Jesus returned to Nazareth from Egypt after the death of Herod, which was in 4 BCE. This means that Jesus was a young boy in 4 BCE, and if he had been born in, say, 7 BCE, he would have been thirty in 23 CE, a date that falls in the crucial period 20–27 CE when Melchizedek was expected to appear.

Many people at the end of the second temple period considered that they were still in exile. The original prophecy of seventy years in exile (Jer. 25.8–14; 29.10–14) was reinterpreted as seventy weeks of years (Dan. 9.24), 'seventy times seven' to suit the new situation, and this longer exile was sometimes described as an era of wicked priests.[46] The *Testament of Levi*, a pre-Christian text preserved and expanded by Christian scribes, has Levi reading in the writings of Enoch – in a passage that is now lost – that his descendants would be wicked: 'For seventy weeks you shall wander away and profane the priesthood, and defile the sacrificial altars . . . Your holy places shall be razed to the ground' (*T. Levi* 14.1; 16.1, 4). Then a new priest would be raised up, whose star would shine brightly. The heavens would rejoice and the earth be glad (*T. Levi* 18.3, 5). Whether this passage is entirely Christian or based on an earlier text cannot be determined. What matters is that the new priest – clearly Jesus – is depicted as replacing the priests of the second temple as the era of wickedness draws to a close.

In the story of Tobias and the angel, set in the seventh century BCE but probably written in the second century BCE, the old man Tobit told his son what would happen in the future. The temple would be burned and ruined for a while. Then the exiles would return and rebuild it

> though it will not be like the former one, until the times of the age are completed. After this they will return from the places of their captivity, and will rebuild Jerusalem in splendour, and the house of God will be rebuilt there with a glorious building for all generations for ever, just as the prophets said of it. Then all the Gentiles will turn to fear the LORD God in truth. (Tobit 14.5–6)

---

[46] There are many 'long exile' texts. See M. A. Knibb, 'The Exile in the Literature of the Inter-Testamental Period', *Heythrop Journal* 17 (1976), 253–72.

Popular belief was that the second temple was temporary, destined to be replaced with a permanent temple to which the converted Gentiles would come. The temporary temple, the corrupted priesthood and the long exile were all part of the same problem.

The new temple would be built by the Messiah, or in the time of the Messiah. Memories persisted in the Jewish community well into the Christian era that the restored temple would be furnished with all that had been missing from the second temple: the fire, the ark, the menorah, the spirit and the cherubim.[47] In John's vision of heaven, he saw the original temple restored: the ark (Rev. 11.19), the seven-branched menorah (Rev. 1.12), the sevenfold spirit (Rev. 4.5) and the cherubim, the living creatures around the heavenly throne (Rev. 4.6).[48] The myrrh oil, kept in the holy of holies for anointing kings and high priests,[49] had been hidden away in the time of Josiah,[50] during the great changes in the temple. This too had to be restored for there to be an anointed one, a Messiah. No high priest of the second temple was anointed; the description of Joshua being made high priest in the second temple mentions only his vestments, but not his anointing (Zech. 3.1–5). Jesus, however, said he was fulfilling the words of Isaiah 61: 'The Spirit of the Lord God is upon me, because he has anointed me . . .' (Luke 4.21, quoting Isa. 61.1), and at his birth he was declared to be 'Christ the Lord', 'the Anointed One' (Luke 2.11). One of the wise men brought him a gift of myrrh oil.

Since about 700 BCE, when Hezekiah had paid tribute to the Assyrians, Jerusalem and Judah had not been independent, apart from the period 142–63 BCE. In 142 BCE 'Simon the great high priest and commander and leader of the Jews' (1 Macc. 13.42) had finally rid his people of their Syrian overlords, and in 63 BCE Pompey captured Jerusalem and entered the temple, the beginning of Roman rule. The period from Pompey to the final war of liberation from Rome was of great significance, because it was the end period of the 490 years, the era of wrath when Jerusalem was dominated by a corrupt priesthood and a defiled temple. The Christians knew and used a stylized

---

[47] *Numbers Rabbah* XV.10.
[48] Ezekiel said that the four creatures were the cherubim (Ezek. 10.20).
[49] Tosefta *Kippurim* 2.15: 'A bottle containing the manna, a flask of anointing oil, Aaron's rod and the chest sent by the Philistines, were all in the house of the most holy of holies.' Another tradition says the oil was kept on the shewbread table, gloss to Targum *Neofiti* Exod. 25.29–30.
[50] Babylonian Talmud *Horayoth* 12a.

account of these years, punctuated by the trumpets of the seven angels that marked the great events. Trumpets and sacred vessels from the holy of holies had been carried by the high priest when the armies of ancient Israel went out to holy war (Num. 31.6), and so seven high priests in white battle vestments, accompanied by seven Levites, carried trumpets in the final battle, according to the *War Scroll.*[51] These seven high priests were probably the 'seven ruling princes of the sanctuary . . . the angels of the King' described in the *Sabbath Songs.*[52]

The early Christians were familiar with this imagery of holy war. The seven angels with trumpets in the book of Revelation (Rev. 8.1— 11.18) mark events on earth as the time draws near for establishing the kingdom of the LORD and Christ (Rev. 11.15–18). What did the shepherds of Bethlehem understand by the title: 'A Saviour who is Christ the LORD' (Luke 2.11)? That this was the angel army coming to liberate their people – but with a message of peace on earth? What did Zechariah mean when he sang of being 'saved from enemies and from the hand of all who hate us' and, being 'delivered from the hand of our enemies, might serve him without fear' (Luke 1.71, 73)? The first trumpet in the book of Revelation marked Pompey taking Jerusalem, the second marked the battle of Actium in 31 BCE, when Mark Antony, who had given the kingdom of Judah to Herod, was defeated by Octavian, later known as the Emperor Augustus. The third trumpet marked the death of Herod in 4 BCE, the fourth his golden eagle that was torn down from the temple when he died, the fifth trumpet marked the army of locusts who ravaged for five months, the reign of Roman terror in 66 CE, and the sixth was the invasion of Palestine by the Roman governor of Syria in the autumn of 66 CE. This prompted the final battle for liberation from Rome. The mighty angel came from heaven, wrapped in a cloud and a rainbow, John was told to measure the temple – it was about to be destroyed – and then the seventh trumpet proclaimed the coming of the kingdom on earth.[53] The seven vessels from the sanctuary poured out the wrath of God on the doomed city of Jerusalem (Rev. 15.1—16.21), and the saints in heaven celebrated the triumph of the holy war and God's judgement on their enemy, the great harlot (Rev. 19.1–8).

---

[51] 1QM VII.
[52] e.g. 4Q 403.1.ii.
[53] For detail see my book *The Revelation of Jesus Christ*, Edinburgh: T&T Clark, 2000, pp. 169–79.

The era of wrath was represented by a harlot ruling in Jerusalem. She was the evil antitype of the Virgin Daughter of Zion, condemned in the sixth century BCE by Ezekiel: 'you played the harlot with the nations, and polluted yourself with their idols' (Ezek. 23.30). The last section of Isaiah also described the temple as a harlot because it had been built with foreign money and yet excluded as impure some of the ancient worshippers of the LORD. In a passage full of words with double meanings, such that their impact is lost in translation, Isaiah condemned the second temple: it was not a tabernacle, *miškan*, but a harlot's bed, *miškab* (Isa. 57.7). The cloud of glory signified the presence of the LORD on Sinai or in the holy of holies; 'The glory of the LORD appeared in the cloud' (Exod. 16.10; also 24.15; 34.5; 1 Kings 8.10–11; Ezek. 1.4), but in Hebrew cloud and sorcerer are written in the same way: '*nn*. Isaiah described the priests of the second temple not as sons of the bright *cloud* of the glory, but as sons of a *sorceress* (Isa. 57.3). Bitter wordplay like this was characteristic of prophetic and temple discourse.

John described the Jerusalem he knew not as the Virgin Daughter of Zion, but as a harlot, the mother of harlots and of the abominations of the earth (Rev. 17.5). The wordplay is lost in the present text of Revelation, but beneath the Greek was a Hebrew original, where the harlot was wordplay on *qdš*, which can mean both harlot and holy one, and abomination, *mšhyt*, was wordplay on anointed one, *mšyh*. Identical wordplay is found in the Qumran Isaiah scroll, where the Servant is described as 'anointed' *mšhty*, but the MT has disfigured, *mšht*.[54] The current Lady of Jerusalem, 'mother' of its people and representing the city and the temple, was a harlot, the mother of harlots and abominations. The true Lady of Jerusalem was a holy one, the mother of holy and anointed ones. In the Christmas story she is Mary.

Just as we should not reckon the date for the destruction of the first temple using only the methods of modern scholarship, so too, the 'background' to the period in which Jesus was born should not be drawn simply from the contemporary 'secular' writers, on the grounds that they are more likely to have been objective and to have recorded what really happened. Reality was in the eyes of those who witnessed events, and the ears of those who heard the story. Those expecting angels probably saw them; those listening for significant words heard them. The priests were reading the prophecies and counting the years and seeking to understand the mystery. Devout

---

[54] The Isaiah Scroll, 1Q Isa^a 52.14.

people were praying for angels to assist them in their struggle, not only against Rome, but also against the corrupted temple in Jerusalem, the harlot. Those who wrote the earliest Christmas stories were far closer in outlook to the visionaries and warriors of Qumran and to Christian prophets like John than to historians like Josephus. They were people waiting for Melchizedek the great high priest to return, and when they wrote the Christmas stories, they described the birth of their great high priest and they described his mother, the Virgin Daughter of Zion, the temple and city of Jerusalem.

2

Other voices

The Gospels of Matthew and Luke tell the Christmas story, but there were other voices. John and Paul both wrote about Jesus coming into the world, and the language they use shows how they imagined what happened, and what it meant. 'But when the time had fully come, God sent forth his Son, born of woman . . .' (Gal. 4.4), wrote Paul. What time? Mark used the same expression to describe the beginning of Jesus' ministry: 'The time is fulfilled, and the kingdom of God is at hand; repent and believe in the gospel' (Mark 1.15). The coming of Jesus was part of a plan. 'God sent forth his Son.' Sent forth from where? John said something similar, but he revealed its context. 'Do you say of him whom the Father consecrated and sent into the world, "You are blaspheming," because I said, "I am the son of God"?' (John 10.36).

In temple tradition, those consecrated and sent out into the world were the royal high priests who had been anointed in the holy of holies – representing heaven – and then emerged into the world. Psalm 89 shows the original setting: 'With my holy oil I have anointed him . . . He shall cry to me, "Thou art my Father" ' (Ps. 89.20, 26). This was the heavenly 'birth' of an already human king, but for Paul, the heavenly 'birth' preceded the human birth; the Son was sent into the world. Paul knew about the human birth of Jesus – 'born of woman' (Gal. 4.4) – and John clearly knew about the Virgin birth and assumed his readers would pick up the irony of his reference. In a debate about true descent from Abraham, some Jews said to Jesus, 'We were not born of fornication. We have one Father, even God' (John 8.41). Thomas, too, attributed a rueful saying to Jesus: 'He who knows the father and the mother will be called the son of a harlot'.[1]

The mysteries of the temple are now largely beyond recovery, and with them, the significance of much early Christian discourse and practice. We can be fairly sure, however, that the birth of Jesus was set within an established world view, and John shows that this was a

---

[1] *Gospel of Thomas* 105.

temple world view. The anointed/consecrated one was sent into the world as the incarnate Son of God.

The distinction between the two births was long emphasized. Augustine, who died in 430 CE, said this in a Christmas sermon:

> Our LORD Jesus Christ, the Son of Man as well as the Son of God, born of the Father without a Mother, created all days. By his birth from a Mother without a Father, he consecrated this day. In his divine birth he was invisible; in his human birth, visible; in both births, awe-inspiring. Hence it is difficult to determine which birth the prophet was speaking about when he prophesied concerning Him: 'Who shall declare his generation?' Was he speaking of the birth in which He, regarding whom it was never true that He was not yet born, has a co-eternal Father? Or of the birth in which He, born in time, has already made the Mother in whom he was made? Or of the birth in which He, who always was, was always born?[2]

Here are the problems facing anyone who tries to describe something that happened in both time and eternity. Augustine knew that the Second Person was the Creator, the traditional Christian understanding of the Old Testament. He knew that the Son of God did not 'originate' in Bethlehem, that the nativity was his incarnation, his coming into the material world. In the language of the temple, he came through the veil from the presence of God into the material world, and the only person who did this was, by definition, the high priest. How the two births related to each other has been lost, as we have seen. The confusion of Psalm 110.3 'in the day of thy power, in the beauties of holiness, from the womb of the morning: thou hast the dew of thy youth' (Ps. 110.3, AV) has in no way been illuminated by the technical terms such as adoptionism which scholars have coined to define what could and could not have been the lost mystery.

The earliest temple description of mingling divine and human is embedded in the prescriptions for the Day of Atonement, when the high priest entered the holy of holies and then emerged, sprinkling blood 'to cleanse and to hallow'. This imagery was immediately adopted by the Christians to explain the meaning of the death and resurrection of Jesus, and gave rise to the hope for his return from heaven. The high priest entered the holy of holies carrying the blood and then he emerged again to complete the renewal of the creation. Jesus' death was the sacrifice, and he entered heaven at his ascension.

---

[2] Augustine, *Sermon 13, Christmas Day.*

Luke hints at the high priestly context for this departure. Jesus blessed the disciples as he left them (Luke 24.50), and 'a cloud took him out of their sight' (Acts 1.9), like the incense cloud that surrounded the high priest as he entered the holy of holies. The two angels spoke to the disciples and said that Jesus would return in the same way. This was authentic early tradition. John knew that Jesus would come again with clouds (Rev. 1.7), and he saw him return: 'Afterwards, I saw a mighty angel coming down from heaven, wrapped in a cloud, with a rainbow over his head' (Rev. 10.1). The rainbow was the sign of the LORD.[3]

When Luke depicted a typical early sermon in Jerusalem, he had Peter describe recent events as fulfilling the Day of Atonement, showing that the early Church was waiting for her high priest to return.

> You denied the Holy and Righteous One . . . and killed the Author of life . . . But what God foretold by the mouth of all the prophets, that his Christ should suffer, he thus fulfilled. Repent therefore, and turn again, that your sins may be blotted out, that times of refreshing may come from the presence of the LORD, and that he may send the Christ appointed for you, Jesus, whom heaven must receive until the time for establishing all that God spoke by the mouth of his holy prophets from of old. (Acts 3.14–15, 18–21)

This imagery shaped much of the later reflection on the meaning of Jesus' death and the Eucharist,[4] and, as we shall see, the way the Christmas story was told.

The high priest represented the LORD. On the Day of Atonement, when he prepared to remove the effects of sin by purifying the temple that represented creation, he had to sacrifice a bull and a goat and to collect their blood which represented their life. The bull was a sacrifice for himself and his family (Lev. 11.16), and the goat was 'for the LORD'. In each case the animal whose blood/life was used to make atonement represented the agent of atonement. Other texts show what all this meant. Two identical goats were chosen, and it was decided by lot which goat should be sacrificed and which sent into the desert as the scapegoat. It seems that the two lots bore the names 'the LORD' and 'Azazel',[5] and that these markers were actually put on each animal. One goat wore the Name.[6] The goat for sacrifice was

---

[3] See my book *The Revelation of Jesus Christ*, Edinburgh: T&T Clark, 2000, pp. 180–99.
[4] See my book *The Great High Priest*, London: T&T Clark, 2003.
[5] The chief of the fallen angels.
[6] Mishnah *Yoma* 4.1.

not 'for the LORD', as usually translated, but 'as the LORD' (Lev. 16.8), a perfectly normal way to read the Hebrew, and how it was understood by Origen.[7] One goat represented the LORD, the other, destined to be banished into the desert, represented Azazel. Before the bull was sacrificed, the high priest placed both his hands on it, indicating, it is thought, that this animal's blood/life was a substitute for his own.[8] Similarly, the blood of the goat *represented* the life of the LORD. After the blood of each animal had been offered separately in the holy of holies, the high priest had to mix them before he could complete the sprinkling that cleansed and healed the creation. 'He emptied the blood of the bull into the blood of the goat and then poured the full into the empty vessel.' He symbolically mingled his own life – the bull's blood – with the life of the LORD – the goat's blood. The order of the pouring shows that the human became divine – the bull into the goat; and then the mingled 'lives' became the high priest – the bloods were poured into the vessel for the bull. Mingled, divine and human, the bloods were sprinkled on the golden altar within the temple and on the great altar outside. This completed the atonement, that is, the restoration of creation. It ritualized the mingling of divine and human. The human did not become divine nor the divine human; both were mingled.

Day of Atonement imagery shaped the accounts of Jesus' death and resurrection. Interpretation was inseparable from the story, and the fulfilment of prophecies and rituals gave significance to the story for those who had witnessed the events and reflected upon them. Hebrews 9.11–14 shows clearly that the death of Jesus was understood as the Day of Atonement sacrifice, and interpreted accordingly. This generation also reflected on the birth of Jesus, originally a story of unusual happenings when the child was born. As Luke said of Mary, they kept all these things and pondered them in their hearts (Luke 2.19). When they told the story of Jesus' birth, they did so in the same way as they told the story of his death, *but using another aspect of the high priestly tradition*: 'The Word became flesh and dwelt among us, full of grace and truth; we have beheld his glory, glory as of the only Son from the Father' (John 1.14) is how John told the Christmas story. 'Dwelt' is, literally, 'tabernacled', indicating immediately that this is a temple scene. As of old, so with the incarnation, the glory came to

---

[7] Origen, *Celsus* 6.43.
[8] Mishnah *Yoma* 3.8; 4.2; 5.4.

the tabernacle with the presence of the LORD, and then emerged into 'the world'. Beholding the glory was the greatest blessing the high priesthood could give to Israel: 'May the LORD make his face/presence[9] shine upon you and be gracious to you: May the LORD lift up his face/presence upon you and give you peace' (Num. 6.25–26, my translation). The birth of Jesus was about beholding the glory, seeing the presence. 'The glory' is the key term here; it leads into a complex web of associations that join together the high priesthood and the temple, Adam and Eve and the lost garden of Eden, and the birth of Jesus.

The Enoch books show something of the high priestly tradition at the end of the second temple period. A man who entered the holy of holies and ascended to stand before the throne of God was taken from his earthly garments – representing his human body – and clothed with 'the garments of the glory of the LORD'. Then he was anointed with myrrh oil 'like dew' – the symbol of resurrection – and transformed into 'one of his glorious ones' (*2 En.* 22). This was one aspect of the mysteries of the holy of holies, how 'Enoch' became the angel high priest, clothed in the glory of the LORD (*2 En.* 22). Such mystical experiences cannot be defined in terms acceptable to philosophers or to literalists who claim to be fundamentalists. They are, however, fundamental to any reading of the New Testament. The memory of this ritual for clothing the high priest persisted: the *Exodus Rabbah*, the great Jewish commentary compiled in the Middle Ages, knew that the garments of the high priest had been the garments of God,[10] and the *Zohar*, an anthology of Jewish mystical lore, remembered that the garments had been called 'the residual garments' because they were 'emanations of supernal mysteries, made after the supernal pattern'.[11] The garments were part of the mystery of the glory. This is why John described the LORD's coming into the world as the coming of the glorious high priest: the LORD, Son of God, consecrated and sent into the world (John 10.36), the glory made visible: 'We have beheld his glory, glory as of the only Son from the Father (John 1.14). The incarnation was the birth and appearance of the great high priest, and for the people of Israel, the realization of the blessing they had long prayed for; the shining of the face and presence of the LORD.

---

[9] The same word in Hebrew, *panim*.
[10] *Exodus Rabbah* xxxviii.8.
[11] *Zohar, Exodus* 229b.

Adam

The first figure to wear the glory was Adam, set as high priest in the garden of Eden. Little of this is now in the Old Testament, but the first Christians knew and used many more stories about Adam, Eve and Eden than are obviously in the Old Testament. They knew the hidden meanings in some of the Eden texts, and may well have known a version of Genesis slightly but significantly different from ours. One, thought to be the scroll formerly kept in the temple as the master copy, said that the LORD had made for Adam and Eve garments of light, presumably before he had made the garments of skin.[12] Temple words were used to describe Adam's role in Eden. When he was put into the garden, he had 'to till it and keep it' (Gen. 2.15), but both these words have a double meaning. They could also mean 'serve' a liturgy in the temple, and 'preserve', perhaps the tradition or the temple.

Other stories known in the first century CE show that the first Christians could have understood the text that way. Adam as the high priest clothed in glory is found in several texts. A broken fragment from Qumran says: '[Adam] our father, you created in the image of your glory . . . you breathed into his nostrils, and with understanding and knowledge . . . '.[13] The aspiration of the Damascus covenant community was to live for ever and be restored to 'all the glory of Adam'.[14] They had returned to the covenant, to the ways of truth, and to all the things in which Israel had gone astray, and so they hoped to be restored to their lost state. Later Jewish Targums remembered Adam's glory: 'The LORD God made clothes of glory for Adam and his wife';[15] 'At first they had had coats of light . . . after their sins they had only coats of skin.'[16] In Christian tradition, Ephrem the Syrian, who died in 373 CE, said that 'God clothed Adam with glory', and Adam knew he was naked only when he had lost his garment of glory through disobedience.[17]

---

[12] Rabbi Meir's scroll, mentioned in *Genesis Rabbah* xx.12. The Hebrew for light, *'r*, is very similar to the Hebrew for skin, *'r*. Before they had garments of skin, Genesis 3.21, they had had garments of light. See J. P. Siegel, *The Severus Scroll*, Missoula: SBL, 1975.

[13] 4Q 504.

[14] CD III.

[15] Both Babylonian and Palestinian traditions knew this: Targum Onkelos and Targum Neophiti to Gen. 3.21.

[16] *Zohar Genesis* 36b.

[17] St Ephrem, *Commentary on Genesis* 2.

Eden as the temple was also widely assumed. Solomon's temple had been decorated with golden cherubim, palm trees and flowers (1 Kings 6.29–32). There was even a serpent, which Hezekiah removed (2 Kings 18.4). In the *Book of Jubilees*, parts of which were found at Qumran, Adam was created and then (later) set in the garden (Gen. 2.7–8). This was because the Creator observed the temple purity laws (Lev. 12.1–6), which in *Jubilees* applied to the child as well as to the mother. Adam was unclean for forty days after being created, and then the angels took him to Eden to work and to keep it, as in Genesis 2.15. Eve, who observed the purity laws for a female child, was set in the garden after eighty days. Only after observing the purity laws could the couple enter 'the sanctuary . . . the garden of Eden, because it is more holy than any land' (*Jub.* 3.10, 12). When they left the garden (*Jub.* 3.27), Adam burned the incense of the sanctuary – frankincense, galbanum, stacte and other sweet spices as specified in Exodus 30.34ff. Now this blend of incense could only be used in the temple; anyone using it privately was 'cut off' from his people (Exod. 30.35).

Another text known in the time of Jesus was the *Life of Adam and Eve*, which gives more detail about their expulsion from Eden. In the garden, Adam and Eve had eaten the food of angels.[18] When Adam was created as the image of God, that is, as Yahweh, all the angels were commanded to worship him: 'Worship the image of the LORD God, as the LORD God has instructed.' This was worship in the heavenly temple, with the angel priests worshipping the Image of God. Only Satan refused to worship, on the grounds that he was older, created before the Image and therefore should receive his homage. Because he refused to worship the Image, he was thrown from heaven and vowed revenge.[19] The account of Jesus' temptations in the desert assumes that readers know this story: Jesus could rule the world if he would worship the devil [and thus the devil would be worshipped at last and have his revenge] (Luke 4.5–7).[20] Hebrews, too, recalls this story: 'When he brings the firstborn into the world, he says, "Let all God's angels worship him"' (Heb. 1.6).[21] There is a

---

[18] *Life of Adam and Eve* 4.2.

[19] *Life of Adam and Eve* 14.1–3. This story underlies Zechariah 3.1, where Satan opposes the new Image, that is, the new high priest.

[20] A fragment from Qumran is similar; the spirits/angels were created to serve Adam, 4Q 381.

[21] This story is also in the Qur'an 7.11: 'We bade the angels bow down to Adam, and they bowed down; not so Iblis, he refused to be of those who bow down . . .'.

dark parody of the story when John describes the reign of the beast. The second beast, the agent of the first beast, deceived those on the earth with an image of the beast that could breathe and speak. All those who would not worship the image of the beast were killed' (Rev. 13.11–15).

Adam and Eve leaving Eden became a description of the older high priesthood leaving the first temple in the seventh century BCE, when Josiah purged it and drove out many priests. The later prophecies in Isaiah show how the older priesthood longed for the day when they could return to their holy place and be recognized again. The LORD would grant to all mourning in Zion the oil of gladness and the mantle of praise, and the ancient ruins [the true temple] would be rebuilt. 'You shall be called the priests of the LORD, men shall speak of you as the ministers of our God . . . I will make an everlasting covenant with them' (Isa. 61.6, 8). This was the section of Isaiah that Jesus read at Nazareth. We do not know how much of the chapter he read, but he did claim to be fulfilling the prophecy. This meant restoring the ousted priesthood and opening Eden. The risen LORD told the Christians at Ephesus: 'To him who conquers I will grant to eat [again] of the tree of life, which is in the Paradise of God' (Rev. 2.7, also 22.14). This was another example of history repeating itself; the expulsions in the seventh century BCE just before the destruction of the first temple were recalled in the events that preceded the destruction of the temple in 70 CE.

Paul described Jesus as the second Adam, and this is the best-known Adam imagery in the New Testament. The original Adam was 'the type of the one who was to come' (Rom. 5.14). He was from the dust, the second Adam was from heaven (1 Cor. 15.47). Philo had understood the two creation stories in this way: Genesis 1.26 described the heavenly Adam,[22] made in the image and after the likeness of God; Genesis 2.7 described the man formed from dust. 'There are two types of men; the one a heavenly man, the other an earthly.'[23] Paul, then, was drawing on contemporary Adam traditions in his exposition of Christianity. The allusions elsewhere in the New Testament – returning to Eden, the rebellion of Satan – show that Adam stories not in the Old Testament were also used in the early Church. Eden imagery became church imagery. The *Book of the Cave of Treasures* is an anthology of lore and legend from the Syriac-speaking church, attributed

---

[22] The Hebrew here has 'Adam'.
[23] Philo, *Allegorical Interpretation* I.31.

to Ephrem in the fourth century, but probably not quite so old. In it we find: 'Eden is the Holy Church, and the Paradise which was in it is the land of rest and the inheritance of life which God hath prepared for all the holy children of men. And because Adam was priest and king and prophet, God brought him into Paradise that he might minister in Eden, the Holy Church.'[24]

Luke described Adam as the son of God (Luke 3.38) immediately after his account of Jesus' baptism, when the voice from heaven said: 'Thou art my beloved Son' (Luke 3.22). He must have had this connection in mind. Irenaeus too, when outlining his version of 'history repeating itself',[25] saw similarities between Jesus and Adam. Adam created 'from the Will and the Wisdom of God, and from the virgin earth' was his interpretation of Genesis 2.7. 'So then the LORD . . . took the same way of entering the flesh, being born from the Virgin by the Will and the Wisdom of God.'[26] He went on to contrast the disobedience of Eve and the obedience of Mary, the tree of knowledge that brought disaster and the tree of the cross that brought life. Here, the birth of Jesus was understood as the beginning of the new creation, and Adam was son of God in the sense that he had no human parents. Exactly the same was said of Melchizedek: 'He is without father or mother or genealogy, and has neither beginning of days nor end of life, but resembling the Son of God he continues a priest for ever' (Heb. 7.3). Jesus was described in Hebrews as Melchizedek (Heb. 7.15–28). Some enigmatic words of the *Gospel of Philip* may show how Jesus' conception was envisaged.[27] 'Adam came into being from two virgins, from the spirit and from the virgin earth. Christ therefore was born from a virgin to rectify the fall which occurred in the beginning.'[28]

The Lady

John did describe the birth of the Son of God, but he did not tell the story of Bethlehem. For him it was a great temple vision (Rev. 11.19—12.6). He saw the temple in heaven open, and he saw the ark returned to its place in the holy of holies. This meant he was seeing a vision of the true temple restored, since the ark was one of the five

---

[24] *Cave of Treasures* Book 1.
[25] Usually called 'recapitulation'.
[26] *Proof of the Apostolic Preaching* 32.
[27] *The Gospel of Philip* was originally thought to be an early Gnostic text, but the boundaries between 'mainstream' Christianity and the various heresies were drawn much later.
[28] *Gospel of Philip*, CGII.3.71.

things that would return with the Messiah.[29] Then he saw a great sign: a regal woman clothed with the sun and crowned with stars. She gave birth to a son who was snatched up to the throne of God. The child was to fulfil the prophecies of Psalm 2: he would rule the nations with a rod of iron (and we assume, be the LORD's anointed, set in Zion as the divinely begotten Son). John saw the conflict in heaven, when Michael drove out the devil – the story in *The Life of Adam and Eve*. The woman's child must have been the Image, the Firstborn, whom the devil refused to worship, an identification so important for the Christians that their proof text, Deuteronomy 32.43, did not survive in its original form. Hebrews 1.6 had it as a key verse to identify Jesus – 'When he brings the Firstborn into the world he says, "Let all God's angels worship him"' – but the complete verse only survived in the Christian Greek Old Testament. The original Hebrew was lost until that fragment of Deuteronomy was found at Qumran.[30]

John's vision implies that Jesus had a heavenly Mother as well as a heavenly Father, and there is plenty of material to suggest that the first Christians thought in this way. If John the Baptist was believed to be an angel on earth, simultaneously a human and a heavenly being,[31] could this have applied to Mary also? Did the early Christians, reflecting on the events of Jesus' birth, conclude that Mary must have had a heavenly counterpart? If not, then who was the woman in John's vision giving birth to the Son of God? Some sayings attributed to Jesus are ambiguous, for example the saying in the *Gospel of Thomas*: 'He who knows the father and the mother will be called the son of a harlot.[32] Others are quite clear: according to the *Gospel of the Hebrews*, quoted by Origen and by Jerome, Jesus called the Holy Spirit his Mother, presumably his heavenly mother. Jesus had an experience of being lifted up – presumably similar to his experience in the desert when the devil took him up and showed him all the kingdoms of the world (Luke 4.5) – and being carried to Mount Tabor. 'Even now did my Mother the Holy Spirit take me by one of my hairs and carried me away to Mount Tabor.'[33] It was the Holy Spirit who spoke at the baptism, and in fact the canonical Gospel accounts do not say whose

---

[29] See above, p. 27.
[30] 4QDeut^q, see M. Abegg, P. Flint and E. Ulraich, *The Dead Sea Scrolls Bible*, Edinburgh: T&T Clark, 1999, p. 193.
[31] See above, p. 13.
[32] *Gospel of Thomas* 105.
[33] Quoted by Origen in his *Commentary on John* ii.12, and in *Homily 15 On Jeremiah*; and by St Jerome in his commentary *On Ezekiel* 16.13.

voice it was. We assume it was the voice of the Father, but some early Christians thought otherwise. Jerome said, in his commentary on Isaiah 11.2: 'In the [*Gospel of the Hebrews*] I find this written: "And it came to pass when the LORD was come up out of the water, the whole fount of the Holy Spirit descended and rested upon him and said to him, 'My son, in all the prophets I was waiting for thee that thou shouldst come and I might rest in thee. For thou art my rest, thou art my first begotten son, that reignest for ever.'[34]

The Spirit as Mother is perfectly understandable among the Hebrews, because the word 'spirit' in Hebrew is a feminine noun, and if it was 'Hebrews' who first reflected on the events of Jesus' birth, this is something they would not have questioned. They could not think or speak any other way. It raised questions in their minds about the manner of the incarnation, which some were treating in the same way as the stories of the Greek gods and their human mistresses. The *Gospel of Philip* asks the obvious question for one thinking of the Holy Spirit as feminine: 'Some said. "Mary conceived by the Holy Spirit." They are in error. They do not know what they are saying. When did a woman ever conceive by a woman?'[35] What, then, might Luke have intended when he attributed those words to Gabriel? 'The Holy Spirit will come upon you, and the power of the Most High will overshadow you' (Luke 1.35). And who was the woman clothed with the sun in John's vision? She appeared when the ark was seen, so she was in the holy of holies (Rev. 11.19—12.1), she was a Queen with crown of stars, and she was the Mother of the Messiah.

Despite the way the Old Testament has usually been read, there was a Lady in the ancient tradition. She appears with names such as the Virgin or the Daughter of Zion. The Lady is found in Isaiah, especially in the second part of the book, where she and the mysterious male figure, the Servant, are the main characters in the prophecies. We are familiar with the Servant passages and the way they were taken up as prophecies of Jesus, but few take any notice of the equally important female figure who also appears in the New Testament. Some examples: in the eighth century BCE, Isaiah wrote of the Daughter of Zion, and this is usually read as no more than a figure of speech, a poetic way of describing Jerusalem: 'the mount of the daughter of Zion, the hill of Jerusalem' (Isa. 10.32; also 16.1 and Mic. 4.8).

---

[34] Quoted in M. R. James, *The Apocryphal New Testament*, Oxford: Clarendon Press, (1924) 1980, p. 5.

[35] *Gospel of Philip*, CG II.3.55.

The virgin daughter of Zion speaks in anger and contempt to the Assyrian king who was preparing to attack her: 'She despises you, she scorns you, the virgin daughter of Zion' (Isa. 37.22). Later she appears as the abandoned city who is about to be restored: 'Awake, awake, put on your strength, O Zion, put on your beautiful garments, O Jerusalem, the holy city . . . Shake yourself from the dust . . . O captive daughter of Zion' (Isa. 52.1). She would be decked with precious stones (Isa. 54.11–12), and would eventually give birth to a son without labour pains (Isa. 66.7). All this could simply describe Jerusalem, but other passages have similar expressions about the LORD. Can 'the mount of the daughter of Zion' be understood differently from 'the hill of the LORD' (Ps. 24.3)? *Zion was the name of the city, but so was 'Yahweh'.* The female figure was as 'real' as the LORD. The last verse of Ezekiel describes the new city and says – despite the English translations – 'Its name shall be the LORD' (Ezek. 48.35). The early Christians read the text this way. Jesus said in the letter to the church at Philadelphia: 'I will write on him the name of my God [i.e. Yahweh], and the name of the city of my God, the new Jerusalem . . . and my own new name' (Rev. 3.12).

Micah, who prophesied in the eighth century BCE at the same time as Isaiah, also knew the Lady. The daughter of Zion, like a woman in labour, would go out of her city into the open country, but the LORD would rescue her. She gasped for breath in the face of murderers (Jer. 4.31). The power and the kingdom would return to her (Mic. 4.8–10). After her labour, she would give birth to the great Shepherd of Israel (Mic. 5.2–4). This is the obvious context for Isaiah's oracle about Immanuel: 'Behold, *the* Virgin shall conceive and bear a son and call his name Immanuel' (Isa. 7.14). The Hebrew has 'the' and the Greek has 'the', Matthew quotes '*the* Virgin' (Matt. 1.23) but the English versions, for some reason, make her an indeterminate figure '*a* virgin shall conceive'. This was the Lady. Presumably this was the context for Zephaniah, another contemporary of Isaiah, calling on the daughter of Zion to rejoice because the King of Israel, the LORD, was within her (Zeph. 3.14–15). Zechariah, too, when the exiles returned from Babylon in the late sixth century, called on the daughter of Zion to sing and rejoice, ' "For lo, I come and I will dwell in the midst of you", says the LORD' (Zech. 2.10). The Lady was the Mother of the LORD.

How they understood the Lady as the city is alien to our ways of thinking, but when we read about the birth of Jesus, we are reading a story told by people who still thought in this way. When Jerusalem was destroyed in 70 CE 'Ezra', writing as though history was repeating itself, had a vision of a weeping woman. Her son, for whom she had waited thirty childless years, had died on his wedding night. 'Ezra' rebuked her for her selfishness; 'Zion the mother of us all' was greatly distressed (2 Esdr. 10.7),[36] so how could this woman think only about her own tragedy? Then the woman was transfigured before him: 'her face suddenly shone exceedingly, and her countenance flashed like lightning' (2 Esdr. 10.25). Ezra no longer saw a woman but a huge city, and he asked the archangel Uriel about the vision: 'This woman whom you saw . . . is Zion.' The archangel explained that her thirty childless years had been the 3,000 years before Solomon built the city and made offerings there, that is, built the temple. 'Then it was that the barren woman bore a son' (2 Esdr. 10.46). *The Lady of Zion's son was born in the temple*, and the destruction of the city and the temple was his death on his wedding night. The Christians interpreted the destruction of the temple differently, since they regarded the second temple as a harlot, and it was only after her destruction that the Lamb could marry his Bride (Rev. 19.1–9).

Here is another situation alien to our ways of thinking. The Lady was both the Mother and the Bride of the Lamb. Isaiah had known this. When Zion was restored and no longer desolate, when her name was changed to Hephzibah, meaning 'My delight is in her', then 'As a young man marries a virgin, so shall your sons marry you' (Isa. 62.5).[37] The lost Lady and her son/consort appear in many places in the New Testament: in the book of Revelation, as we have seen, but also in the prophecy linked to Palm Sunday: 'Rejoice greatly, O daughter of Zion! Shout aloud, O daughter of Jerusalem! Lo, your king comes to you' (Zech. 9.9, quoted in Matt. 21.5 and John 12.15). John adds at this point: 'His disciples did not understand this at first, but when Jesus was glorified, they remembered that this had been written of him and had been done to him.' Looking back on the life, death and resurrection of Jesus, they had reflected and seen significance in many things. Jesus had spoken 'in figures' (John 16.25), and only later did the disciples come to understand what had been happening. The Christmas stories were told in this way too, and we shall see how Mary, Mother of the Messiah, was depicted as the lost Lady, just as John the Baptist had been both a man and an angel.

---

[36] 2 Esdras is a Jewish text from about 100 CE that has been reworked and preserved by Christians.

[37] Sometimes this is translated 'builders'. The words look the same in Hebrew.

As late as the sixth century CE, a Jewish apocalypse about rebuilding the temple was written and attributed to Zerubbabel – again history repeating itself, since Zerubbabel had built the second temple. The *Book of Zerubbabel* has, as one of its key figures, the Mother of the Messiah who would do battle with two evil kings and restore her city. Her name was Hephzibah, the name Isaiah had given to the restored city: 'My delight is in her'.[38] The mother and the city were interwoven images.

The hidden descent

Another cluster of images depicted the descent of the Son into the world, often described as the hidden or secret descent. Both the conception and the actual birth were mysteries, and no attempt was made to explain them. Even the angels did not know about them or understand. The unexpected descent of the Word from heaven was part of the plan to overcome evil and especially magic, the work of the evil angels. This was not a Christian innovation. The Wisdom of Solomon[39] described the Exodus in the same way. In the silence at midnight, 'thy all-powerful Word leaped from heaven, from the royal throne, into the midst of the land that was doomed, a stern warrior carrying the sharp sword of thy authentic command' (Wisd. 18.15). This image of the unexpected descent of the warrior Word was used by the Church to describe the return of the LORD, who would be greeted by his watching army of the faithful, clad in breastplates of faith and love, and helmets of hope (1 Thess. 5.1–11). The unexpected appearance of the Word, however, was also a theme in the nativity story.

The most familiar reference to the descent of the Word is in the Nicene Creed: 'Who for us men and for our salvation, came down from heaven', but the earliest detailed description of the descent is found in the *Ascension of Isaiah*, a collection of pre-Christian Jewish material about the prophet. It is impossible to know exactly how much of the present text is Christian addition, but an allusion to

---

[38] See M. Himmelfarb, 'Sefer Zerubbabel', in *Jewish Fantasies*, ed. D. Stern and M. J. Mirsky, New Haven and London: Yale University Press, 1990, pp. 67–90.

[39] *The Wisdom of Solomon* was probably written in the Jewish community in Egypt in the first century BCE. Nobody can be sure of the origin of this and many other texts. In the Muratorian Canon, a list of books recognized by the Church in Rome in the late second century CE, the Wisdom of Solomon is included in the New Testament.

Nero – 'the king of this world and murderer of his mother'[40] – suggests a date in the early 60s CE.[41] For our purposes, this text is important because it shows how some of those who read, and even wrote, the Christmas stories were picturing the birth of Jesus. First, they were thinking in terms of history repeating itself. The *Ascension of Isaiah* tells a story set in the eighth century BCE, predicting events in the seventh century BCE. In fact, it is a thinly veiled account of the early years of the Church in Palestine. The 'Isaiah' who ascended to heaven and reported his visions was probably James, the first bishop of Jerusalem and a relative of Jesus. The *Infancy Gospel of James* is attributed to him.[42] He and many other Christians left Jerusalem during the persecution led by Saul (Acts 9.1), and took refuge in the desert. Eventually James, like Isaiah, was killed by the wicked ruler in Jerusalem, 'Manasseh'. The reason was that 'Isaiah' claimed that he had seen the LORD, something that Moses said was impossible.[43] Hence, perhaps, John's emphasis on the Christian claim: 'We have beheld his glory' (John 1.14), and his saying that in Isaiah's vision of the glory of the LORD the prophet had seen Jesus (John 12.37–41).

The second vision recounted by 'Isaiah' tells how he ascended through the ranks of angels in the six heavens until he stood in the seventh, where he saw Enoch and all the righteous ones standing like the angels in their robes of glory. What follows is not clear, possibly because the picture differs from later Christian teaching. It seems that 'Isaiah' and the angels worship the LORD and the Holy Spirit, and then they all worship the Great Glory.[44] Then he heard God Most High say to 'My LORD Christ who will be called Jesus', 'Go out and descend through all the heavens . . . And you shall make your likeness like that of all who are in the five heavens . . . And none of that world shall know that you are the LORD with me of the seven heavens and of their angels.'[45] The descending LORD did not conceal himself in the sixth heaven, and there the angels praised him. In the other heavens,

---

[40] *Ascension of Isaiah* 4.2–3.

[41] Nero murdered his mother in 59 CE and instigated the great persecution of the Christians in Rome in 65 CE.

[42] See below, p. 128.

[43] See my book *The Revelation of Jesus Christ*, Edinburgh: T&T Clark, 2000, pp. 193–4.

[44] *Ascension of Isaiah* 9.27–42. This is 'subordinationism' – the Second and Third Persons of the Trinity being of lower rank that the First Person – and was later excluded from Christian belief as set out in the Athanasian Creed: Unity in Trinity and Trinity in Unity, co-eternal and co-equal.

[45] *Ascension of Isaiah* 10.7–16.

none recognized him, and so none praised him. He took the form of an angel with the angels, and took the form of a man on earth, implying, as is also implied in Hebrews 1.5, that the Son was more than an angel. He had to change his form in order to resemble the angels, and then 'take the form of a Servant, being born in the likeness of men . . . found in human form' (Phil. 2.7–8). More extreme versions of this position were later known as 'docetism' that Jesus only *seemed* to be a man.

'Isaiah' saw a scene in Bethlehem, with Mary, a virgin of the family of David, and Joseph, a carpenter. 'And when she was betrothed, she was found to be pregnant, and Joseph wished to divorce her.'[46] Then the angel of the Spirit appeared in the world and spoke to Joseph, who then stayed with Mary. Two months later, when Mary and Joseph were alone, Mary saw a baby, apparently in a vision. Curiously, there is no description of the birth, as there is in Luke, with the swaddling bands and the manger cradle. Joseph apparently did not see the baby, but when his eyes had been opened, he too saw the child and praised the LORD because he [the LORD] had come to him. There was a voice that said: 'Do not tell this vision to anyone.'[47] News of the miraculous child spread, however, a child born without pain. Everyone knew about the child but 'they were blinded concerning him' and did not recognize where he had come from. The family then moved to Nazareth, where the baby Jesus suckled like a normal infant, again so that nobody would recognize him.

The 'hidden Messiah' was well known to Jews in the first century CE. When 'Ezra' asked the archangel Uriel to explain a vision he had received of a man rising from the sea, he was told: 'This is he whom the Most High has been keeping for many ages, who will himself deliver the creation' (2 Esdr. 13.26). When certain signs had been observed – not unlike the sequence in the synoptic Gospels (for example Mark 13) – then the Son of the Most High would be revealed. John, too, wrote about the descending Messiah and his unknown origin: the crowd in Jerusalem were perplexed because they knew where Jesus came from, 'and when the Christ appears, no one will know where he comes from' (John 7.27). Others said Jesus could not be the Messiah because he did not come from Bethlehem (John 7.40–43). John had Jesus say: 'No one has ascended into heaven but

---

[46] *Ascension of Isaiah* 11.3.
[47] *Ascension of Isaiah* 11.12.

he who descended from heaven' (John 3.13). John the Baptist said: 'He who comes from heaven is above all. He bears witness to what he has seen and heard' (John 3.31–32).

At about the same time as the *Ascension of Isaiah* was being expanded with Christian material, Ignatius, bishop of Antioch, described the coming of the LORD with the same image of descent in secrecy and silence to escape the notice of the hostile powers.

> Mary's virginity was hidden from the prince of this world; so was her childbearing, and so was the death of the LORD. All these mysteries, about to be loudly proclaimed, happened in the deep silence of God. How were they made known in the world? High in the heavens a star shone out, brighter than all the rest. Words could not describe its brilliance. It was so strange that men were bewildered. Everywhere magic crumbled away before it, all the spells of witchcraft were broken, and superstition was dealt the fatal blow. The ancient empire of evil was destroyed, because God was now appearing in human form to bring a new order – eternal life. Now everything that had been perfectly prepared in the counsel of God began, and all creation was in turmoil at this plan for the complete destruction of death.[48]

These words of Ignatius are very like those of Paul, and give a context for what he was explaining to the Corinthians: 'But we impart a secret and hidden Wisdom of God, which God decreed before the ages for our glorification. None of the rulers of this age understood this, or they would not have crucified the LORD of Glory' (1 Cor. 2.7–8). Paul went on to allude to Isaiah: 'From of old no one has heard or perceived by the ear, no eye has seen a God besides thee, who works for those who wait for him' (Isa. 64.4). The context of Isaiah's assurance was the LORD *coming down* from heaven: 'O that thou wouldst rend the heavens and come down' (Isa. 64.1). The great mystery was not the 'wisdom of this age or of the rulers of this age who are doomed to pass away' (1 Cor. 2.6) but concerned the descent of the LORD and the incarnation. Despite this warning from Paul, future generations did try to clarify the mystery of the holy of holies and define the descent and incarnation.

The *Epistle of the Apostles*[49] is a text that has survived only in Coptic and Ethiopic,[50] and is accepted as representing mainstream Christian

---

[48] Ignatius, *Letter to the Ephesians* 19.
[49] English version in M. R. James, *The Apocryphal New Testament*, Oxford: Clarendon Press, (1924) 1980.
[50] There is single leaf of a fifth-century Latin manuscript also.

thinking in the mid-second century.[51] It was written as a warning against the Gnostics, and begins: 'Cerinthus and Simon . . . are enemies of our LORD Jesus Christ, for they pervert the word and the truth.' It tells how the risen LORD appeared to his disciples in Galilee, and explained to them about his origin, about his descent through the ranks of angels, robed in the wisdom and power of God, and becoming an angel when among the angels. He then explained what happened at the annunciation; the angel was the LORD himself, but in the form of Gabriel:

> On that day whereon I took the form of the angel Gabriel, I appeared unto Mary and spake with her. Her heart accepted me and she believed, and I formed myself and entered into her body. I became flesh, for I alone was my own messenger in that which concerned Mary, in the appearance of the shape of an angel.[52]

Towards the end of the second century, Irenaeus, who saw himself as the guardian of true teaching in the face of the threats from Gnosticism, wrote a summary of Christian belief: the *Proof of the Apostolic Preaching*. He too accepted the hidden descent as fundamental belief.

> But because the LORD descended invisible to created things, he was not made known in his descent to them. Because the Word was made flesh he was visible in his ascent, and when the powers saw him, the angels below cried out to those on the firmament, 'Lift up your heads, ye gates, and be ye lift up ye everlasting doors, that the King of Glory may come in . . .' (Ps. 24.7)[53]

And in the enigmatic Sibylline oracles, in this case a Jewish text with Christian additions from mid-third-century Egypt, we read: 'But whenever a bright star most like the sun shines forth from heaven in midday, then indeed the secret Word of the Most High will come, wearing flesh like mortals.'[54]

The *Gospel of Philip* too:

> Jesus took them all by stealth, for he did not reveal himself in the manner in which he was, but it was in the manner in which they would be able to see him that he revealed himself. He revealed himself to them all. He revealed himself to the great as great. He revealed him-

---

[51] There would be 120 years from Easter to the return of the Lord, *Epistle of the Apostles* 17.
[52] *Epistle of the Apostles* 13–14.
[53] *Proof of the Apostolic Preaching* 84.
[54] *Sibylline Oracles* 12.32, text in OTP 1.

self to the small as small, he revealed himself to the angels as an angel and to men as a man. Because of this, his word hid itself from everyone. Some indeed saw him thinking they were seeing themselves, but when he appeared to his disciples in glory on the mount he was not small. He became great, but he made the disciples great, that they might be able to see him in his greatness.[55]

The earliest Christian writers claimed that Jesus, as the great high priest, had revealed the secrets of the holy of holies: 'To Jesus alone as our high priest were the secret things of God committed';[56] 'We enter in through the tradition of the LORD, by drawing aside the curtain.'[57] There is a saying of Jesus not in the New Testament that was known in the early Church. 'Keep the mysteries for me and the sons of my house.'[58] What mysteries? The greatest mysteries were those set out in the Creeds: the incarnation and birth of the LORD, and his death and resurrection, and both the 'incarnation and birth' and 'death and resurrection' of the high priest had been mysteries of the holy of holies. From the mid-fourth century, the period when the Nicene Creed was being formulated and refined, there is the statement of Basil the Great: 'Of the dogma and kerygma which are preserved in the Church, we have some from teachings in writing, and others we have received from the tradition of the apostles, handed down in a mystery.'[59] The examples he gave concerned the epiclesis at the Eucharist, baptism and anointing, and the nature of the Holy Spirit, which was the subject of his treatise. The Church in which Basil grew up – he was born in 330 CE – was led by bishops who produced this creed at Nicaea in 325 CE. How did they relate these affirmations to the story of the nativity in the New Testament – the shepherds, the star and the magi?

> Our LORD Jesus Christ, the Son of God, the only begotten of the Father, God of God, Light of Light, true God of true God, begotten not made, consubstantial with the Father, by whom all things were made, which are both in heaven and on earth: who for us men and for our salvation descended, became incarnate and was made man.

There is more than an echo here of the tradition of the holy of holies.

---

[55] *The Gospel of Philip*, CGII.3.57–8.
[56] Ignatius, *Letter to the Philadelphians* 9.
[57] Clement, *Miscellanies* 7.17.
[58] Quoted in *Clementine Homilies* 19.20 (attributed to Clement of Rome) and Clement of Alexandria, *Miscellanies* 5.10.
[59] St Basil, *On the Holy Spirit* 66.

3

Luke

Luke's Gospel has two beginnings: there is an 'opening' statement at the start of chapter 3, as well as the more obvious introduction in the first chapter. The second introduction marks the point where Luke's Gospel begins to resemble Mark's, often said to be one of his sources. 'In the fifteenth year of Tiberius Caesar, Pontius Pilate being governor of Judea and Herod being tetrarch of Galilee . . .' (Luke 3.1) John the Baptist started preaching. Jesus came to him to be baptized, and then according to the oldest surviving versions of Luke's Gospel,[1] the voice at the Jordan said to him: 'You are my son. Today I have begotten you' (Luke 3.22 quoting Ps. 2.7). The present text here and in the other synoptic Gospels is, 'You are my beloved son. With you I am well pleased.' The older text is one of the royal birth texts from the temple, and implies that Jesus, in one sense, was 'born' at his baptism. *The baptism is one of Luke's birth stories.*

The evidence for this version of the text is impressive:[2] the *Gospel of the Hebrews*,[3] the earliest Latin translations before the work of Jerome; Justin in Rome,[4] Clement of Alexandria,[5] Origen,[6] and the early baptism prayer, 'the LORD in baptism, by the laying on of the bishop's hand, bore witness to each one of you and caused his holy voice to be heard that said: "You are my Son. This day I have begotten you." '[7] Each Christian was born at baptism and became a son of God. The most important witness is the Codex Bezae, which has a very early and characteristically 'Jewish' version of Luke and Acts.

---

[1] Ps 2.7 as quoted in the Codex Bezae, is 'virtually the only reading that survives from the 2nd and 3rd centuries'. See B. D. Ehrman, *The Orthodox Corruption of Scripture*, Oxford: Oxford University Press, 1993, p. 62.

[2] Ehrman, *The Orthodox Corruption of Scripture*, p. 62.

[3] Quoted in Jerome, *Commentary on Isaiah* 11.2.

[4] Justin, *Trypho* 88.

[5] Clement, *Instructor* 1.25.

[6] Origen, *Commentary on John* 1.29; *Celsus* 1.41.

[7] The *Didascalia Apostolorum*, ii.32, an early third-century text from Syria, in R. H. Connolly, ed., *Didascalia Apostolorum*, Oxford: Clarendon Press, 1929, p. 93.

The narrator is viewing the incidents he relates and the characters that participate in them from within the context of first century Judaism, and is adopting a typically Jewish approach to the theological debate. There is frequent evidence of a first hand familiarity with the Jewish world in which the events unfold that is considerably less visible in the manuscripts of the Alexandrian tradition. Our conclusion is that the Bezan text was written at a time when there *were still people who had known Jesus and the first generations of his disciples* . . .[8]

Since it is the oldest texts of Luke that have the 'birth' reading, it is likely that later scribes changed the text to make it agree with Matthew and Mark and to remove a considerable problem. Jesus 'born' at his baptism, however, would be consistent with the formula quoted[9] by Paul at the beginning of Romans: '[Jesus Christ] designated Son of God in power by the Spirit of holiness by his resurrection from the dead' (Rom. 1.4).[10] Birth *was* resurrection in the context of the holy of holies, and so Paul could have been taught that Jesus experienced the high priestly 'birth' at his baptism, the moment when he was empowered by the Holy Spirit as the Son. In the early third century CE Origen was to link Jesus' baptism experience with Ezekiel's vision of the throne. He may have made this link himself, or he may have been drawing on a traditional interpretation – we cannot know. Ezekiel, he said, saw by the River Chebar what Jesus saw at the River Jordan.

Origen was a great biblical scholar who had contact with learned Jews, and so is unlikely to have made this link without good reason. Ezekiel, he said, on the fifth day of the fourth month in the thirtieth year (Ezek. 1.1), saw the throne and the Living One (Ezek. 1.20–22[11]). Origen linked the thirtieth year to Jesus' age at his baptism – recorded only by Luke, and so presumably a significant age (Luke 3.23).[12] It was the age when young Levites began their service (Num. 4.3),[13] and the fifth day of the fourth month[14] was close to Epiphany, which came to be the date commemorating Jesus' baptism. The question is: did Luke know that Jesus had received a vision of the throne when

---

[8] J. Ruis-Camps and J. Read-Heimerdinger, *The Message of Acts in Codex Bezae*, vol. 1, London: T&T Clark, 2006, p. 1.

[9] Alas, in translation, so we have lost the nuances of the original.

[10] See above, p. 7.

[11] At this point the Hebrew word is singular, 'the Living One'.

[12] Origen, *On Ezekiel Homily 1*.

[13] And the minimum age for the 'bishop' of the Damascus Covenant Community, CD XIV.

[14] The fourth month in the old temple calendar that started in the autumn.

he saw the heavens open at his baptism? The open heavens implies such an experience – and this was the high priest's experience when he was born as the Son before being sent out into the world: he stood before the throne. Luke is usually identified as a companion of Paul on some of his travels; what did they talk about? If Paul could write of the Son of God being 'sent forth' when the time had fully come (Gal. 4.4), was this in any way reflected in the way Luke wrote his account of Jesus? The 'sending forth' at the beginning of the high priest-hood could be implicit in what Luke wrote about the voice at the baptism. In his description of Jesus' departure, he also used high priestly imagery: Jesus blessed the disciples (Luke 24.50) and 'a cloud took him out of their sight' (Acts 1.9).

'But Luke was writing for Gentiles, and all this subtlety would have been lost on them.' That is what everyone was taught for many years. Recent scholarship, however, has questioned this, and taken a very obvious starting point. Who was 'the most excellent Theophilus' (Luke 1.3) for whom Luke was writing? Was he in fact Theophilus the high priest, who held office from 37 to 41 CE and was closely involved with the turmoil of the Church's early years in Jerusalem?[15] His immediate family had been involved in the trial of Jesus, because he was the son of Annas and the brother-in-law of Caiaphas. The allusions to high priestly lore would not have been lost on Theophilus. Even Jesus' genealogy has seventy generations from Jesus back to Enoch (Luke 3.23–38). In the time of Enoch, the fallen angels and their offspring had been bound for seventy generations, until the time of the great judgement (*1 En.* 10.12), and Luke knew that Jesus' generation was the seventieth and would not pass away until the temple had been judged and destroyed, and the kingdom established (Luke 21.32).

'But Luke's Gospel was written long after the destruction of Jerusalem.' That is another hypothesis that became a 'fact' in the mid-twentieth century. If Luke was 'the brother famous among all the churches for his preaching of the gospel' (2 Cor. 8.18),[16] his Gospel was probably written during his active ministry. And was Luke a Gentile? This is another assumption. He came from Antioch, was a doctor by profession, and he wrote good Greek, but he could easily

---

[15] R. A. Anderson, 'Theophilus: A Proposal', *Evangelical Quarterly* 69.3 (1997), 195–215.

[16] J. W. Wenham, *Redating Matthew, Mark and Luke*, Downers Grove: InterVarsity Press, 1992, pp. 230–7.

have been a Jew.[17] The subtle allusions to temple tradition indicate, at the very least, a well-informed temple source that he understood.

Luke knew that 'many' had composed accounts of the recent events, suggesting that he himself had access to them (Luke 1.1). Perhaps this accounts for the two beginnings in his Gospel. The first edition began with the baptism, and the final version incorporated the birth story. Luke may have written the first two chapters himself, or he may have incorporated an existing text or oral tradition. The Greek here is more 'semitized', so perhaps it was a translation from Hebrew. Others have suggested that Luke was able to write in different styles to suit his subject. It is easy to separate the two chapters into various sections: stories about John, stories about Jesus, and both presented in parallel forms, with an annunciation for each and a birth story, and the meeting of the two mothers set between them. The whole composition is punctuated by psalms, suggesting that in its final form it was a stylized production. Perhaps it was even performed. Many speculations are possible, but repeating them does not transform them into facts. All we have, in the end, is the text of the Gospel, and the variant forms of it that are known from ancient manuscripts and quotations.

The first annunciation: the birth of John

Zechariah was a priest of the division of Abijah, the eighth division of the priests, and he was married to Elizabeth, who was from the family of Aaron. She had high priestly blood, and so in every sense the story begins in the temple. Zechariah's division of the priesthood was on duty in the temple twice a year: for one week at some time between mid-April and mid-May, and for one week between mid-October and mid-November. When the lots were cast, as was the custom, he was chosen to burn the afternoon incense. This happened only once in each priest's lifetime; when he had made the offering, his name was never again included in the lots. The Mishnah describes what happened: five priests were involved in the ritual, cleaning the incense altar, trimming the lamps, carrying the burning cinders, and then the chosen priest took the golden ladle in which was the incense dish. It is difficult to see how Zechariah could have

---

[17] Paul came from Tarsus and wrote good Greek.

been alone in the temple.[18] When the duty priests emerged, all the other priests joined with them to give the blessing in unison.[19]

The only time a priest functioned alone in the temple was on the Day of Atonement, when the high priest entered the holy of holies with the incense. This probably gave rise to the later belief that Zechariah had been a high priest officiating on the Day of Atonement, which fitted the later church calendar. If John the Baptist was conceived around the Day of Atonement, he was born in June, with the annunciation to Mary in the spring and Jesus born the following midwinter. But there was no high priest called Zechariah. The date of John's birth is not known for certain, but the high priest until 5 BCE was Simon, and he was followed by Matthias. Luke, correctly, describes Zechariah as 'a certain priest'. Matthew's story of the nativity, as we shall see,[20] favours an autumn date for Jesus' birth.

While he was offering incense, Zechariah saw an angel of the LORD standing by the altar (Luke 1.11) and he learned that his wife would bear a child. The angel was Gabriel. In the biblical story, the last time Gabriel had appeared was with a message to Daniel. 'At the time of the evening sacrifice' – the time he appeared to Zechariah – he revealed to Daniel the future of his people, that after seventy weeks of years the prophecies would be fulfilled and the Most Holy One would be anointed. Zechariah would have known the calculations of the temple priests and that the time for the Messiah was near. The angel told him that the child would be named John, and that he would grow up to be the new Elijah, the herald of the day of the LORD (Luke 1.8–17).

The words of the angel, translated into Hebrew, show that this passage could have been poetry, perhaps a psalm, as could several other passages in the Lucan account that are not usually recognized and printed as poetry. Putting the texts 'back' into Hebrew poetry often reveals patterns that are not so clear in the Greek. Nothing can be proved, but Gabriel's two addresses to Mary at the annunciation, Elizabeth's welcome to Mary, the words of the angel to the shepherds, the song of the angel host, and Simeon's words to Mary, together with the familiar canticles – the Song of Mary (the Magnificat), the Song of Zechariah (the Benedictus), and the Song of Simeon (the Nunc

---

[18] Mishnah *Tamid* 5.2—6.3.
[19] Mishnah *Tamid* 7.2.
[20] See below, p. 115.

Dimittis) seem to form a sequence of ten hymns, and raise a question as to the original role of the Lucan birth stories.[21] Five songs from angels and five from humans: who might have written them? There is another temple drama in the New Testament, punctuated by psalms, where angels travel between earth and heaven: the book of Revelation. And there is debate about some of the Qumran texts; did the *Songs of the Sabbath Sacrifice*, for example, describe the angels worshipping in heaven, or an angel priesthood worshipping on earth?[22]

There were various people at that time, as we have seen, who distinguished themselves from the Jerusalem establishment, people who were still living in 'exile', for whom the era of the second temple was a time of divine wrath.[23] They may well have been the descendants, literally or culturally, of those voices in the closing chapters of Isaiah: the servants who would eat, drink and rejoice while their oppressors were deprived and would leave their name as a curse (Isa. 65.13–16); those who had been cast out and were waiting to hear the LORD coming into the temple for the day of judgement (Isa. 66.5–6); those who would at last be recognized (again?) as priests of the LORD and enjoy the double portion of the first-born (Isa. 61.5–7). Luke is the only Gospel writer (why?) to record the incident in the synagogue at Nazareth, when Jesus proclaimed the fulfilment of Isaiah 61 (Luke 4.16–21). Perhaps he knew that 'good news to the poor' had a particular meaning in the early Church; perhaps he even knew some of 'the poor' and their psalms. Familiar lines such as 'he has put down the mighty from their thrones' (Luke 1.52) and 'that we should be saved from our enemies' (Luke 1.71) are clearly political, and Luke thought them (or even *knew* them) to be appropriate for the Christmas stories.

Isaiah's other oracles for the 'poor' were very similar to the passage Jesus read at Nazareth, and were taken up by him in the Beatitudes. Who were the poor in spirit, those who mourn, those hungering and thirsting for righteousness, the merciful, the pure in heart, the peacemakers, those persecuted for the sake of righteousness, reviled and misrepresented? Their promised rewards are interesting

---

[21] See R. A. Aytoun, 'The Ten Lucan Hymns of the Infancy in their Original Language', *Journal of Theological Studies* 18 (1916–17), pp. 274–88. All the analyses of the hymns as poetry are from this article.

[22] The debate around the proposals of C. T. Fletcher Louis, set out in his book *All the Glory of Adam: Liturgical Anthropology in the Dead Sea Scrolls*, Leiden: Brill, 2002.

[23] See above, p. 26.

too: the kingdom of heaven, inheriting the land, seeing God and being called sons of God (Matt. 5.3–12). John the Baptist was to turn the disobedient to the wisdom of the righteous ones (Luke 1.17, my translation), who sound like a defined group, so who were they? The privilege of the high priest was to see God and to become a son of God, and certain people had lost their lands and their rights in the temple when the exiles had returned from Babylon in the sixth century BCE. History is full of people who remembered wrongs for centuries, and never gave up their claim to certain land or status.

It has been suggested that the 'poor' in the Gospels were close to, or even identical to, the 'poor' at Qumran.[24] The singer of the eighth hymn described himself as the poor one, whom 'they' planned to kill, but God defended him against those who were stronger;[25] and in the thirteenth hymn his afflictions have been his sevenfold purification, and the soul of the poor one was delivered from the mouth of lions.[26] At other times, the poor are a group, 'the well loved poor who rise up together'.[27] In the War Scroll, the redeemed 'poor' defeat the hordes of Belial.[28] The fragment of a commentary on Psalm 37 identifies the 'meek', *'nwym*, who will possess the land and delight in great peace, as the 'poor' (Ps. 37.11). 'The wicked borrows and cannot pay back, but the righteous is generous and gives; for those blessed by the LORD shall possess the land, but those cursed by him shall be cut off' (Ps. 37.21–22) was interpreted to mean: 'This concerns the [congregation of] the poor, *'bywnym*, who [shall possess] the whole world as an inheritance. They shall possess the high mountain of Israel [for ever], and shall enjoy [everlasting] delights in his Sanctuary.'[29] A small piece known as the 'resurrection fragment' has several similarities to Gospel material.[30] 'Over the poor his spirit will hover, and he will renew the faithful with his power . . . He who liberates captives, restores sight to the blind' (cf. Luke 4.18). He will heal the wounded, revive the dead and bring good news to the poor . . . (cf. Jesus' reply to John the Baptist, Luke 7.22 and Matt. 11.5).

---

[24] For a good summary, see R. E. Brown, *The Birth of the Messiah*, updated edition, London: Cassell, 1993, pp. 350–5.
[25] 1QH X.
[26] 1QH XIII.
[27] 1QH XIII.
[28] 1QM XI.
[29] 4Q 171.
[30] 4Q 521.

It was in such a context of long memories and political ferment – not just against the Romans but against the long established regime of the second temple – that we must read the story of the birth of John the Baptist, the son of a priest. The angel said to Zechariah: 'Do not fear', the usual way for the LORD to begin when speaking through his angel or his prophet. 'Do not fear,' said Isaiah to Ahaz (Isa. 7.4). 'Do not fear,' said the angel to the women on Easter morning (Matt. 28.5). 'Do not fear,' said Gabriel to Mary (Luke 1.30). The promised child would be filled with the Holy Spirit from birth, even though Luke says that his prophetic ministry actually began when the word of God came to him in the desert (Luke 3.2). This is a parallel situation to the birth of Jesus in Bethlehem and his subsequent 'birth' at the start of his ministry.

The angel told Zechariah that his wife would bear a son, to be named John.

> And you will have joy and gladness
> And many will rejoice at his birth.
> He will be great before the LORD,
> And shall drink no wine or strong drink,
> And with the Holy Spirit he shall be filled
> even from his mother's womb.
> And many of the sons of Israel
> He will turn to the LORD their God,
> And he himself will go before him,
> In the spirit and power of Elijah,
> To turn the hearts of the fathers to the children,
> And the disobedient to the wisdom of the righteous ones,
> To make ready for the LORD a people prepared.
>   (Luke 1.14–17, as in the 'Hebrew original')

John was to prepare the 'sons of Israel' for the LORD, and the synoptic Gospels all quote the same passage from Isaiah to describe his ministry: 'The voice crying in the wilderness: "Prepare the way of the LORD . . . and all flesh shall see the salvation of our God"' (Isa. 40.3–5 quoted at Luke 3.4–6).[31] John was to preach repentance before the day of the LORD, that is, the day of judgement, but also to fulfil the hopes of the sixth century BCE, that the LORD's people would return to their city, and the LORD himself would appear to lead them: 'Behold the LORD God comes with might, and his arm rules for him; . . . he will gather his flock like a shepherd' (Isa. 40.10, 11). The

---

[31] The Isaiah passage reads: 'The voice crying, "In the wilderness prepare the way . . ."'.

day of the LORD was the recurring hope of second-temple voices: 'On that day the LORD their God will save them, for they are the flock of his people' (Zech. 9.16); 'On that day there shall be a fountain opened for the house of David and the inhabitants of Jerusalem to cleanse them from sin and uncleanness' (Zech. 13.1); 'On that day his feet shall stand on the Mount of Olives' (Zech. 14.4); 'On that day there shall no longer be a trader in the house of the LORD' (Zech. 14.21). There were many such hopes.

For the Christians, the day of the LORD was the coming of Jesus, whom they recognized and proclaimed as the LORD. *Much confusion has been caused by failing to realize that the early Christians proclaimed Jesus as Yahweh.* That is what 'Jesus is LORD' meant, and so the day of the LORD, with all its established expectations of the LORD appearing in glory in the temple to bring judgement on his enemies (for example, Isa. 66.6), was interpreted of Jesus as a human baby, who also appeared in the temple. John's role was to prepare for the coming of Yahweh, the LORD, and so the Gospels show his ministry pointing to the adult Jesus. Here, his birth story shows that from the beginning John was his forerunner, his Elijah. Gabriel echoed Malachi's words about Elijah, but replaced the curse with a message of hope: 'He will turn the hearts of the fathers to the children and the hearts of the children to their fathers, lest I come and smite the land with utter destruction' (Mal. 4.6), became: 'He will turn the hearts of the fathers to the children, and the disobedient to the wisdom of the righteous ones, to make ready for the LORD a people prepared for him' (Luke 1.17, my translation). The expected becoming the unexpected is a theme of the Christmas story. The 'righteous ones' suggests that the composer of this song was one of the 'righteous ones' and that the birth of John was seen as part of the plan to restore them to their former place. Luke knew that the first Christians had called Jesus the Holy and Righteous One (Acts 3.14), and the *Damascus Document* described a community 'who have listened to the Teacher of Righteousness and have not despised the precepts of righteousness'.[32]

Zechariah asked for a sign that this would happen, and Gabriel told him he would be unable to speak until the child was born and named John. The people waiting outside wondered at his delay in the temple, and realized, when Zechariah could not speak to them, that he had seen a vision. Zechariah was dumb and deaf – they spoke to

---

[32] CD XIV.

him with signs (Luke 1.62) – until his son was born. He could not give the blessing that day, but did so later when John was born.

The second annunciation: the birth of Jesus

In the sixth month of Elizabeth's pregnancy, the angel Gabriel brought news to Mary that she would have a son. The angel's words became some of the most repeated in the New Testament: 'Hail favoured one, the LORD is with you. Blessed are you among women' (Luke 1.28).[33] Mary was a virgin promised in marriage to Joseph, and she lived in Galilee. Nazareth does not appear in some old versions of the Gospel, for example the Codex Bezae, nor is there any mention of Mary's family, nor of her being descended from David, even though these elements appear in later writings, perhaps because of the formula: 'descended from David according to the flesh' (Rom. 1.3).[34] If Mary was the Virgin mother of Jesus, the Davidic descent must have been through her. Nor does the text say that Mary saw Gabriel. The angel appeared to Zechariah, but only 'came in' to Mary, and she was frightened by the voice. Despite all the familiar annunciation pictures of a visible Gabriel coming to Mary, the memory that she did not see the angel survived in the tradition that she conceived through her ear. 'The archangel said, "The Holy Spirit shall come upon you, and the Power of the Most High shall overshadow you . . ." She conceived by the hearing of her ears, and she spent three months in the house of Joseph . . .'[35] Ephrem bears witness to a similar belief in the Syriac tradition: 'By her ear did Mary behold the Hidden One who had come in the utterance; the Power who had come to embodiment was thus conceived in her womb.' 'Ephrem's allusion to the characteristically Syriac idea of conception through the ear perhaps reflects an early polemic . . .'[36] A beam of light coming into Mary's ear, or even a dove, can often be found in pictures of the annunciation.

---

[33] The second half of the greeting is omitted by several modern versions, but appears in the Codex Bezae, the fifth-century Codex Alexandrinus, many Old Latin texts and in the Vulgate, and was included in the AV. Other ancient texts do not have it.

[34] Mary's being of the house of David appears in the *Ascension of Isaiah* 11.2; the *Infancy Gospel of James* 10.1; Ignatius' *Letter to the Ephesians* 18; and Justin's *Trypho* 45.

[35] The Coptic *Life of the Virgin*.

[36] S. P. Brock, 'Passover Annunciation and Epiclesis: Some Remarks on the Term *aggen* in the Syriac Versions of Luke 1.35', *Novum Testamentum* 24.3 (1982), pp. 222–33, p. 227, quoting Ephrem, *Memra on the Prologue of John*.

Gabriel's greeting has been much pondered: is there any signi-ficance in the 'Hail', or was it just the ordinary greeting of the time? Some have linked it to Zephaniah's words to the daughter of Zion to rejoice, 'because the LORD is in your midst' (Zeph. 3.14–15), but without the Hebrew original of Gabriel's words, there is no way of knowing. The remainder of this first speech goes easily into five lines of Hebrew poetry:

> Do not fear Mary for you have found favour with God;
> For behold you will conceive and bear a son, and call his name Jesus.
> He will be great, and will be called Son of the Highest,
> And the LORD God will give to him the throne of David his father,
> And over the house of Jacob he will reign for ever, and his kingdom
>   will have no end.

(Luke 1.28–33 as in the 'Hebrew original')

The words of Gabriel are the key to the original story of the birth of Jesus. What did it mean to be 'Son of the Highest', that is, to be Yahweh the LORD? The context is the royal rituals of the old temple, when the new king was enthroned and became the human presence of the LORD. Since the first Christians knew that the LORD was the Son of God Most High, and that God Most High had allotted Jacob to him as his special people, this is how we should understand Gabriel's message. The child, like the ancient kings, would be given the Name (Yahweh the LORD), and established as his presence and his king on earth. The two stages of sonship, the two births, are assumed here, not explained: the relationship within the divine – the Most High and the Son, the eternal generation of the Son; and then the relationship of the divine and the human – the Son and his earthly manifesta-tion, the Virgin birth and the incarnation.

There is a good description of the two aspects of sonship in the *Gospel of Philip*, an early Christian text rediscovered in Egypt in 1945 at Nag Hammadi. This shows the ultimate temple origin of the great debate in the early fourth century about the nature of the Second Person, which resulted in the credal affirmation 'begotten not created'.

> There is the Son of man and there is the son of the Son of man. The LORD is the Son of man, and the son of the Son of man is he who is created through the Son of man. The Son of man received from God the capacity to create. He also has the ability to beget. He who has received the ability to create is a creature. He who has received the ability to beget is an offspring. He who creates cannot beget, but he who begets also has power to create. Now [others] say 'He who

creates begets', but his so called offspring is merely a creature, therefore his children are not offspring but creatures.[37]

Here, the Second Person, 'the Son of man' has a son, the human being.
The Second Person is the Creator – an established Christian belief –
but he also 'begets' a son. This means that the son of the Son is not
his creature but also part of the divine unity expressed by the language of begetting. It was the LORD who spoke to the king and said:
'You are my son, today I have begotten you' (Ps. 2.7).

Another aspect of this temple mystery is seen also in Revelation,
but not explained. In visionary texts like this, human beings are
described as animals and heavenly beings as men, and the whole text
is permeated by temple wordplay. Thus when the Lamb approaches
the throne, it indicates a human figure in heaven, almost certainly
depicted in temple rituals as a man taking his place on the throne
of the LORD in the holy of holies. The Lamb is wordplay for the
Servant,[38] and so what we see here is the Servant of the LORD
approaching the throne and taking the scroll. Then John describes
the heavenly host worshipping: 'To him who sits upon the throne and
to the Lamb be Glory' (Rev. 5.13). 'Him-who-sits-upon-the-throne-
and-the-Lamb' are one figure, not two, with the divinity mentioned
before the human. Later in the vision, His servants stand before the
throne of 'God-and-the-Lamb' and worship *him* (Rev. 22.3). Peter
caused consternation when he told the crowd at Pentecost: 'God has
made him both LORD-and-Christ, this Jesus whom you crucified' (Acts
2.36). The one figure who is both divine and human. There are many
examples of this divine and human fusion followed by singular
forms,[39] the earliest being Solomon's coronation, when he sat on
the throne of the LORD, and Israel worshipped him (1 Chron.
29.20–23[40]). This temple way of understanding the divine-and-
human is implicit in Gabriel's first words to Mary. 'He will be great
and will be called the Son of the Most High; and the Lord God will
give him the throne of his father David' (Luke 1.32). Her son would
be given the Name and then set on the throne, becoming, in a way
we do not understand, the LORD. The divine and human are worshipped as one. Jesus in Revelation said that his own new name, that

---

[37] *Gospel of Philip*, CG II.3.81.
[38] In Aramaic, both words would be *talya'*.
[39] See my book *The Revelation of Jesus Christ*, Edinburgh: T&T Clark, 2000, p. 140.
[40] The Hebrew of 1 Chron. 29.20 is, literally, '. . . they worshipped the LORD, the king'.

is, Yahweh the LORD, was the same as the name of his God (Rev. 3.12), and Paul knew an early Christian formula, perhaps a hymn, that described Jesus as the servant who was exalted, given the great Name, and then worshipped by all creation (Phil. 2.7–11), which is the scene in Revelation 5.

It used to be said that 'Son of God' was an anachronism, something imported into the stories by non-Jewish converts to Christianity, as the phrase 'son of God' could never have been used by Jews. Then a small piece of text was found in cave 4 at Qumran. 'The Son of God fragment',[41] as it is often called, has Gabriel's words: 'The son of God he will be proclaimed . . . the son of the Most High they will call him.' These seem to be titles that an imposter gave himself, since his kingdom was like sparks and so presumably short-lived. Nevertheless, the titles are there. The *Messianic Rule* from Qumran also mentions the birth of the Messiah: 'When God begets the Messiah, he shall come with them [at] the head of the whole congregation of Israel'.[42]

Son of God and sons of God became a sensitive issue for Jews in the early years of the Church. The line in Deuteronomy that identifies the LORD as Son of God Most High does not appear in the post-Christian Hebrew text, though a fragment of the Hebrew text has been found at Qumran showing that the 'sons of God' version was pre-Christian, and the basis for the Old Greek translation, which has 'angels of God'. In the older text, the LORD was one of the 'sons of God' who guarded the nations of the earth. Another pre-Christian fragment found at Qumran, a piece of Deuteronomy 32.43[43] has the *'elohim* summoned to worship the LORD on the Day of Atonement; in the Old Greek they became 'the sons of God', but they, too, do not appear in the post-Christian Hebrew text. The lines that disappeared were used as a Christian proof text in Hebrews 1.6 to establish that Jesus was the LORD.

Mary questioned Gabriel: 'How can this be?' Gabriel spoke again and described the process of divine birth.

> The Holy Spirit will come upon you
> And the power of the Most High will overshadow you.
>
> (Luke 1.35)

---

[41] 4Q 246.

[42] 1Q 28a II.

[43] 4Q Deut^q.

'The Holy Spirit will come upon you, and the power of the Most High will overshadow' seems to be parallelism characteristic of Hebrew poetry. Paul has a similar 'double' description of the incarnation: 'Christ the Power of God and the Wisdom of God' (1 Cor. 1.24), so how did the incarnation of the LORD come to be described as twofold, two aspects of the divine? This is not the 'two births', but another aspect of temple lore. John described the LORD as the Word, Logos, and he described the incarnation as 'the Word became flesh and dwelt among us' (John 1.14). He gave no further detail. Philo, however, his exact contemporary, wrote a great deal about the Logos, and even though he was often expressing his Jewish traditions in Greek terms, he shows how the Logos was perceived when the Christmas stories were written.

First, Philo's retelling of the Old Testament in contemporary terms shows that the LORD was the Logos.[44] This is very important. Second, the Logos was understood to be two powers, represented by the two cherubim over the ark in the holy of holies. This is where Moses heard the LORD: 'from between the two cherubim that are upon the ark of the testimony, I will speak with you' (Exod. 25.22). The two powers, said Philo, were indicated in the Old Testament by the two names *Yahweh*, the LORD, representing the ruling power, the source of justice, and *'elohim*, God, representing the power of creativity and mercy. 'The cherubim are the symbols of the two first powers of God, namely the creative and the kingly, of which the one is called God and the other LORD.'[45] He continues here by explaining their attributes. Then, early in the second century CE, Jewish scholars completely reversed these attributes, making the LORD the one who loves and God the one who judges. This change was due to 'religious movements which necessitated such a discarding of an older teaching' – presumably the advent of Christianity. The LORD could not be interpreted as the judge after the horrors that had befallen the Jews at the hands of the Romans, and so the LORD was presented as the loving and creating aspect of God.[46]

The two names and what they indicated were known in the Christian community. Thomas, when he saw the risen LORD with his wounded hands and side, used the twofold form: 'My LORD and

[44] See my book *The Great Angel*, London: SPCK, 1992, pp. 114–33.

[45] Philo, *Questions on Genesis* I.57.

[46] A Marmorstein, 'Philo and the Names of God', *Jewish Quarterly Review* 22 (1931), 295–306.

my God' (John 20.28). Gabriel's words to Mary declare this twofold presence: the Holy Spirit and the Power would overshadow her, such that her son would be, in Paul's words, both the Wisdom and the Power of God. Thus Gabriel's promise of 'overshadowing' indicates *the coming of the Glory to the holy of holies.*[47] Philo understood the coming of the Glory to be coming of the powers. He had Moses say 'By thy Glory, I understand the powers that keep guard around thee.'[48] The image of the Glory coming to the holy of holies became an important part of how the Christmas story was told, as we shall see.[49] 'Between the cherubim' is reflected in the (later) Christian use of a difficult verse in Habakkuk, describing the LORD recognized 'between the creatures', which was eventually linked to the ox and the ass at the manger. The verse reads in the Old Greek: 'Be known in the midst of the two creatures, recognized in the drawing near of the years, manifested in the coming of the time' (LXX Hab. 3.2) As the LORD had appeared to Moses between the two creatures, the cherubim, this was symbolic of how the incarnate LORD would appear. The current Hebrew of this verse, again, is not easy to decipher, and somewhat different.

This twofold aspect of incarnation was known to Irenaeus. When he described the birth of Jesus as a recapitulation of the birth of Adam – history repeating itself – he said that Adam was formed from the Will and Wisdom of God, and from the virgin earth.[50] The Will corresponds to the power of God, and the Wisdom to the Holy Spirit. For Irenaeus, the virgin earth corresponds to the physical body of Mary, but there were other and earlier Christian interpretations which said that Adam was born from two virgins: Wisdom and the earth.[51] There was a heavenly Virgin called Wisdom with an earthly counterpart called Mary, just as John the Baptist had been both a man and an angel.[52]

Gabriel then said: 'Therefore the child to be born will be called holy, Son of God' or: 'Therefore the holy child to be born will be called Son of God.' The line can be read either way, but there is no

---

[47] The Syriac text here shows an additional understanding of 'overshadow' as 'protect' that is reflected also in the Targums, e.g. Neofiti Num. 10.34, where the cloud of the Glory of the Shekinah 'covers over/shields by day'. See Brock (n. 36 above), pp. 222–33.
[48] Philo, *The Special Laws* 1.45.
[49] See below, p. 146.
[50] Irenaeus, *Proof of the Apostolic Preaching* 32.
[51] See below, p. 104.
[52] See below, p. 13.

real difference in the meaning. It does not seem to be poetry, and could have been a later explanation added to Gabriel's words.

Then there are four more lines that could easily have been poetry:

> Behold Elizabeth your kinswoman
> She also has conceived a son in her old age
> And this is the sixth month
> For her who was called barren.
> (Luke 1.36, as in the 'Hebrew original')

'For nothing is impossible with God' may be another insertion, as it seems not to be poetry. It is an echo of the LORD's words to Abraham, when he was told that the aged Sarah would have a child (Gen. 18.14).

The nature and process of the incarnation was an early and persistent focus of misunderstanding and scandal. The *Gospel of Philip* implies this: 'Some said: "Mary conceived by the holy spirit." They are in error. They do not know what they are saying. When did a woman ever conceive by a woman?'[53] 'Spirit' is a feminine noun in Hebrew [and related languages], and the *Gospel of Philip* bears witness to the early tendency to understand the incarnation in the manner of the classical myths – the gods mating with human women. Justin had to deal with the same problem:

> But lest some . . . should charge us with the very things we have been laying to the charge of the poets who say that Jupiter went in to women through lust, let us try to explain the words. [The prophecy of the Virgin means] that a virgin should conceive without intercourse.[54]

The meeting of Elizabeth and Mary

Mary went to visit Elizabeth, and when she greeted her, the unborn John 'leaped in her womb'. The angel had promised Zechariah that his son would be filled with the Spirit from the womb, and here the baby recognizes the coming of the unborn Jesus.[55] Elizabeth too is filled with the Spirit and utters a psalm of welcome. 'Utters' is an interesting verb. In the Old Greek Bible, it was used to describe the music of the Levites in the temple, and the English translates it in various ways: they *made loud music* (1 Chron. 15.28); *invoking* (1 Chron. 16.4);

---

53 *Gospel of Philip*, CG II.3.55.
54 Justin, *Apology* 1.33.
55 See Brown (n. 24 above), p. 333.

sounding the cymbals (1 Chron. 16.5); and cymbals *for the music* (1 Chron. 16.42). Elizabeth's welcome was liturgical, and translates well as Hebrew poetry.

> Blessed are you among women,
> And blessed is the fruit of your womb!
> And why is this granted me,
> That the mother of my Lord should come to me?

Then the metre changes:

> When the voice of your greeting came to my ears,
> the babe in my womb leapt for joy.
> And blessed is she who believes there will be fulfilment
> of what was spoken to her from the LORD.
>   (Luke 1.42–45, as in the 'Hebrew original')

Why should this greeting be a 'liturgical' piece? We can guess from the political situation at the time why some elements of the Lucan hymns should have political elements, but what context might there have been for a liturgical greeting for the mother of the LORD? Had there been an earlier temple context for the greeting, 'Blessed are you among women and blessed is the fruit of your womb'?

This question is closely related to another: what did Luke mean by 'the mother of my Lord'? Had Elizabeth recognized, with the prophetic gift of the Spirit, that the LORD was present? She cannot have used the Name, because it was only spoken in the temple on the Day of Atonement. Further, the form Yahweh cannot take a suffix to give the form 'my Yahweh', that is, 'my LORD'. But had she used the customary substitute form ''Adonai' to avoid uttering the Name, it was possible to say '*my* Lord'. 'The mother of the LORD' was not an unthinkable idea, and here we must bear in mind the belief that important human beings like John the Baptist had heavenly counterparts, their angels. Isaiah's prophecy spoke of the Virgin who would bring forth a son named 'God with us'; Micah knew of the woman in labour who was about to give birth to the great shepherd Ruler of Israel. Was this woman human or divine? And was her son human or divine? Or were each of them both human and divine? John saw in heaven the woman clothed with the sun whose son was born and then snatched up to the throne; in other words, she was in the holy of holies where she gave birth, and her son was born onto the earth and then taken up. There were to be prolonged controversies in the later Church over the title Theotokos, the Bearer of God, often translated as 'Mother of God'. The book of Revelation suggests that the human birth of Jesus to Mary was also the birth of the LORD to his heavenly Mother.

At this point the holy of holies is covered by the veil of time and generations of familiarity with certain texts, without asking what they meant. In the holy of holies, John saw a royal Lady crowned with stars (Rev. 12.1–6), who gave birth to a son. This Lady – now clearly Mary – was depicted in the apses of many great churches, for example, the Hagia Sophia in Constantinople. Why did the Church make this connection? The eighth-century prophets Isaiah and Micah knew of this woman and of her son who would be the guardian and saviour of his people. From the surviving glimpses of the royal 'birth' ceremonies, we can see that the newly 'born' king emerged from the holy of holies. What about his mother, earthly or heavenly? Were there ever liturgical acclamations about her? 'Fruit of the womb' is a Hebraic expression (for example, Deut. 7.13; Ps. 127.3), and so, 'Blessed are you among women and blessed is the fruit of your womb' could well have been quoting or alluding to something well known, a greeting for the mother of the LORD. In some early Christian texts, Jesus called the Holy Spirit his mother, but from the Old Testament we can recover another of her names.

'Mother of the LORD' is not a title found in the Old Testament today, but the Qumran community had a significantly different version of Isaiah[56] – only a few letters, but very important letters.[57] The Virgin mother of Immanuel was described as the *mother of the LORD*. Where the LORD asks Ahaz: 'Ask a sign from the LORD your God' the complete Qumran Isaiah scroll has: 'Ask a sign from *the mother of the LORD your God*' (Isa. 7.11). This tells us who the Qumran community believed the Virgin to be; she was not just the mother of Immanuel, she was the mother of the LORD. How this form of the prophecy relates to the better-known versions is not relevant here; what matters is that some people in the time of Jesus were reading Isaiah in this way. Elizabeth's greeting to Mary fits best in this context: that the Virgin was expected to give birth to the LORD.

Mary responded to Elizabeth's greeting with the Magnificat – or so the text now reads. Several early texts attributed the Magnificat to Elizabeth, but the Roman Catholic Church forbade such thinking in 1912, when the Pontifical Biblical Commission decreed that the

---

[56] 1Q Isa³, which is the only known pre-Christian text of this verse. In other ancient portions of the Hebrew Isaiah, this section has not survived.

[57] In the Qumran scroll, there is an *aleph*, where the later Hebrew texts have an *'ayin*.

Magnificat had to be attributed to Mary.[58] The real problem is that the Magnificat does not obviously fit either woman. It resembles Hannah's song of thanksgiving for the birth of her son Samuel (1 Sam. 2.1–10), but the 'low estate of his handmaiden' (Luke 1.48) fits Elizabeth's situation better than Mary's, since she was childless. The poem mentions the handmaiden (Luke 1.48) and the servant (Luke 1.54), the two figures in Isaiah's prophecy about the future of Jerusalem, and then the children of Abraham (Luke 1.55). The words of the LORD through Isaiah were: 'You, Israel my servant, Jacob whom I have chosen, the offspring of Abraham my friend . . . I have chosen you and not cast you off, fear not for I am with you' (Isa. 41.8–9). The Lady was comforted and told that her time of hard service – the Greek has 'humble status' – was over (Isa. 40.2). The Lady comforted and restored, the Servant remembered and the children of Abraham reinstated are themes from the latter part of Isaiah, the voices of the people in the long exile.[59] This was history repeating itself, and here they are part of Mary's song.

The Magnificat is a traditional psalm of praise; words of acclamation, followed by the reasons for the praise.[60] It is full of allusions to other texts, as are the hymns in the book of Revelation, which probably originated in the same milieu as the hymns of Luke's nativity story. Mary speaks as does Isaiah's Jerusalem, the city abandoned by the LORD and then restored (Isa. 54.1–8).

> My soul magnifies the LORD [my God]
> And my spirit rejoices in God my Saviour
> For he has indeed seen the low estate of his handmaiden.
> For behold from henceforth all generations will call me blessed;
>
> For the mighty one has done great things for me,
>   And holy is his name.
> And his mercy is from generation to generation
>   For those who fear him.
> He has shown strength with his arm
>   He has scattered the proud,
> He has put down the mighty from their thrones,
>   And exalted the lowly;
> The hungry he has filled with good
>   And the rich he has sent away empty.

---

[58] Brown (n. 24 above), p. 334.
[59] See above, p. 26.
[60] Psalm 33 shows the pattern.

He has helped Israel his servant
Remembering his mercy,
As he spoke to our forefathers,
To Abraham and his children for ever.
(Luke 1.46–55, as in the 'Hebrew original')

The first reason for her praises is that she has been restored: 'He has done great things for me, and holy is his name.' 'Holy is his name' could well have been Isaiah's characteristic description of the LORD, 'The Holy One of Israel',[61] and so the sense of the original might have been: 'He has done great things for me. The Holy One is his name.'

Her second reason to praise is that enemies have been defeated and the proud have been brought low (cf. Isa. 2.12–17). Mary's words are like the angel's words to Enoch in the holy of holies: 'This son of man . . . shall put down kings from their thrones and kingdoms, because they do not extol and praise him and acknowledge whence the kingdom is bestowed upon them' (*1 En.* 46.5). Was 'Enoch' alluding to the source that Mary knew? The Enoch books are a repository of high priestly tradition.

Her third reason to praise is 'filling the hungry', whether in a literal or spiritual sense. In a spiritual sense, the promised food was the fruit of the tree of life (Rev. 2.7), described as food for the chosen ones, the righteous and the holy (*1 En.* 15.4–5). Their drink was to be the water of life (Rev. 22.17), described as the inexhaustible fountain of righteousness, surrounded by fountains of wisdom, 'and all the thirsty drank of them' (*1 En.* 48.1). Isaiah contrasted the future state of the servants and their enemies:

> Behold, my servants shall eat but you shall be hungry, behold, my servants shall drink but you shall be thirsty, behold my servants shall rejoice but you shall be put to shame . . . You shall leave your name to my chosen for a curse . . . but his servants he will call by a different name. (Isa. 65.13–15)

Her fourth reason to praise was because God had not forgotten his people, another theme in Isaiah and the Psalms. 'But Zion said, "The LORD has forsaken me, my LORD has forgotten me. Can a woman forget her sucking child, that she should have no compassion on the son of her womb? Even these may forget, yet I will not forget you"' (Isa. 49.15). And, significantly because the context is the destruction of the temple: 'Do not forget the life of thy poor (plural) for ever . . .

---

[61] There are many examples: Isa. 12.6; 43.3; 47.4; 60.9, 14; also Pss. 71.22; 89.19.

Have regard for the covenant . . . Let the poor and needy[62] praise thy name' (Ps. 74.19–21).

One of the characteristics of Luke's stories of the birth is that he never quotes prophecy, unlike Matthew who constantly cites the texts: 'All this took place to fulfil what was spoken by the prophet' (Matt. 1.22). As in the book of Revelation, Luke's allusions are woven through the text, sometimes with changes to the familiar form as when Gabriel spoke to Zechariah, where one line of the Malachi prophecy was changed. There may be far more allusions than we now recognize, since Gabriel's words to Mary include contemporary messianic titles only recently discovered at Qumran: 'He shall be called Son of the Most High.' Other Qumran texts show that their body of holy texts was larger than our present Old Testament. Here in the Magnificat there is a new psalm, woven together from the hopes and aspirations of the rejected, the voice perhaps of that community but put into the mouth of Mary, because she and her child personified the hope of that community to bring an end to the age of wrath.

The birth of John

John was born, and on the eighth day the neighbours gathered for the circumcision and naming of the child. Elizabeth named him John, which caused some surprise as this was not a family name. They made signs to Zechariah, which assumes he had become deaf as well as dumb after seeing the angel. He confirmed that the child would be called John, and immediately he was able to speak again. Everyone talked about the strange events and wondered what they meant. Then Zechariah, filled with the Spirit, prophesied by singing a psalm based on the blessing that he never gave in the temple. The priest as a prophet was well known: the Spirit of the LORD came upon Jahaziel, a Levite and temple musician, and he prophesied before the crowd in the temple court (2 Chron. 20.13–19); the Spirit of God 'clothed itself' with Zechariah when he was in the temple, and he too prophesied a condemnation of the people. They stoned him (2 Chron. 24.20–22).

The prophecy of Zechariah is now called the Benedictus (Luke 1.67–79). He spoke of the Davidic house and the holy covenant with Abraham, with no mention of Moses and the law. His people wanted

---

[62] The word is *'ebyon* whence the name of the early Christian group, the Ebionites.

'to serve'[63] the LORD without fear in holiness and righteousness, reminiscent of the voices of the long exile who had been excluded from the priesthood and the temple. His enemies might not have been just the Romans; they might have been elements in the temple where he served. A possible liturgical context for this piece is the day of the LORD, the final Day of Atonement. That mutilated passage in Deuteronomy 32.43 depicts the LORD emerging to avenge the blood of his sons, to punish his enemies and purify the land of his people; and the Qumran Melchizedek text also looked forward to the final Day of Atonement, when the heavenly high priest appeared to rescue his people and punish their enemies.

Zechariah's Benedictus celebrates the birth of the forerunner, and falls into two sections.[64] The first, vv. 67–75, is a psalm of praise, but some parts of it (vv. 69b–70, 'in the house of his servant David, as he spoke through the mouth of his holy prophets from of old', and v. 73, 'the oath which he swore to our forefather Abraham') disrupt the metre and are probably 'Zechariah's' own topical additions to the original.

> Blessed be the LORD God of Israel
> For he has visited his people and made redemption for them
> And has raised up for us a horn of salvation.
> Salvation from our enemies, and from the hands of all who hate us.
>
> To perform the mercy (promised) to our forefathers
> To remember his holy covenant
> To grant that we should be without fear
> To set us free from the hands of our enemies
> To serve him in uprightness and righteousness
> Before him all the days of our lives.

The second section, vv. 76–79, is a prophecy about the new child.

> And you child
>   shall be called the prophet of the Highest,
> For you will go [as a messenger[65]] before the face of the LORD
>   to prepare his ways,
> To give knowledge of salvation to his people,
>   in the forgiveness of their sins,

---

[63] The term for priestly service in the temple.
[64] What follows has been developed from M. Gertner, 'Midrashim in the New Testament', *Journal of Semitic Studies* 7 (1962), pp. 267–92.
[65] This addition is necessary for the metre in Hebrew.

Through the tender mercies of our God,
  in which the rising light will dawn upon us from on high
To give light to those in darkness and in the shadow of death
And to guide our feet into the way of peace.
                    (Luke 1.68–79 as in the 'Hebrew original')

The whole is woven as a midrash around the Aaronites' priestly blessing which prays that the people might see the presence of the LORD (Num. 6.24–26). A contemporary example of such an adaptation was found in the *Community Rule* at Qumran,[66] and a comparison of the biblical form of the blessing with the Qumran form will show how Zechariah wove his words together.

May the LORD bless you | and keep you.
May he bless you with all good | and preserve you from all evil.

May the LORD make his face shine on you | and be gracious to you.
May he enlighten your heart with life giving wisdom | and grant you
  eternal knowledge.

May the LORD lift up his face upon you | and give you peace.
May he raise his merciful face towards you | for everlasting bliss.

The LORD's shining face here means intellectual enlightenment, his graciousness is the gift of knowledge, and lifting up his face means showing mercy.

May the LORD bless you and keep you became the first section of the Benedictus: a blessing of the LORD and an account of how he had protected his people. He had visited them, redeemed them and fulfilled the prophecies, a key element in early Christian proclamation (for example, Acts 3.21). The LORD had promised they would be saved from their enemies, and he had remembered the covenant with Abraham that they would possess the land. 'Remembering the covenant of the forefathers' appears in the *Damascus Document* as the reason why their community was saved during the era of wrath.[67] The *War Scroll* blesses God for his great marvels: 'Thou hast kept thy covenant with us from of old, and hast shown us the gates of salvation many times . . . For thou didst know the time appointed for us and it has appeared.'[68] Tightly woven into Zechariah's lines are the names of the chief characters of the story. In verses 71–73,

---

[66] 1QS II.
[67] CD I, IV.
[68] 1QM XVIII 7–11.

'saved from our enemies' alludes to Jesus, whose name means 'Saviour' (Matt. 1.21); 'the mercy promised to our forefathers' alludes to John, whose name means 'the Lord has been gracious'; 'remembering' the covenant alludes to Zechariah, whose name means 'the Lord has remembered'; and 'the oath which he swore' alludes to Elizabeth, whose name means 'the Lord has sworn'.

May the Lord make his face shine on you and be gracious to you became 'You will go before the *face* of the Lord *to prepare* his way.' 'Face' and 'prepare' sound almost the same in Hebrew,[69] and so with the wordplay characteristic of temple discourse, Zechariah links this to the prophecy always associated with John: 'Prepare in the wilderness the way of the Lord' (Isa. 40.3). The contemporary understanding of the second line of the blessing – enlightenment and eternal knowledge – became 'to give knowledge of salvation to his people in the forgiveness of their sins'. Here, too, there is wordplay: John would give knowledge of salvation and also of Jesus – almost the same word – for the forgiveness of sins.

May the Lord lift up his face upon you and give you peace, understood to mean the Lord's face shining with mercy and bringing peace, becomes 'the tender mercy of God', 'light for those who sit in darkness' and 'guide our feet into the way of peace'. The light to those 'who sit in darkness and in the shadow of death' is a close allusion to 'the people who walked in darkness . . . and in the shadow of death . . .' (Isa. 9.2, AV), which precedes the announcement of the birth of the royal child. The 'rising' light is sometimes translated 'the dayspring'. It was a title for the Messiah (Zech. 3.8; 6.12) and in Hebrew the word also means 'a branch'. Here, the Messiah is the rising light, the dawn light which is mentioned in Matthew: 'We have seen his star *at its rising*' (Matt. 2.2, my translation) and also in John's vision of the great angel with the seal of the living God appearing from *the rising* of the sun (Rev. 7.2). The reference to the rising light at this point could indicate the first appearance of the star, six months before the birth of Jesus; this is what Ephrem believed: 'The rising from on high refers to the star of the magi.'[70]

John grew up, 'and he was in the wilderness till the day of his manifestation to Israel' (Luke 1.80). His elderly parents may have died when he was still young and he may have become a member of the

---

[69] His face is *panaw* and prepare is *pannu*.

[70] Ephrem, *Commentary on the Diatessaron* 1.32, in C. McCarthy, trans., *Saint Ephrem's Commentary on Tatian's Diatessaron*, Oxford: Oxford University Press, 1993.

community at Qumran. There is no evidence beyond the fact that Luke includes the detail and so it must have been important.

The birth of Jesus

The basic story is simple: during a census, Mary and Joseph went to Bethlehem, found nowhere to stay, and were outside the town when the child Jesus was born. Some shepherds visited the family while they were there. Where Luke gives detail, it is to emphasize significant points that could be linked to prophecies or other expectations. He does not spell out these links, but no detail in Luke's account is there without a reason.

There was a census – and this is the first problem, since Quirinius became the governor of Syria in 6 CE and conducted a census of Judaea but not Galilee in 6–7 CE. This is too late for the birth of Jesus. Caesar Augustus had called for a census of all Roman citizens in 8 BCE, but Luke implies this was a general census: 'all the world should be enrolled'. Tertullian, however, writing about 200 CE in north Africa, said that the governor who took the census was Sentius Saturninus. No New Testament manuscript today has this name, but Saturninus did hold office from 9 to 6 BCE. Tertullian, refuting the followers of Marcion who said that Jesus was not born as a human baby but appeared as a fully grown man, said they could find details of Jesus' family if they consulted the census records. 'A census had been taken in Judaea by Sentius Saturninus which might have satisfied their enquiry in respect of the family and descent of Christ.'[71]

Luke, or later scribes, may have confused the names of the governors, perhaps because the census under Quirinius was the much hated landmark in Jewish history that prompted the revolt of Judas the Galilean. Or it may be that this census, like others, took many years to complete, and this one was completed in the time of Quirinius. Justin, writing for the emperor Antoninus Pius in the mid-second century CE, said that he could check the details of Jesus' birth 'from the registers of the taxing you made under Cyrenius, your first procurator in Judaea'.[72] Pursuit of the details of Roman history does not, however, establish the truth or otherwise of the Christmas story. The census was a significant detail for another reason; it fulfilled prophecy, and

---

[71] Tertullian, *Against Marcion* IV.19.
[72] Justin, *Apology* 1.34.

showed that Christ had been born among men.[73] Psalm 87 has Yahweh registering all those who were born in Zion, and he records: 'This one was born there' (Ps. 87.6). The Old Greek read the Hebrew differently, or read different Hebrew for verse 5: 'Mother Zion, the man will say, even the Man will be born in her, and the Most High himself will establish her.' Eusebius,[74] quoting from Origen, said there was another Greek translation: 'In the census of the peoples, this one will be born there.' Since it was the LORD who was registering the peoples, it was the LORD himself who prophesied that he would be born there.

Mary's child was born, and Luke gives four details: the first-born son (v. 7), wrapped in swaddling clothes (vv. 7, 12), lying in a manger (vv. 7, 12, 16), because there was no place in the inn (v. 7). Each was significant, especially since there is repeated reference to the manger and the swaddling clothes.

The 'first born' sets the scene because in the temple, Firstborn is the title for the human person who has become the presence of the LORD on earth. The original Firstborn had been the LORD himself, the first of the angel sons of God. Paul assumed knowledge of this when he explained: 'For all who are led by the Spirit of God are sons of God . . . in order that he might be the Firstborn among many brethren' (Rom. 8.14, 29). The newly anointed Davidic king was given this title; he cried out to the LORD, 'You are my Father' and the LORD appointed him the Firstborn, the highest of the kings of the earth (Ps. 89.26–27). This was the liturgical counterpart of the promise made to David through Nathan: 'I will raise up your offspring after you . . . I will be his Father and he shall be my son' (2 Sam. 7.12, 14). Paul shows that this divine sonship was central to the gospel, and all Christians being one in Christ meant that they all shared his status. They would be the assembly of the Firstborn in the heavenly Jerusalem (Heb. 12.23).

She wrapped him in swaddling clothes is, literally, 'she wrapped him around'. Why mention the baby's clothes? Because the clothing of the 'newly born' high priest was an important part of his becoming the Son. Enoch was taken from his earthly garments – his human body – and clothed with garments of God's Glory because he had become part of the Glory.[75] The new child is clothed with earthly

---

[73] Thus Origen, *On Luke Homily 11*.
[74] Eusebius, *Commentary on the Psalms*, in Patrologia Graeca Latina, XXIII.1048–9.
[75] See above, p. 35.

garments, and so the process is reversed. The Glory is incarnate. The *Epistle of the Apostles* said that at his incarnation, the LORD was robed in Wisdom and Power. In an early Christian wisdom text, Wisdom the Mother gives to her son 'a high priestly garment that is woven from every Wisdom'.[76]

Then the child is set in a manger. The Hebrew word for manger, *'ebus*, is almost the same as the ancient name for Jerusalem, *y^{e}bus*, and so the scene Luke describes is almost, but not quite, the Virgin who clothes the first-born and sets him in ancient Jerusalem. 'I have set my king in Zion' (Ps. 2.6). This manger/Jerusalem wordplay appears in the opening verses of Isaiah.[77] In its original context it was part of a complex oracle about the rebellious sons of God, the fallen angels. They are corrupted sons, *mšḥtm*, which echoes their intended title: anointed sons, *mšḥm*.[78] The whole passage is political, a condemnation of the princes and priests of Jerusalem, woven through with wordplay. The ox, *šor*, knows its owner, *qoneh*; this is very similar to the prince, *śar*, knows his begetter, *qoneh*; and the ass, *ḥamor*, is very like a word for priest, *komer*.[79] The humble animals recognize their master but the rulers of Jerusalem have not understood. In the Christmas story, this was comment on the current rulers and priests. By the mid-second century, Justin was using this prophecy to explain why so many Jews had not recognized Jesus. 'Wherefore the prophetic spirit, censuring the Jews through Isaiah, said: "The ox knows its owner and the ass its master's crib, but Israel has not known me and my people has not understood me."'[80] Origen interpreted the verse differently: the ox was a clean animal and the ass unclean, and even an unclean animal recognized the LORD.[81] The two animals eventually came to symbolize both Jews and Gentiles worshipping the LORD.

---

[76] *The Teaching of Silvanus*, CG VII.4.89.

[77] See my book *The Hidden Tradition of the Kingdom of God*, London: SPCK, 2007, pp. 5–6.

[78] See above, p. 7.

[79] The priest/ass wordplay was widely known. There was a story that Antiochus Epiphanes had found a golden ass's head in the temple (Josephus, *Against Apion* 2.7), and Tacitus, writing in 109 CE, knew this too (*Histories* 5.3). Tertullian, defending Christianity from pagan criticism about 200 CE, wrote, 'You are under the delusion that our God is an ass's head' (*Apology* 16.1). Clearest of all is the graffito found in Rome, dated anywhere from the late first century to the third, which crudely depicts the crucifixion of a man with an ass's head and says, 'Alexamenos worships his God'.

[80] Justin, *Apology* 1.63.

[81] Origen, *On Luke Homily 13*.

The ox and the ass looking into the manger were part of the nativity scene from the very beginning, even though they are not mentioned in the text – testimony to the importance of sources other than written. They do not appear in a nativity text until the *Gospel of Pseudo-Matthew*, compiled perhaps in the eighth century, but which had been widely used in Christian art.[82] The Habakkuk prophecy, 'Be known in the midst of the two creatures, be recognized in the drawing near of the years, be manifested in the coming of the Time' (LXX Hab. 3.2)[83] assumed these two creatures, but linked them to the two cherubim of the ark and the throne where the king had sat as the Lord. Early depictions of the nativity show no more than the two animals looking into a manger;[84] the icon of the nativity has the two animals and the manger in the centre, and even when European art in the second millennium moved away from the old icon style, the two animals remained for a long time. They are a good example of an ancient tradition about the nativity that was not put in writing until the mid-second century, and yet carried important prophecies.

The Firstborn was robed and set between the two creatures. Luke's few details about the birth were remembered as allusions to the holy of holies and the temple birth of the royal high priest. This is also implicit in his final detail: 'There was no room for them in the inn.' The word translated 'inn', *kataluma*, is also used for the location of the last supper (Luke 22.11). It is not a common word, and in conjunction with 'place', *topos*, seems also to allude to the holy of holies. This latter is a common enough word, but in the first century CE, it had acquired a special meaning in temple and mystical discourse. Philo used 'place', *topos*, to indicate the Logos, something very similar to the early rabbinic practice of using the Hebrew equivalent, *mqwm*, to indicate the *shekinah* or Glory of God. 'When "place" refers to something divine revealed to man, . . . it may mean God's image . . . This doctrine allows that "place" is a divine creature called Lord'.[85] Comparing those who serve God to the elders who ascended Sinai with Moses, Philo wrote: 'For then they shall behold the place which is in fact the Logos, where stands God the never changing'.[86] In Bethlehem, the Logos has no 'place' in the 'inn'.

---

[82] See D. R. Cartlidge and J. K. Elliott, *Art and the Christian Apocrypha*, London: Routledge, 2001, esp. pp. 15–23.

[83] See above, p. 64.

[84] See Cartlidge and Elliott (n. 82 above), pp. 18–20.

[85] A. F. Segal, *Two Powers in Heaven*, Leiden: Brill, 1978, p. 162.

[86] *On the Confusion of Tongues* 96.

Inn, *kataluma*, may be an approximation to a technical temple term. These were often transliterated rather than translated into Greek, imitating the sound of the original Hebrew word. In the account of Solomon's temple, for example, the porch, Hebrew *'ulam* became in Greek *ailam*; the inner sanctuary, *d*ᵉ*bir*, became *dabeir*; and the holy ones, *q*ᵉ*dešim*, became *kadeseim*.[87] The inn, *kataluma*, sounds very like the Hebrew *ta'alumah*, which means the hidden or secret (place).[88] Related words mean conceal or eternal, and the word translated 'virgin', *'almah*, implies the hidden or secret woman. The secret place of the temple was the holy of holies. 'No place in the inn' could well have been an allusion, there being no 'Logos' in the holy of holies. The Firstborn and the Glory, the Logos, was not 'born' in the holy of holies and did not appear in his garments of Glory in Jerusalem. He was swaddled in a manger elsewhere.[89] The expected in the unexpected.

The annunciation to the shepherds

Luke does not say where the shepherds were grazing their flocks, and so we look for a location with links to prophecy. The most likely is Migdal 'Eder, meaning 'the tower of the flock', which was near Bethlehem.[90] In an enigmatic oracle, Micah had linked it to the daughter of Zion in labour in the open country outside the city, and to the restoration of royal power:

> And you, O Tower of the Flock, hill of the daughter of Zion, to you it shall come, the former dominion shall come, the kingdom of the daughter of Jerusalem . . . Writhe and bring forth, O daughter of Zion, like woman in travail; for now you shall go forth from the city, and dwell in the open country.   (Mic. 4.8, 10, my translation)

There follows the prophecy of the birth of the great shepherd of Israel, coming forth from Bethlehem: 'Therefore he shall give them up until she who is in travail has brought forth; then the rest of his brethren shall return to the people of Israel. And he shall stand and feed his

---

[87] Respectively, 1 Kings 6.33 = LXX 3 Kms 7.6; 1 Kings 6.23 = LXX 3 Kms 6.22; 2 Kings 23.7 = LXX 4 Kms 23.7.

[88] In the LXX 2 Kms 7.6, i.e. the Greek of 2 Sam. 7.6, *kataluma* means the dwelling place of the LORD in the desert wanderings.

[89] None of these suggestions constitutes proof, but together, they seem too much to be just coincidence.

[90] Rachel's tomb was nearby, Gen. 35.19–21.

flock in the strength of the Lord, in the majesty of the Name of the Lord his God' (Mic. 5.3–4). The Lady would give birth to a son, and the people would return; this was the hope of the long exiled. The Targum, however, did not mention the daughter of Zion, the mother of the Messiah, or the tower of the flock; only the Messiah and the restoration of the kingdom. In the Targum the daughter of Zion became the congregation of Israel, so was the mother of the Messiah a sensitive issue? The Targum to Micah 4.8 became: 'And you, O Anointed One of Israel, who have been hidden away because of the sins of the congregation of Israel, the Kingdom shall come to you, and the former dominion shall be restored to the congregation of Jerusalem.' Micah 5.2 became: 'from you shall come forth before me the Anointed One, to exercise dominion over Israel, whose name was mentioned from of old, from ancient times'. The birth of the Messiah was elsewhere linked to the tower of the flock, but this is not obvious in English translations. After burying Rachel near Bethlehem, Jacob moved on to 'the tower of Eder', that is, the tower of the flock, and the Targum adds here: 'the Tower of the Flock, the place from which the King Messiah will reveal himself at the end of days'.[91]

The tower of the flock, however, was not only a place near Bethlehem. It was an ancient name for the holy of holies, the place where the Lord of the sheep stood, and where his prophets received revelations (for example, Isa. 21.8; Hab. 2.1). Details about the tower and the flock are found in *1 Enoch*, where the history of Israel is the story of the flock and of the Lord of the sheep, who leaves his tower when the flock forsake him. The Lord allowed other angel shepherds to rule them (that is, foreign rulers), but an angel scribe kept a record of their deeds and begged the Lord to intervene (*1 En.* 89.50–77). A birth among the shepherds outside Jerusalem but near the 'tower of the flock' was a sign pointing to the birth in the original tower of the flock among the shepherds, in the holy of holies among the angels. The angel announced to the Bethlehem shepherds the birth of the Davidic king, in other words, the return of the Lord to his people in this time of danger. Origen knew that the shepherds represented the guardian angels 'keeping watch over their flocks by night', and that the angel of the Lord had announced the coming of the good shepherd to help them in their struggle.[92]

---

[91] Targum Pseudo Jonathan Gen. 35.21.
[92] Origen, *On Luke Homily 12.*

A later prophecy, heralding the return to Jerusalem after the exile, set the herald of *good tidings* to Jerusalem on a high hill near the city. The form of the verb shows that the herald was female. 'Get you up to a high mountain, O herald of *good tidings* to Zion . . . Say to the cities of Judah, behold your God' (Isa. 40.9). The Greek translation here uses the same word[93] as does the angel to the shepherds: 'I bring you good news!', and it is interesting that the traditional nativity icon depicts the birth of Jesus in a cave in the side of a mountain.

An angel of the LORD appeared to the shepherds, and the Glory shone around them, and they were afraid.[94]

> Do not be afraid, for behold
>   I bring good news to you
> Great joy
>   Which will be for the whole people,
> For there is born to you
>   This day a Saviour
> Who is the LORD's Christ,
>   In the city of David.
> And this for you
>   You will find as a sign
> A child wrapped around
>   And lying in a manger.
>   (Luke 2.10–11, as in the 'Hebrew original')

The angel's message is given in the traditional form: reassurance, the message itself, and then the sign to confirm it. Isaiah had given Ahaz the sign of the Virgin's child: before he was grown, Jerusalem would be free from her enemies (Isa. 7.14–16). The angel brought the shepherds good news of great joy for the whole people, and the political aspect must not be overlooked because of later ways of reading the story. Herod knew that a Davidic king meant trouble for him. The Greek titles that follow here, 'Christ the LORD', probably represent the Hebrew 'the LORD's anointed', and so the angel says: 'Today the LORD's Anointed has been born for you in the city of David, a Saviour.' The underlying prophecy here is Isaiah 9.1–7: 'The people who walked in darkness have seen a great light; those who dwelt in a land of deep darkness, on them has light shined' – Luke mentioned that the shepherds were out at night. 'You have made great the rejoicing, you have increased the joy' (Isa. 9.3), is represented by the angel

---

[93] *Evangelizomai.*

[94] Origen noted that the angel did not take the message to Jerusalem, *On Luke Homily 12.*

giving the shepherds news of great joy.[95] The Isaiah oracle then describes a great triumph over enemies, before announcing the birth of the child. Since the voices in Isaiah seem to be the angel host, this is the divine 'child' who is about to become king. 'For unto us a child is born . . . and his name will be called Wonderful Counsellor, Mighty God, Everlasting Father, Prince of Peace . . . Upon the throne of David and over his kingdom, to establish it'. The titles of this royal child are to be Saviour and LORD's Anointed, or, in the more familiar form: LORD Jesus Christ. Since the royal child was born in the holy of holies, he would have emerged into the world through the temple veil, and so Luke described how the heavens opened at that point. This was all God's angels worshipping the Firstborn as he came into the world (Heb. 1.6).

When the heavens opened, the angels sang as the Glory of the LORD shone round about them.

> Glory in the highest [heavens] to God
> And on earth peace among men.

There are various versions of this text, depending on the form of the word *eudokia*, goodwill. Some have the genitive form – 'Peace on earth among men *of goodwill*'; some have the nominative – 'God's *favour* to men on earth'. One of the Qumran hymns shows that the chosen community were 'the sons of his favour' who had been illuminated, given the knowledge of God's marvellous mysteries and returned to the covenant,[96] but 'great joy for the whole people' suggests that this was not limited to one group. The lines read best as Hebrew poetry if the word *eudokia* is omitted: 'On earth peace among men.'[97]

The song of the heavenly host was a sign of the new creation, the restoration of the covenant that meant the renewal of the earth. Whenever the angels or the heavens sing in the Old Testament, it is a sign of the new creation. At the beginning of creation, 'the morning stars sang together and all the sons of God shouted for joy' (Job 38.7). When the LORD called the Servant and announced a new beginning, there was a new song, or possibly a 'renewing' song (Isa. 42.10).[98] Praise renewed the earth. When Isaiah heard the angels singing 'Holy, holy, holy is the LORD of hosts', he knew that the

---

[95] Following the emendation proposed in *Biblia Hebraica Stuttgartensia*.

[96] 1QH XII.

[97] The cry of the crowd when Jesus entered Jerusalem has a similar form to the song of the angels: 'Peace in heaven and Glory in the highest' (Luke 19.38).

[98] See my book *The Great High Priest*, London: T&T Clark, 2003, p. 119.

whole earth was full of his Glory (Isa. 6.3). Gregory of Nyssa, in a Christmas Sermon,[99] linked the birth of the Saviour to the restoration of creation and its hymns of praise. He preached from Psalm 118.26, 'Blessed is he who enters in the name of the LORD', and said that sin had silenced the voice of praise on earth. The human creation no longer joined with heaven. With the coming of the Saviour – 'not by boat or some sort of chariot, but through a pure Virgin he comes into human life' – heaven and earth formed one choir again, and harmony was restored. Peace on earth among men.

The shepherds went to find the child, and then reported what they had heard and seen. 'And all who heard it, wondered at what the shepherds told them.' Mary '*kept* all these things, *pondering* them in her heart' (Luke 2.19). Both the verbs here imply comparing things, putting things together. The first implies putting together and keeping, the second implies interpreting. Was it Mary who first recognized the fulfilment of prophecies in the events surrounding the birth of her son? Mary, as we shall see, was presented as Wisdom, whose characteristic was that she held all things together in harmony' (LXX Prov. 8.30). On the eighth day, the baby was circumcised and named Jesus.

The LORD in his temple

The scene then moves to the temple in Jerusalem and the two rites observed by every young family. When he was one month old, the first-born son had to be redeemed with a payment of five shekels of pure silver. The first-born male of every clean animal was deemed to belong to the LORD and had to be sacrificed, but the first-born son was redeemed with a money payment to the temple (Num. 18.15–16).[100] Luke does not mention that Jesus was redeemed with five silver shekels; Mary and Joseph 'brought him up to Jerusalem to present him to the LORD' (Luke 2.22). Since every detail in Luke's account is significant, it would be strange if this was just an omission. Perhaps it is the first indication of his death, the ultimate sacrifice of the Firstborn. The same word for 'present', *paristemi*, is used by Paul to mean 'present as a sacrifice' (Rom. 12.1), and the closest parallel in the Old Testament is Daniel's night vision, when he sees one like a son of man *presented* before the Ancient of Days.

---

[99] Gregory died in 395 CE. *Oratio in Diem Natalem Christi*, Patrologia Graeca 46 1128–37. I do not know of an English version.
[100] Mishnah *Bekhoroth* 8.7.

In that context, the man is presented as a sacrifice before he is enthroned.

The young mother had to be purified from the blood of giving birth. Luke's text is not entirely clear here, as 'their' purification is treated as though one action. 'Every male that opens the womb shall be called holy to the LORD' (Luke 2.23) describes the sacrifice or redemption of the first-born, but offering 'a pair of turtle doves or two young pigeons' is the ritual for the new mother. The ancient law was that 40 days after the birth of a son and 80 days after the birth of a daughter, the mother took to the temple a lamb as a burnt offering and a pigeon or dove as a sin offering. Those who could not afford a lamb used a bird for each offering (Lev. 12.1–8). The priest had to wring the neck of the sin offering and sprinkle some of the blood on the altar; the rest was poured out at the base. The burnt offering was burned, and thus the mother was purified from the blood shed during childbirth. We are not told why Mary needed this purification, nor was there any need to take the child to the temple, unless his being 'offered to the LORD' really did mean that he was not redeemed with money. The focus of this story is the mother and child, *the LORD and his mother coming to the temple.*

In the court they met Simeon and Anna, and even though Luke says little about them, they afford a glimpse of temple life. Simeon was 'righteous and devout' and waiting for 'the consolation, *paraklesis*, of Israel' (Luke 2.25). Luke says nothing of his family or his age, only that he received revelations when the Spirit came upon him. The word used, *chrematizo*, implies that he had received a prophetic oracle and knew he would live to see the coming of the LORD's Anointed.[101] He spent his time in the temple because they believed that the LORD would appear there, emerging from the holy of holies with the earth in silence before him, to rescue his sons and judge their enemies, bestriding the earth in fury and trampling the nations in anger (Hab. 3.12). The surviving parts of the Qumran commentary on Habakkuk[102] show how those prophecies were understood in Simeon's time. There were the Spouter of Lies and the Wicked Priest who attacked the Poor, and the last priests in Jerusalem who had piled

---

[101] Jesus made a similar promise to his disciples, that they would see the kingdom of God before they died (Luke 9.27), and immediately afterwards, Peter, James and John saw Jesus transfigured. In other words, they saw beyond the temple veil into the light of the holy of holies, and had a vision of the heavenly Jesus.

[102] 1Qp Hab. VIII, IX, X.

up wealth through plunder. Simeon probably knew these people. Isaiah had prophesied a voice in the temple announcing the LORD coming to judge those who had corrupted the temple (Isa. 66.1–6), and the final sections of the Book of the Twelve Prophets give some idea of what they were expecting. The messenger/angel[103] of the Day of the LORD would appear, Elijah with his final warning (Mal. 4.5) to prepare the way (Mal. 3.1). The Hebrew text of Malachi is not clear here, but seems to say that the LORD himself would then come to his temple as the angel of the covenant, bringing judgement first on the wicked priests and then on all those who practise witchcraft, sexual immorality, falsehood and oppression. 'Who can endure the day of his coming?' (Mal. 3.2). Their expectation of the day of the LORD in the temple was probably like John's vision in the book of Revelation: the heavens opening, the throne, angels with trumpets. That is what Simeon was hoping to see.

Simeon and Anna were symbolic figures, which is why they are included. We assume that Anna was one of those who were 'looking for the redemption, *lutrosis*, of Jerusalem' (Luke 2.38). Zechariah had sung of the LORD visiting and redeeming his people (Luke 1.68); the disciples on the road to Emmaus had hoped that Jesus would 'redeem Israel' (Luke 24.21). It was a widely cherished hope. But Anna, unlike Simeon, is described in some detail: she was a very old widow of the tribe of Asher, a daughter of Phanuel, a prophet who spent all her time in the temple, worshipping, fasting and praying. What might these details mean? Phanuel is not a biblical name; it is the name of one of the archangels,[104] who was also known as Uriel. Phanuel means the presence or face of God, Uriel means the light of God. Daughter of Phanuel may have been a description of her status as a prophet, just as the apostle Joseph was given the name 'Son of Encouragement' and always thereafter known as Bar Nabas (Acts 4.36). The singer of the Qumran hymns proclaimed: 'Thou hast revealed thyself to me in thy Power as perfect light . . . Through me thou hast illumined the face of the congregation.'[105] He could easily have been called a son of the light of God, and so perhaps Anna was a daughter of the light of God. She had special prophetic gifts to understand what she was seeing.

---

[103] The same word in Hebrew.
[104] e.g. *1 En.* 40.9; 54.6, together with Gabriel, Michael and Raphael.
[105] 1QH XII.

Nor was the tribe of Asher an important group, but the name Asher has interesting associations, and the Hebrew word for 'tribe' has other meanings such as 'stem' or 'branch'. When Ezekiel, again in that crucial period in the sixth century BCE, described the deported queen as a vine that had been cast down, its withered *stems* were the royal children who were no more (Ezek. 19.11, 12, 14). Was Anna a stem from a tree known as Asher, or even Asherah? The tribe of Asher would have been more recognizable to a translator than a stem of Asherah, but two other random survivals do suggest this latter as a possible understanding. First, there was an incident in the reign of Asa, when he tried to eradicate from Jerusalem the veneration of Asherah, the ancient tree symbol for the Mother. The king deposed his own mother who had made one of these images (1 Kings 15.13). Her name was Maʿacah, but in the Greek translation her name was changed to Anna. Why? Second, there is a curious reference in one of Juvenal's satires, written early in the second century CE, in which he ridiculed a poor Jewish woman, possibly a refugee. She was 'a fortune teller, an interpreter of the laws of Jerusalem, a high priestess of the tree, a reliable mediator with highest heaven'.[106] This is not the usual picture we have of a Jewish woman of the time, but it must have been recognizable to Juvenal's readers or there would have been no point to his satire.

The Lady and her tree symbol were an issue for the Jerusalem authorities in the time of Jesus, as can be seen from some of the regulations in the Mishnah. Trees pruned in a special shape and used in worship were forbidden, and anything made from their wood was forbidden.[107] The branch of such a tree could not be used in a Tabernacles procession, nor could a branch from an apostate city be used – that is, from a city that had adopted a different form of Judaism.[108] The Enoch tradition, however, cherished the hope that in the time of the Messiah a certain tree would return to the temple. Enoch had seen it on one of his heavenly journeys, fragrant, growing on the mountain of the throne of the Great Holy One, and with fruit in clusters like the fruit of a palm.[109] One day, that fruit of that tree would give life to the chosen ones. The archangel Michael told him that after the great judgement, the tree would be transplanted

---

[106] Juvenal, *Satires* 6.543–5.
[107] Mishnah *ʿAbodah Zarah* 3.7, 9.
[108] Mishnah *Sukkah* 3.1–3.
[109] The palm tree is significant, see p. 144.

northwards to the house of the LORD (*1 En.* 24.1—25.7). In other words, the tree of life from which Adam had been barred was somewhere in the south but would return to the temple, and the chosen would eat from it just as Jesus promised his own faithful followers (Rev. 2.7). In his vision of the land around Jerusalem, Enoch also saw branches sprouting from a felled tree (*1 En.* 26.1; the early Church regarded *1 Enoch* as Scripture), and the Qumran community described themselves as the branches of the Council of Holiness.[110] Was Anna, with her gift of prophecy, one of these branches?

Certain symbols were also forbidden at that time, according to the Mishnah. 'If a man finds an object on which there is a figure of the sun, a figure of the moon or a figure of the dragon, he must throw them into the Dead Sea.'[111] Now the sun, the moon and the dragon sound very like the image of the Lady that John saw in his vision, the Lady appearing in the holy of holies to give birth to her son the Messiah (Rev. 11.19—12.6). Who was using her symbols so extensively that there had to be a law against them? Her other symbol was the tree of life, and John saw this too: the tree of life restored to the holy of holies, its fruit for the faithful and its leaves to heal the nations. From its base flowed the river of life (Rev. 22.1–2).

Who might Anna have been? Whom did she represent? Juvenal's 'fortune teller and high priestess of the tree' could well have been a prophet whose sacred symbol was the tree, whose face had been illuminated by the light of God, and who was looking for the tree/the Lady to return to the temple. What did Anna 'see' when she saw Mary and her child entering the temple court? When her people imagined the LORD coming to the temple, they did not envisage a small child and his young mother, and yet this is what Simeon has 'seen'. Anna spoke about the child Jesus to all who were looking for the redemption of Jerusalem, which means that she knew people who were expecting the great high priest to perform the final rite of redemption.

Both Simeon and Anna were temple prophets, so they knew about the birth of John some six months earlier, and of his father being struck dumb in the temple. They knew the prophecy at his birth. Since she was a very old woman, Anna had lived through Herod's murder of the temple priests in 32 BCE, when they had been calculating the date of the Messiah. She knew the risks in making such a claim. Both Anna and Simeon probably knew the Qumran calcula-

---

[110] 1QH XV.
[111] Mishnah '*Abodah Zara* 3.2.

tions that Melchizedek the great high priest was returning for the final Day of Atonement at the beginning of the tenth jubilee. The tenth jubilee, however, was not due until 20 CE,[112] and they were probably hoping for something rather more spectacular than a mother and her new baby son. The expected and the unexpected.

What is less often noticed in the Old Testament prophecies, and in John's vision, is that the Lady also appears with the LORD. Malachi's prophecy of the LORD coming to his temple is accompanied by a prophecy of the Lady: 'For you who fear my name, the Sun of righteousness [or the true Sun] shall rise with healing in her wings' (Mal. 4.2). 'Sun' is a feminine noun in the Hebrew here, and she rises on her people on the Day of the LORD. Isaiah's warning of the voice in the temple is accompanied by a much longer passage about Zion, the mother with her sons (Isa. 66.7–14). The LORD God Almighty taking power on earth and bringing the judgement (Rev. 11.15–18) is accompanied by the woman appearing in the holy of holies, 'clothed with the sun' (Rev. 12.1) and later flying with the wings of a great eagle (Rev. 12.14). Given the expectations of the time, the woman in John's vision is likely to have been the Sun of Malachi's prophecy and the birthing woman in Isaiah. Simeon and Anna may well have been expecting the LORD to return to the temple and the Lady to appear.

Isaiah had foreseen the light rising on Jerusalem. The city was told to rise and shine, 'for the Glory of the LORD has risen upon you . . . Nations shall come to your light and kings to the brightness of your rising' (Isa. 60.1, 3). Ezekiel had seen the light of the Glory of the LORD returning to the temple (Ezek. 43.1–5), but had described it as the fiery chariot throne and the living creatures (Ezek. 1.4–14). Daniel had seen a vision of political turmoil and oppression – the four monsters – and then the 'one like a son of man' who was offered before the Ancient of Days and then enthroned to establish the Kingdom (Dan. 7.13–14). Gabriel had explained to Daniel that there would be seventy weeks of years before the city and the holy people would see an end to sin and transgression. Then there would be the great atonement, visions and prophecies would be fulfilled, everlasting righteousness established, and the Most Holy One would be anointed (Dan. 9.24). The Qumran community knew this figure as Melchizedek, the King of Righteousness.

All this, and a good deal more that has been lost to us, would have been in the minds of Simeon and Anna as they looked for the

---

[112] Using our calendar!

consolation of Israel and the redemption of Jerusalem. Now 'consolation and redemption' are two recurring themes in Isaiah. The great
exhortation to return from exile begins: 'Comfort, comfort my
people, says your God', and then, in words that are taken up in the
Magnificat, 'say that her humble estate/time as a servant is over'.
'For he has regarded the low estate of his female servant' (Luke 1.48,
translating literally) echoes both the Hebrew, which has 'her time of
service is completed' and the Greek, which has 'her time of hard
service is completed' (Isa. 40.2). Mary is presented as the female
figure/Jerusalem whose time of hardship has ended, and the LORD is
the Redeemer: 'I will help you, says the LORD. Your redeemer is the
Holy One of Israel' (Isa. 41.14: there are many examples).

Closest to the scene in the temple are the words of Isaiah 52: Zion
has to put on her beautiful garments again for she is no longer a
captive. 'How beautiful upon the mountains are the feet of him who
brings good tidings,[113] who publishes peace, who announces good
tidings of good, who publishes salvation, who says to Zion, "Your
God reigns" . . . They see the return of the LORD to Zion.' And then
the two great themes: 'The LORD has comforted his people, he has
redeemed Jerusalem. *The LORD has bared his holy arm*, before the eyes
of all the nations; and all the ends of the earth shall see the salvation
of our God' (Isa. 52.7–10). Two Greek texts of Isaiah, both from
Egypt,[114] have this line differently. '*The LORD will reveal his Holy One*
before all the nations . . .', suggesting that at some stage the Hebrew
letters *zrw'*, which can mean arm, were given their other meaning:
scion, planting. We cannot know how Simeon and Anna understood
the line, but it is easy to see how it came to be read in that way. Part
of the comfort and redemption of Jerusalem would be the coming
of the Holy One.

Simeon took the baby in his arms and blessed God:

> Now let your servant depart
> According to your word, LORD, in peace;
> For my eyes have seen your salvation
> Which you have prepared before the face of all peoples
> A light for revelation to the Gentiles
> And for the Glory of your people Israel.
> (Luke 2.29–32 as in the 'Hebrew original')

---

[113] The Greek uses the word *evangelizo*, bring good news.
[114] The fifth century Codex Alexandrinus, and the sixth century Codex Marchalianus.

His lines echo Isaiah: 'the Glory of the LORD shall be revealed, and all flesh shall see it together' (Isa. 40.5); 'a light to the nations' (Isa. 42.6); 'a light to the nations that my salvation may reach to the end of the earth' (Isa. 49.6); 'You shall go out in joy and be led forth in peace' (Isa. 56.12). Simeon's song has a broader vision than the earlier songs in the Christmas story. Gabriel's words to Zechariah and to Mary, Mary's song and Zechariah's prophecy at the naming of John were all concerned with the Davidic king and the redemption of Israel. The song of the angels at Bethlehem was the first to extend the good news beyond Israel: 'On earth peace among men'. It was Simeon who blessed God with the words: 'Mine eyes have seen thy salvation which thou hast prepared before the face of all peoples, a light for revelation to the Gentiles', thus fulfilling the prophecy of the first Zechariah: 'Many nations shall join themselves to the LORD in that day, and shall be my people; and I will dwell in the midst of you' (Zech. 2.10) and the words of Isaiah: 'All the ends of the earth shall see the salvation of our God.'

The light of the Glory had returned to the temple, and Simeon's prophetic inspiration was that he recognized the Glory in the mother and child. Simeon has *seen* the Glory, and so his words join with those of John: 'We have beheld his Glory' (John 1.14). At this point the definition of Israel was broadened and changed, and there would be many difficult times in the early years of the Church as the new Israel was emerging. When the Christians were emphasizing that they had *seen* the Glory, the name 'Israel' was said to mean 'the one who has seen God', and so the emphasis in the Christmas stories was a claim to being the new Israel. Philo often used the expression; it was fundamental to his Judaism. He never explained it nor argued for it; it was something he could assume. 'The nation that sees, that is, Israel'[115]; 'For Israel means seeing God'.[116] 'The sons of Israel' (Lev. 15.31) for him became 'the sons of the seeing one'.[117] Almost all the early Christian writers adopted this explanation of Israel and claimed it for the Church.[118] It was used in prayers: 'For by [Christ] thou hast brought home the Gentiles to thyself for a peculiar people, the true Israel beloved of God and seeing God';

---

[115] Philo, *On Dreams* II.44.
[116] Philo, *Preliminary Studies* 51.
[117] Philo, *Allegorical Interpretation* III.15.
[118] See C. T. R. Hayward, *Interpretations of the Name Israel in Ancient Judaism and Some early Christian Writings*, Oxford: Oxford University Press, 2005, esp. pp. 156–93.

'the God of Israel, Thy people which truly see and which have believed in Christ'.[119]

The story of Simeon was later developed to emphasize this link with the temple and its liturgy. Simeon saw the child as he really was, 'shining like a pillar of light' in the arms of Mary. The angels, praising him, encircled him around, 'like guards before the king'.[120] Jesus coming to the temple was the LORD coming with the angels on the Day of Atonement, the first-born coming into the world (Heb. 1.6). The cherubic hymn, incorporated into the eastern liturgy in the sixth century, describes the procession with the bread and wine in the same way: 'That we may receive the king of all, invisible escorted by the host of angels'.

Then Simeon spoke again, an oracle of the judgement that the LORD was bringing.

> Behold this one is set for the fall and the rise
> Of many in Israel, and for a sign that will be spoken against.
> And you also, a sword will pierce your soul
> So that the hostile thoughts of many hearts are revealed.
> (Luke 2.34b–35 as in the 'Hebrew original')

Israel would change. Some would fall, some would rise, and Jesus would be the point of division, the 'sign spoken against'. Luke recorded an incident in Jesus' ministry when he spoke of the division he would cause: 'Do you think I have come to give peace on earth? No, I tell you, but rather division; for henceforth in one house there will be five divided, three against two and two against three' (Luke 12.51–52). Families would betray each other even to death (Luke 21.16), and the divisions would eventually bring the fall of the temple. Josephus wrote about an ancient oracle that the city and temple would fall when Jews began to kill each other,[121] and it seems that Jesus' talk of division caused by his presence was referring to that prophecy.[122]

The sword to pierce Mary's soul has been much debated and there is no agreement as to Simeon's meaning. Given the temple and judgement context of his oracle, the sword was probably the sword of the Messiah on the day of judgement. The Word of God who rode

---

[119] *The Apostolic Constitutions* 7.36 and 8.15. For detail see my book *Temple Themes in Christian Worship*, London: T&T Clark, 2008, pp. 154–60.

[120] *Arabic Gospel of the Infancy* 6.

[121] Josephus, *War* 6.110.

[122] We no longer have this in the Old Testament, but it is unlikely that Josephus would have described a new teaching of Jesus as an ancient oracle.

out from heaven with his army of angels had a sharp sword coming from his mouth (Rev. 19.15); the risen LORD whom John saw as the great high priest in the temple had a two-edged sword in his mouth (Rev. 1.16); and the Servant, called from his mother's womb, had a mouth like a sharp sword (Isa. 49.1–2). It represented his teaching and his judgement. John had to write to the erring Christians at Pergamum 'the words of him who has the sharp two-edged sword' (Rev. 2.12). They were warned to abandon the false teaching lest the LORD come in judgement 'and war against them with the sword of my mouth' (Rev. 2.16). The clearest exposition was for the Hebrews: 'For the Word of God is living and active, sharper than any two-edged sword, piercing to the division of soul and spirit, of joints and marrow, and discerning the thoughts and intentions of the heart. And before him no creature is hidden, but all are open and laid bare to the eyes of him with whom we have to do' – the great high priest (Heb. 4.12–13). Since Simeon's words were addressed to Mary, the sword could have been the sorrow that some of Jesus' teaching would cause her: he declared that his true mother and brothers were those who heard and did the word of God (Luke 8.20–21), and rebuffed a blessing on his mother with similar words: 'Blessed is the womb that bore you and the breasts that you sucked.' But he said, 'Blessed rather are those who hear the word of God and keep it!' (Luke 18.27–28). And Mary had to watch her son die.

Thus there were three prophecies in Luke's Christmas story: Gabriel to Mary, that her child would be the Son of the Most High and inherit the throne of David; Gabriel to the shepherds, that the child would be the Saviour, the LORD's Anointed; and Simeon to Mary, that the child would bring division, sorrow and hostility.

The family then returned to Nazareth, and Jesus grew up, filled with wisdom and blessed with the favour of God. The only glimpse of his childhood is the story of his Passover visit to Jerusalem when he was twelve, how he was separated from his anxious family, and reunited with them after three days. They found him in the temple with the teachers: 'Did you not know that I must be in my father's house?' *And they did not understand what he meant* (Luke 2.49–50).

We can only speculate about the temple teachers who were so amazed at Jesus' understanding (Luke 2.47). One clue may lie in the rule that certain texts could not be read in public, or could be read but not explained.[123] Ezekiel's vision of the throne was one such

---

[123] Mishnah *Hagigah* 2.1.

passage; it could not be discussed unless the other person already understood it 'of his own knowledge'. Nor could the blessing of the priests – 'May the LORD make his face shine upon you' (Num. 6.24–26) – be explained. Was it knowledge like this that amazed the temple teachers? Memories surviving in much later Jewish mystical texts show that people who studied the mysteries of the heavenly throne, the 'merkavah mystics',[124] did meet in the temple area, and the visions that Jesus entrusted to John – 'the revelation of Jesus Christ which God gave him to show to his people what must soon take place' (Rev. 1.1) – show that Jesus was one of them. These were the secrets of the holy of holies, the ancient teachings of the high priesthood. The *Hekhalot Rabbati*[125] describes how Rabbi Nehunya ben Ha-Qanah[126] sat on a marble bench in the temple precincts, with his disciples around him, an inner group and then others who listened at a distance. In his visions he saw the very bonds of the covenant that held the creation in place, and his disciples recorded what he saw.[127]

Perhaps Luke's enigmatic words: 'He was filled with wisdom, and the favour of God was upon him' (Luke 2.40) hint at the development of Jesus' awareness of his future role. What did Mary tell her son about her own experiences? To what extent did she shape his ideas? Luke simply says, as he did of the birth story, that 'his mother kept all these things in her heart' (Luke 2.51). Jesus astounding the teachers of the high priestly tradition would have been a fitting conclusion to the story of the birth of the great high priest, and maybe that is why Luke chose to include the episode.

---

[124] The chariot throne was called the *merkavah*.

[125] A collection of Jewish mystical texts. I do not know of an English translation, though there are extracts in P. Schaefer, *The Hidden and Manifest God*, New York: SUNY Press, 1992. The name means 'The Greater Palaces'.

[126] An anachronism, as he was second-generation teacher, around the end of the first century CE and so after the temple was destroyed. The memory could have been of earlier teachers.

[127] *Hekhalot Rabbati* sections 201–3, 228.

4

Matthew

Matthew records different parts of the Christmas story and in his own characteristic style. All through his Gospel he emphasizes the fulfilment of prophecies and quotes them. He cites 14 passages of which eight are from Isaiah,[1] suggesting that Isaiah was especially important. He may even have had a collection of messianic prophecies, like the one found at Qumran that was written early in the first century BCE. Messianic prophecies, whether or not they existed as a formal list, determined how Matthew told his story; he selected incidents that corresponded to the prophecies, but that does not mean he invented the incidents. He was telling a story that was both symbolic and cosmological, and so the two narratives were fused. John begins his Gospel with a theological statement and ends it with the reminder that he has made a selection from his material to show that 'Jesus is the Messiah, the Son of God' (John 20.31). Matthew has no clear statement like this, but his work was no less selective and no less theological. He worked with a scheme of prophecy and fulfilment which he attributed to the teaching of Jesus himself. Luke did the same in his account of the sermon at Nazareth where Jesus said he was that day fulfilling Isaiah's prophecy (Luke 4.21). When refusing to resist arrest in Gethsemane, Matthew had Jesus say, 'But how then should the scriptures be fulfilled that it must be so? . . . But all this has taken place that the scriptures of the prophets might be fulfilled' (Matt. 26.54, 56). Fulfilling prophecies is how Jesus was remembered, and so it is consistent with other early records that this should be emphasized by Matthew.

Matthew is not now considered an eyewitness of the ministry; he collected his materials from various sources. The usual assessment today is that he drew on Mark, on a lost collection of Jesus' teachings that

---

[1] 1.21–23 quotes Isa. 7.14; 2.5–6 quotes Mic. 5.2; 2.15 quotes Hos. 11.1; 2.18 quotes Jer. 31.15; [2.23 quotes Isa. 11.1]; 3.3 quotes Isa. 40.3; 4.15–16 quotes Isa. 9.1–2; 8.17 quotes Isa. 53.4; 12.17–21 quotes Isa. 42.1–4; 13.14–15 quotes Isa. 6.9–10; 13.35 attributes to Isaiah Ps. 78.2; 21.4–5 quotes Isa. 62.11 and Zech. 9.9; 27.9–10 attributes to Jeremiah Zech. 11.12–13 and alludes to Jer. 32.6–15.

modern scholars have designated 'Q', and on material he gathered from communities he knew. His Christmas story belongs with the latter as it is unique to his Gospel. The traditional view of Matthew is different. Eusebius, bishop of Caesarea early in the fourth century, said that Matthew was one of the twelve disciples, and that Matthew and John were the only ones who 'left memoirs of the LORD's doings'. Matthew preached to the Hebrews, and when he was called to preach elsewhere, he 'committed his own gospel to writing in his native tongue'.[2] This implies that when Matthew was with his community, nothing was in writing.[3] Presumably he was able to use the full range of techniques available to oral teaching: wordplay, intentional ambiguity, and knowing what knowledge he could assume on the part of his hearers. They would have known the prophecies, they would have been familiar with parables, and known how to understand the real meaning of a parable: the parable, *mashal*, and its application, *nimshal*. Jesus said this to his disciples: 'To you has been given the secret of the kingdom of God, but for those outside everything is in parables.' Those 'outside' heard the story but did not know what it was about, and this may well have been the fate of the Christmas stories once they passed outside a Hebrew milieu.

There was a Hebrew Gospel in the library at Caesarea, and Jerome thought it was the original Matthew. Whether Matthew's Gospel or something like it had existed in Hebrew is important for reading the Christmas story. Jerome quoted the Hebrew Gospel in his study of the LORD's Prayer and noted that the Hebrew word used for 'daily' bread, was in fact 'tomorrow's' bread.[4] In other words, it was a prayer for the bread of the Kingdom, the great tomorrow, and thus a eucharistic prayer. If recovering one Hebrew word can illuminate so familiar and important a text as the LORD's Prayer, there may be places where the Christmas story is also illuminated, for example the magi from the east, where 'east' and 'ancient times' are the same word in Hebrew.

Matthew tells the story in terms of the three dreams when an angel of the LORD appeared to Joseph. First, he was told that Mary had conceived by the Holy Spirit (Matt. 1.20–21); then he was told to take Mary and Jesus to Egypt (Matt. 2.13); finally, he was told to take them

---

[2] Eusebius, *Church History* 3.24.

[3] New Testament texts imply oral transmission, as we should expect in the early period, e.g. 2 Tim. 1.13; 2.2.

[4] Jerome, *On Psalm 135*, see M. R. James, *The Apocryphal New Testament*, Oxford: Clarendon Press (1924) 1980, p. 4.

back to the land of Israel (Matt. 2.20). In each case, the dream was linked to a prophecy and its fulfilment: that the Virgin should bear a son, that the son should be called from Egypt, and that the child should be called a Nazarene. Is this how Joseph himself interpreted the events into which he was drawn? Dreams – often described as night visions – were a recognized way of receiving prophetic revelation. 'I saw in the night' said Zechariah (Zech. 1.8); Daniel 'saw in the night visions' (Dan. 7.13); Jacob dreamed at Bethel and saw the ladder to heaven (Gen. 28.12); and the original Joseph was the most famous dreamer of all (Gen. 37.5–11). Zechariah learned the meaning of his dream from the angel who spoke to him or spoke *within* him – the Hebrew can be read either way (e.g. Zech. 1.19; 2.3; 4.1, 4). Perhaps Joseph had been wondering about events, looking for fulfilment of prophecy as were so many at that time, and had his questions answered in a dream. Linking prophecies to events may have been part of the story from the beginning. If Jesus was aware of who he was and what he was doing [*and the opposite has been the unacknowledged assumption of New Testament scholarship for a long time!*], then reflecting on the events of his birth and childhood as fulfilment of prophecy could have been what Matthew received from the community that had known Jesus, and not simply what he chose as his 'style'.

Some have suggested that Matthew had the story of Moses' birth in mind when he was writing the Christmas story; not the story in Exodus, but the story as told by Josephus. One of Pharaoh's magi foretold that a Hebrew child about to be born would defeat the Egyptians and raise up the Israelites. Pharaoh commanded that every male Hebrew child should be thrown into the river. Amram, father of the unborn Moses, feared for the future of his people, but God spoke to him in a dream and said his expected child would be the promised Saviour of his people. His mother bore him in secret with little pain so that her cries were not heard, and, as in the biblical story, the infant was found by Pharaoh's daughter and taken to be her child. When the wise man who had foretold the dangerous child identified Moses as the one destined to destroy Egypt, Pharaoh protected him for his daughter's sake.[5] There are some similarities, but not enough to account for the way Matthew told the Christmas story.

Nobody knows where Matthew's Gospel has its roots. There are many Jewish concerns in the rest of the Gospel, which suggest that

---

[5] Josephus, *Antiquities* 2.10.

Matthew drew his unique material from a community of Hebrew Christians. The Sermon on the Mount is presented like new teaching from Moses on Sinai, with the commandments written on the heart as Jeremiah prophesied (Jer. 31.31–34). The light was set on a stand to give light to all *in* the house (Matt. 5.15), whereas Luke has the same light illuminating those who *enter* (Luke 11.33). The story that Jesus' body had been stolen from the tomb and the guards bribed came from the temple authorities (Matt. 27.62–66; 28.11–15). Matthew's Jesus addresses Jewish concerns: 'Think not that I have come to abolish the law and the prophets' (Matt. 5.17); 'Every scribe who has been trained for the kingdom of heaven is like a householder who brings out of his treasure what is new and what is old' (Matt. 13.51); Jesus and his disciples paid the temple tax (Matt. 17.24–27); the parable of the workers in the vineyard who all received the same wage addressed the relative status of Jewish and Gentile converts (Matt. 20.1–16); the parable of the sheep and the goats reminded an already religious people of the true priorities of the Kingdom (Matt. 25.31–46).

The 'Jewishness' of Matthew's Gospel suggests a particular cultural context for the people who told these Christmas stories, but it does not identify where they lived. Why did they tell him the story of the magi? Did his informants live in the same area as the magi, or had they memories of them passing through their land? This could point to a community in Syria, or to one east of the Jordan. Or did the community have memories of the holy family living in Egypt? There is no way of knowing. What can be observed is that Matthew does not obviously link the story to the temple, nor does he have the songs and new prophecies that characterize Luke's account. He seems to be dealing with the hostile gossip implied in the story of Jesus' body stolen from the tomb, and reflected in some of John's observations – 'For fear of the Jews no one spoke openly of him' (John 7.13; 19.38, 39). Consider the remarks that John put into the mouth of his Jewish characters. 'Can anything good come out of Nazareth?' (John 1.46); 'Is the Christ to come from Galilee? Has not the scripture said that Christ is descended from David, and comes from Bethlehem, the village where David was?' (John 7.41–42). 'We were not born of fornication. We have one Father, even God' (John 8.41); 'Do not write "The King of the Jews", but "This man said I am the King of the Jews"' (John 19.21). 'King of the Jews' is one of Matthew's key themes, as is the birth in Bethlehem, the family living in Nazareth, and Joseph not being his father. He was writing for Hebrew converts to Christianity whose faith was being undermined by other stories that were circulating. Matthew could well have prefaced his Gospel as did Luke: 'That you may know the truth concerning the things of which you have been informed' (Luke 1.4).

The genealogy

Matthew and Luke both give Jesus' genealogy: Luke after his baptism (Luke 3.23–38), and Matthew as the preface to his Gospel. They are different, and countless attempts have been made to harmonize them. Early in the fourth century, Eusebius said that the disparity between the genealogies had led to much ill-informed speculation, and recommended a letter written by Sextus Julius Africanus to Aristides, which he thought was the true explanation of the differences. Africanus, a highly educated Christian writing about one hundred years before Eusebius, was a native of Palestine. Of his considerable output only two letters survive. Eusebius quoted thus:

> The names of the families in Israel were reckoned either by nature or by law; by nature, when there was genuine offspring to succeed; by law when another man fathered a child in the name of a brother who had died childless[6] . . . thus the memory of both was preserved, the real and nominal fathers . . . the two families, descended from Nathan and Solomon respectively, were so interlocked by the remarriage of childless widows and the 'raising up' of offspring, that the same persons could rightly be regarded at different times as the children of different parents, sometimes the reputed fathers, sometimes the real.
>
> (*History* 1.7)

He went on to explain that when Luke wrote 'Jesus being the son, as was supposed, of Joseph' (Luke 3.23), he was referring to this custom. This explanation was widely accepted in the Church and, in the eighth century, was used by John of Damascus in his *On the Orthodox Faith* 87. Philo had an interesting contemporary observation on the birth of Isaac, which he believed to be a supernatural conception: 'Moses shows us Sarah conceiving at the time when God visited her in her solitude (Gen. 21.1), but when she brings forth it is not to the Author of her visitation, but to him . . . whose name is Abraham.'[7] Abraham was deemed to be the father of Isaac, even though the child was a supernatural conception.

---

[6] The Jewish custom known as levirate marriage.
[7] Philo, *Cherubim* 46.

Jesus' human family, said Africanus, had preserved their geneal-ogy and used to travel the country reciting it. The family of David were well aware of their heritage, as were the Roman authorities. Hegesippus, a Hebrew Christian in Palestine early in the second cen-tury, wrote the story of the church of which only extracts survive. He said that Domitian ordered the execution of all the descendants of David, and that enemies denounced the relatives of Jesus. The emperor was 'as afraid of the advent of Christ as Herod had been', but when the magistrate saw that the Davidic line were only labour-ing farmers with rough hands, he dismissed them as harmless. Hegesippus was writing only a few years after these events.[8] Rabbi Simeon ben Azzai, a contemporary in Palestine, said he had found a family genealogy in Jerusalem in which someone had been declared of illegitimate birth and, since the 'someone' is not named but must have been well known, the reference was probably to Jesus.[9] Such a surviving genealogy is interesting, since Africanus said that records of pure Hebrew families and of those descended from proselytes were destroyed by Herod. He 'had no drop of Israelitish blood in his veins, and stung by the consciousness of his base origins, burnt the regis-ters of their families thinking that he would appear nobly born if no one was able to trace his line back'.[10] It is likely that people knew the genealogy of the line of David, and that the Christians preserved it. Why Luke should have given a parallel genealogy to the main royal line is a mystery, unless it was a precaution against persecution.

The genealogies in Matthew and Luke correspond for the genera-tions from Abraham to David (Matt. 1.2–6; Luke 3.31–34), apart from Admin (Luke 3.33) and two variant spellings. After David, the genealogies separate, Matthew following the main royal line through Solomon, and Luke following another branch of the royal line through Nathan, an older brother of Solomon (2 Sam. 5.14) and assumed in later tradition to have been Nathan the prophet (Luke 3.31).[11] Jesus was thus literally a son of David, but no more. The sec-tion after the exile, from Shealtiel and Zerubbabel to Jesus is com-pletely different in the two genealogies. In addition, Luke traces the line back to Adam the son of God (Luke 3.38), whereas Matthew traces it only to Abraham, and states that Jesus was the son of David, the

---

[8] Domitian was emperor 81–96 CE. This extract is in Eusebius, *History* 3.19–20.
[9] Mishnah *Yebamoth* 4.13.
[10] Eusebius, *History* 1.7.
[11] This would have made him a much older brother, as he condemned David for the affair with Bathsheba, Solomon's mother.

son of Abraham. Luke has seventy generations from Enoch to Jesus, which shows that his genealogy was not so much to trace the family line as to mark Jesus' place in history. The day of eternal judgement would happen seventy generations after Enoch, according to that tradition (*1 En.* 10.12). Matthew's genealogy, however, divides into three sections each of 14 generations, but the significance of this is not known. The names after Abraham, Isaac and Jacob correspond to the list in 1 Chronicles 2.1–15, the names from David to Jehoiachin are the kings as they appear in 1 and 2 Kings [although the monarchs from Ahaziah to Amaziah, 842–783 BCE are omitted], and the names after the exile, apart from Shealtiel and Zerubbabel, are otherwise unknown.

Matthew also mentions four women: Tamar, Rahab, Ruth and 'the wife of Uriah', that is, Bathsheba. Each of these women was a matriarch in the line of Abraham and David, but each bore her son in irregular circumstances. The widowed Tamar was wronged by her father-in-law and not given another of his sons as her husband, so she seduced her father-in-law and thus bore twin sons (Gen. 38.12–30). Six generations later, Rahab, the prostitute who had hidden the Hebrew spies in Jericho (Josh. 2.1–7), bore a son to Tamar's descendant Salmon. He was Boaz, the wealthy man of Bethlehem (Ruth 2.1) who was seduced by Ruth (Ruth 3.6–13). She became the mother of Obed and the great-grandmother of David (Ruth 4.18–22, which lists the descendants of Tamar). David then seduced Bathsheba, the wife of Uriah the Hittite, who became the mother of Solomon. Thus was the royal line recorded from Jacob through to Solomon. Might Matthew have been answering the critics who said that Jesus was born of fornication?

Jewish tradition remembered Jesus as 'the son of the harlot', and the Jews' remark recorded by John – 'We were not born of fornication' – shows that this was an early slander. Jesus was sometimes known, unusually, as the son of his mother not of his father: 'the carpenter, the son of Mary' (Mark 6.3). At other times, he was the son of Joseph: 'Is this not Joseph's son?' (Luke 4.22); 'Is not this Jesus, the son of Joseph whose father and mother we know?' (John 6.42). The question of his parentage was a source of scandal for centuries, as can be seen from the Christians' increased emphasis on Mary's virginity. A well-known saying attributed to Rabbi Hija bar Abba[12] was: 'If the son of the harlot shall say to you "These are two Gods"

---

[12] He was teaching around 300 CE.

say to him "I am He of the Sea, I am He of Sinai"',[13] a reference to the debate about two powers in heaven. There were reports of people in Palestine healing in the name of Yeshu ben Pandira,[14] which must have been Jesus. The name Pandira or Panthera is unusual, perhaps a mockery of the Greek title Virgin, *parthenos*. Jesus was variously said to have been the son of Pandira or Panthera, even though his mother was married to Stada. Thus 'Ben Stada is the same as Ben Pandira. Rabbi Hisda said, "The husband was Stada, the paramour was Pandira."'[15] Of Mary herself, Rab Papa[16] said: 'She was the descendant of princes and rulers, she played the harlot with carpenters.' Mary's Davidic descent was acknowledged.

The emphasis on Mary's virginity, in contrast to the mothers of the royal house of David, may be one of the reasons for Matthew's genealogy. It begins, 'The book of the genealogy of Jesus Christ, the son of David, the son of Abraham' and ends, 'Joseph, the husband of Mary, of whom Jesus was born, who is called Christ' (Matt. 1.16). There is, however, a clear contrast made between that genealogy and the account of the birth of Jesus that follows: '*But* the birth of Jesus was like this' (Matt. 1.18, my translation). It was different.

The Virgin birth

Mary conceived her child in mysterious circumstances; Joseph was worried, but an angel told him in a dream what was happening. That is the outline of Matthew's story, but his great emphasis on the Virgin birth shows where his community's concern lay. Where, in the expectations of a Hebrew community, was there place for a Virgin birth? Not in the Old Testament as it is usually read today. Had there been no expectation of a Virgin giving birth, then Jesus' origin would not have been so hotly contested, nor would the Virgin birth have been significant and emphasized in the story of his birth.

Matthew presents the mysterious conception as fulfilling Isaiah's prophecy: 'Behold, the Virgin shall conceive and bear a son' (Isa. 7.14). The key word is '*almah*, a word with various meanings. Traditionally Christians have translated it Virgin, but more recently 'young woman' has become popular. The translators of the Hebrew Scrip-

---

[13] *Pesikta Rabbati* 21.
[14] Tosefta *Hullin* 2.23.
[15] Babylonian Talmud *Shabbat* 104a. Rabbi Hisda was teaching around 300 CE.
[16] He was a distinguished teacher in Babylon in the mid-fourth century CE.

tures into Greek[17] chose the unambiguous word 'virgin' *parthenos* for *'almah* and they must have had a reason for this. In other words, the Jewish community in Egypt had a memory that *'almah* in this prophecy meant Virgin. Philo, their most distinguished scholar, said that when the Greek translation was made it was so accurate that people called it the sister of the Hebrew 'one and the same both in matter and words'. 'Virgin' was part of the accuracy. Each year the Jewish community in Alexandria crossed to the island of Pharos where the translation was made, and held a festival 'to honour the place where that version first shone out' and to thank God for it.[18]

After the Christians had adopted the Greek Old Testament, Jewish opinion changed: 'The day of its translation was as grievous for Israel as the day the golden calf was made, for the Torah could not be adequately translated.'[19] In the second century CE new Greek translations were made for the Jewish communities by Aquila, Theodotion and Symmachus, to correct the perceived inaccuracies. The translators adopted various styles, but they were unanimous that the word 'virgin' had to go. They all used instead the word for young woman, *neanis*, instead of *parthenos*. Justin, debating with a learned Jew named Trypho just after these translations were made, protested that the scriptures had been edited and altered: 'I certainly do not trust your teachers', he said, 'when they refuse to admit that [the old Greek translation] is a correct one and attempt to make their own. You should know that they deleted entire passages.' One of the examples of alteration was the Virgin prophecy: ' "Behold the Virgin shall conceive", but you say it ought to be read "Behold the young woman shall conceive".'[20] Mary, as we have seen, was being described at this time as a harlot and Jesus as the son of Panthera.

Matthew's emphasis in the Christmas story suggests his readers had a particular interest in Egypt, and there are several indications that the Virgin was important to the Jewish community there – but under another name. The first glimpse of a Jewish community in Egypt is in the sixth century BCE when refugees from the fall of Jerusalem protested at Jeremiah's preaching. It was not their sin, they said, that had caused the disaster, but neglect of the Lady, the Queen of Heaven who had protected the city until her devotees had to reject

---

[17] The scriptures were translated into Greek in Egypt during the third and second centuries BCE.

[18] Philo, *Life of Moses* II.40–1.

[19] Mishnah *Soferim* 1.7.

[20] Justin, *Trypho* 71.

her (Jer. 44.15–19). Isaiah's oracle to Hezekiah in 701 BCE had described the Lady, the Virgin, protecting her city from the invading Assyrians: 'She despises you, she scorns you, the virgin daughter of Zion' (Isa. 37.22). She must have been a victim of Josiah's purge in 623 BCE, but the Egyptian community did not forget her, nor did others forget where she had gone. Enoch saw the fragrant tree – her symbol – growing somewhere south of Jerusalem,[21] and said that just before the temple was burned, Wisdom was abandoned (*1 En*. 93.8). The reference is clear. The Lady – also known as Wisdom and the Queen of Heaven – was banished from her city. Holy books written centuries later and used by Egyptian Jews[22] also described the Lady as Wisdom. Sometimes she was the heavenly Jerusalem, an ambiguity found also in the Old Testament,[23] sometimes an angel figure sharing the throne of the LORD in heaven (Wisd. 9.10) and called the Holy Spirit (Wisd. 9.17). Now 'Holy Spirit' was Jesus' name for his heavenly mother,[24] and an early Christian using the pseudonym 'Isaiah' saw the angel of the Holy Spirit enthroned in heaven.[25]

Philo knew a great deal about the Lady, *more than he could have deduced from the present Old Testament*. Where did he learn this? How 'Jewish' was it? He must have been a good Jew or his community would not have asked him to represent them before the Roman emperor.[26] The Logos was the son of Wisdom,[27] he said, and Wisdom was the first-born mother of all things.[28] Now if Jesus was identified as the Logos, what was said of his mother? That Mary was Wisdom? Texts found at Nag Hammadi in Egypt, which have been labelled 'Gnostic' even though their original owners probably considered themselves Christian, describe a divine mother, the Virgin Holy Spirit enthroned in heaven, on the left of the throne of God.[29] She was Wisdom and her daughter was Eve.[30] Eve was 'the first virgin, not having a husband'. When she gave birth, she was the one who healed herself, and a mysterious poem declared of her: 'I am the woman / and I am the virgin . . . My husband is the one who begot me and

---

[21] See above, p. 85.
[22] The Wisdom of Solomon, The Wisdom of Jesus ben Sira.
[23] See my book *The Great High Priest*, Edinburgh: T&T Clark, 2003, pp. 234–8.
[24] See above, p. 40.
[25] See above, p. 45.
[26] He was their ambassador to Caligula in 39–40 CE.
[27] Philo, *On Flight* 109.
[28] Philo, *On Genesis* IV.97.
[29] *On the Origin of the World*, CG II.5.105.
[30] *The Hypostasis of the Archons*, CG II.4.95.

I am his mother'.[31] This is like the woman in Revelation who gives birth to the Messiah and then comes from heaven as his bride (Rev. 12.1–5; 21.9). In the New Testament, this woman is also the Spirit, as can be seen from John's characteristic pairing: 'The Spirit-and-the-Bride say "Come"' (Rev. 22.17), which is the divine and the human as one.[32] The 'Gnostic' texts cannot be dated, but the book of Revelation preserves the very oldest stratum of Christianity and has a major role for the Mother and Bride of the Son of God.

The Gnostic texts are strange to our eyes and very complicated, often hostile to conventional readings of the Old Testament, but the setting for their speculation [they would have called it theology] is clearly the temple, the holy of holies, and the Eden stories. There is a great chariot throne with cherubim and seraphim, heavenly beings with names such as Yao [Yahweh] and Sabaoth, and then Wisdom, the great mother figure who sent her breath into Adam while he was still a man of dust and then sent him her daughter Eve.[33] There are several versions of the stories, but one is of special interest: Wisdom-Faith wanted to create something without her consort – *virgin birth* – and she produced a heavenly being. Its shadow existed outside the veil [of the temple] and was formed of matter. It proclaimed itself the only God, and eventually made a throne chariot of cherubim surrounded by angels.[34] Despite their bizarre detail, these texts remember Wisdom as the Virgin Mother of the one enthroned in the holy of holies and as having a role in the creation of Adam.

The *Gospel of Philip* also presents early Christian teaching in a temple context, for example the Son wears the Name of the Father and thus becomes the Father (cf. Rev. 3.12).[35] The Lady with her many titles has a role in the *Gospel of Philip*: Mary was 'the *Virgin* whom no power defiled'; *Wisdom* was the mother of the angels;[36] and the *Spirit* given to Adam was his mother.[37] The Virgin's role in the creation of Adam is clear: 'Adam came into being from two virgins, from the Spirit and from virgin earth. Christ, therefore, was born of a virgin, to rectify the fall which occurred in the beginning.'[38] Note there

---

[31] *On the Origin of the World*, CG II.5.114.

[32] See above, p. 61.

[33] The first part of *On the Origin of the World*.

[34] The final sections of *The Hypostasis of the Archons*.

[35] *Gospel of Philip*, CG II.3.54.

[36] Cf. Rev. 12.17 the other children of the Woman clothed with the sun, and the Lady at Ugarit who was the mother of the seventy sons of God, see below, p. 104.

[37] *Gospel of Philip*, CG II.3.55, 63, 70.

[38] *Gospel of Philip*, CG II.3.71.

are two virgins: a heavenly and an earthly, a divine and a human. Wisdom and Mary? Irenaeus has a [later?] version of this his *Proof of the Apostolic Preaching*, a compendium of basic teaching to distinguish Christianity from heresy: 'Whence then is the substance of the first formed man? From the Will and the Wisdom of God, and from the virgin earth . . . So then the LORD, summing up afresh this man, took the same dispensation of entry into the flesh, being born from the Virgin by the Will and the Wisdom of God.'[39] The teaching about the virgin birth was not part of the heresy, nor were the two virgins: the birth from Mary was by the Will and Wisdom of God, where Wisdom is the Lady, the divine Virgin.

The heavenly Virgin was known in ancient Jerusalem, as can be seen in Isaiah. She had also been the great mother goddess in the neighbouring [and earlier] culture of Ugarit and known as *ǵlm/ ǵlmt*, the equivalent to the Hebrew *'almah*, virgin. It is in Ugarit that we glimpse something of the original Lady. She was the virgin mother of seventy sons of God, known as 'the woman who creates the gods'.[40] She was the sun goddess Shapsh who had several other names to describe her many aspects: one was Athirat, like the Hebrew Asherah; another was Rahmay, meaning womb[41] – one of the untranslatable words in Psalm 110.3 that described the birth of the divine son: 'In the glory of the holy ones . . . from the womb [or was it 'from the Lady'?] I have begotten you.'[42] The son of the Great Lady was known as the Morning and Evening Star, and the human heir to the throne of Ugarit was suckled with the milk of the Virgin Asherah.[43] One of her symbols was a spindle, which later became a symbol of Mary.[44]

There are clear similarities between Ugarit and Jerusalem. The mother of the king was the key figure at the Jerusalem court, known as the Gebirah, the Great Lady (1 Kings 15.13, RSV 'queen mother'). When the ancient kings of Jerusalem are listed, their mothers are mentioned (1 Kings 14.21; 15.2, 10; 2 Kings 12.1; 14.2; 15.2, 33; 18.2; 21.1, 19; 22.1; 23.31, 36). Queen Ma'acah (1 Kings 15.13), who

---

[39] Irenaeus, *Proof of the Apostolic Preaching* 32. See above, p. 64.

[40] Wisdom was the mother of the angels according to the *Gospel of Philip*, CG II.3.63.

[41] See N. Wyatt, *Religious Texts from Ugarit*, Sheffield: Sheffield Academic Press, 1998, pp. 324–38.

[42] See above, p. 6.

[43] N. Wyatt, 'The Stela of the Seated God from Ugarit', *Ugarit-Forschungen* 15 (1983), pp. 271–7, at p. 273.

[44] Wyatt, *Religious Texts*, p. 93.

venerated Asherah, was the mother of two successive kings who were themselves father and son. In other words, she became the bride of her own son, as did the Lady in the book of Revelation. When Ezekiel had a vision of the abominations of the temple, he saw 'the seat of the image of jealousy that provokes to jealousy' (Ezek. 8.3). Removing one Hebrew letter from this unlikely title gives something more familiar: 'the seat of the image of the lady who creates' – the same title as the virgin mother goddess at Ugarit.[45] The fate of her title was the fate of most references to her: they were removed or disguised by the spiritual heirs of those who purged the temple at the end on the seventh century BCE. The refugees in Egypt remembered her, as did many others, including Matthew's community and those who heard and understood the vision of the Woman clothed with the sun.

The Virgin in Isaiah's prophecy was the Lady and her current human counterpart, the woman who was pregnant with the next Davidic king. We have to think in terms of incarnation: the human queen 'was' the Virgin, just as the human king 'was' her son the LORD.[46] She was *The* Virgin not a virgin, as in so many modern versions of the Bible. Both the Hebrew and the old Greek of Isaiah 7.14 have *The* Virgin, as does Matthew 1.23, but the AV has *a* virgin in both places, the RSV and GNB have *a* young woman in Isaiah and *a* virgin in Matthew. A vital piece of evidence has thus been removed by 'translators'. The problem with this oracle in Isaiah is not which particular young woman in his time was pregnant, and whether such an oracle could have had any relevance to the remote future and the birth of Jesus; it is far more serious: how did all memory of *The Virgin* come to be removed from the Old Testament and lost to so many of those who interpreted it?

The *'almah* implies a woman associated with the *'olam*, the hidden or eternal place, in other words, with the holy of holies, and that is exactly where the Woman clothed with the sun appeared. The translators of the old Greek Bible knew that the *'almah* was *The* Virgin, and the translators of the new Greek versions knew that the title had to be removed because it was a vital part of the Christian claims about Jesus. Mark, who wrote the earliest Gospel, did not need to mention the Christmas story, but as Christianity grew in strength and influence, so did the need to discredit the claims made for Jesus.

---

[45] For detail see my book *The Great Angel*, London: SPCK, 1992, p. 54.

[46] The icon of the Communion of the Apostles shows the apostles around the table, with Mary at its head, and hovering above her is Wisdom.

One was birth from the Virgin as the true Davidic king,[47] and so the Christmas story was told – never just as a story, but always interwoven with prophecies and other signs. It was the story of the meeting of heaven and earth, just as the Psalmist was able to say: the LORD is in his holy temple; the LORD's throne is in heaven (Ps. 11.4).

Joseph, said Matthew, was a 'just' man who did not wish to put Mary to shame. The word could also be translated 'righteous' and indicate that Joseph was one of 'the righteous' identified by Gabriel (Luke 1.18) and hymned by Zechariah, those who longed to serve the LORD in holiness and righteousness (Luke 1.75). At that time the punishment for Mary's condition was death by stoning, as can be seen from the story of the woman brought to Jesus (John 8.1–11). The Law of Moses was clear; a man and woman caught in the act of adultery were put to death (Lev. 20.10). If a man suspected his wife of infidelity but had no proof, she was taken to the temple and made to drink 'bitter water', in which there was dust from the floor of the tabernacle and ink from the curses that had been written against her. If the water had no effect, the woman was innocent (Num. 5.28). If a young woman was found not to be a virgin at her marriage, she was brought to the door of her father's house, and the men of the place stoned her to death (Deut. 22.20–22).

The story of the woman taken in adultery does not appear in several early manuscripts of John, and is found in various places in others: after John 7.36 and even at the very end of the Gospel after 21.25, or after Luke 21.38. There must have been some unease about the passage, or maybe it was not understood. It appears in the Codex Bezae, suggesting that it was significant to a Hebrew community.[48] When Papias[49] made a collection of the sayings of Jesus, he said the *Gospel of the Hebrews* told of 'a woman falsely accused before the LORD of many sins',[50] another indication that this was important for Hebrew Christians. The woman was brought alone, so this was not adultery as covered by the law in Leviticus which applied to both man and woman. 'Caught in the act' perhaps meant that she was visibly pregnant, with no man acknowledged as the father to marry her. The woman was brought *to the temple* to be stoned by the scribes and Pharisees, and they asked Jesus to pass judgement. Now a woman

---

[47] Members of Jesus' family were arrested.
[48] See above, p. 51.
[49] Papias was bishop of Hierapolis in Asia Minor at the beginning of the second century CE.
[50] Eusebius, *History* 3.39.

brought alone to be stoned implies that she was no longer virgin at her marriage, and had to be stoned at the door of her father's house – *but here it is the temple*. Was this story originally a parable Jesus told about Wisdom-and-Mary, with the current custodians of the Law wanting her dead? Had Mary spoken to Jesus or to John about what her fate might have been? These questions can have no answers, but they are worth pondering.

Gabriel told Joseph in his dream: 'You shall call his name Jesus' – a Hebraic expression. The name Jesus, *Yešuaʿ*, is the short form of *Yᵉhošuaʿ*, Joshua, popularly said to mean 'Yahweh saves'.[51] Jesus also means 'Yahweh saves', as does Isaiah, *Yᵉšaʿyahu* – all variants of the same name, and interesting in the light of Jesus' frequent use of Isaiah's prophecies. The sermon at Nazareth (Luke 4.16–21) implies that Jesus claimed for himself Isaiah's words 'The Spirit of the LORD is upon me . . .' (Isa. 61.1), and the story of Isaiah was taken over by the Christian community as a vehicle for their own prophecies.[52] The original Joshua, who led the Israelites into Canaan, was well named: 'He became according to his name, a great man for the salvation of (God's) chosen ones, to take vengeance on the enemies that rose against them, so that he might give Israel its inheritance' (Ben Sira 46.1, my translation).

Mary's son, however, was to be called Jesus for another reason: he would save his people from their *sins*, not from their enemies. Salvation from enemies had been the hope of Mary – 'He has shown strength with his arm . . . He has scattered the proud . . . He has put down the mighty' (Luke 1.51–52); and of Zechariah – 'that we should be saved from our enemies and from the hand of all who hate us' (Luke 1.71). It was also the hope of those who shouted 'Hosanna' as Jesus rode into Jerusalem: 'Hosanna! . . . Blessed is he who comes with/in the Name of the LORD' (Matt. 21.9). Hosanna, *hošiyʿah na* is another word from the same Hebrew root as 'Jesus', and means 'Save us!'. The crowds were quoting Psalm 118.25, a psalm which sang of victory in the tents of the righteous, of the reversal of their fortunes, of entering the gates of righteousness, and of the rejected stone which became the head of the corner. They were welcoming the one who bore the Name of the LORD, the Davidic king, the Immanuel. It is small wonder that the city authorities were worried at what they heard. The name Jesus was linked in the popular imagination

---

[51] It probably meant 'Yahweh helps'.
[52] See above, p. 45.

to political liberation, and so what did Matthew mean when he gave it the new meaning, 'He will save his people from their *sins*'? The expected and the unexpected.

The Virgin's son would be called Immanuel (Matt. 1.23), meaning God, *el*, with us, *immanu*. This was a royal title of the Davidic kings, as can be seen in one of Isaiah's oracles warning the king that his land would be overwhelmed by enemies: 'The king of Assyria and all his glory . . . will fill the breadth of your land, O Immanuel' (Isa. 8.7–8). The detail of this verse '*His name shall be called* Immanuel' is a good example of how translations can change. The Hebrew of Isaiah 7.14 could be read as 'she will call his name' [the sense adopted by the AV] or 'you (singular) will call his name'; the Greek manuscripts have 'you (singular) will call his name', 'you (plural) will call his name', 'he will call his name'; the great Isaiah scroll from Qumran has 'his name will be called', and Matthew's Greek has 'they will call his name'. The RSV of Matthew 1.23 '*his name shall be called* Immanuel' does not translate Matthew's Greek but gives the form found in the Qumran Isaiah, albeit with no note to this effect.

The star

Jesus was born 'in the days of Herod the king', which ended in 4 BCE. Josephus says he died after an eclipse of the moon and shortly before Passover.[53] Since there was an eclipse of the moon on the night of 12/13 March in 4 BCE, one month before Passover that year, this is the most likely date for his death. It is also the only way to begin working out the year of Jesus' birth. Herod ordered all children less than two years old to be killed, and the holy family sought safety in Egypt. Matthew did not say how old Jesus was when the family fled, only that it was immediately after the visit of the magi, nor did he say how long they stayed in Egypt. The tradition of the Coptic Church is that the holy family lived in central Egypt at Mount Qusqam for 185 days, but they had spent time travelling before that, and Jesus' age when they left Bethlehem is not known. The more precise date of Jesus' birth has then to be established by 'the fifteenth year of the reign of Tiberius Caesar' (Luke 3.1) when Jesus was baptized 'at about thirty years of age' (Luke 3.23). Since 'the fifteenth year' was 27–28 CE, this only shows that he was born before 3 BCE. If he was, say, two or three years old when Herod died, he would have been born in 7/6 BCE. The

---

[53] Josephus, *Antiquities* 17.6 and 17.9.

other possible way to establish the date of his birth is to identify the star.

Herod was a ruthless ruler, declared king of the Jews by the Romans in 40 BCE. A story was told about Herod's boyhood, that Menahem the Essene had told him he would one day become king of the Jews and reign for thirty years. As a result, Herod always honoured the Essenes and gave them special privileges because they received divine revelations.[54] He was not Jewish and so had to fight to gain control of his kingdom. His reign eventually began in 37 BCE, the year that Virgil wrote his *Eclogues*. Herod's close contact with Rome means that he probably knew the prophecy in the fourth *Eclogue*: 'Now the Virgin returns, now the reign of Saturn returns, now a new generation returns from heaven to earth, smile on the birth of the child'. Virgil's lines are but one of the many factors that made Herod, who was superstitious and had no right to the throne in Jerusalem, fear the birth of a significant child. There is no archaeological evidence for the massacre of the children in Bethlehem, but there is plenty of evidence that this was not out of character.

The *Assumption of Moses*, probably written during the lifetime of Jesus, said Herod was a wanton king and not of a priestly family; 'He will shatter their leaders with the sword, and he will (exterminate them) in secret places, so that no one will know where their bodies are. He will kill both old and young, showing mercy to none.'[55] He burned the genealogies, as we have seen,[56] and Josephus, reflecting on his death, said he was 'a man of great barbarity towards all men equally and a slave to his passions'.[57] When the temple priests were in despair at his behaviour – and this was in 32 BCE, quite early in his long reign – they scrutinized the prophecies for some hope of when the reign of terror might end, but 'they dared not do this openly for fear of Herod and his friends'. They were waiting for the Anointed One, 'but of Herod, we know that he is an Arabian, uncircumcised'. They knew he could not be the promised ruler, because he was violent and plundered his people. They counted the 490 years of Daniel's prophecy, and worked out that 34 years remained. Josephus' text here is not clear, nor is the process of their calculations, but they did expect something to happen in 2 CE. Herod had an informer who reported the priests' deliberations and despair, and so 'he sent

---

[54] Josephus, *Antiquities* 15.10.
[55] *Assumption of Moses* 6.3–4.
[56] See above, p. 98.
[57] Josephus, *Antiquities* 17.8.

by night and had them all killed without the people knowing about it lest they revolt'.[58]

He styled himself 'king of the Jews',[59] and tried to settle the succession among his sons. This was a sensitive issue. He announced to his subjects: 'Caesar has appointed me lord of the realm and arbiter of the succession . . . and I now declare these my three sons kings and I beseech first God and then you to ratify my decision.'[60] He had executed all three before he himself died. Alexander and Aristobulus were tried and executed in 7 BCE, as the result of the plotting of their brother Antipater, whom the people hated. Herod continued to manipulate the succession by arranging the marriages of his dead sons' children, but Antipater successfully plotted to have these rearranged. There was bribery and torture, and a plot was uncovered that several Arabs were planning to assassinate Herod. All this was happening in 7–6 BCE, when the thirty years prophesied for his reign came to an end. The last of the three designated as future kings of the Jews was executed five days before Herod himself died in 4 BCE.[61] It is small wonder that when Herod heard of magi from the east in Jerusalem in 7 BCE seeking the one who had been *born* king of the Jews, 'he was troubled and all Jerusalem with him' (Matt. 2.3).

Herod was the great star Wormwood who fell from heaven like a blazing torch, causing many to die in the bitter waters – a reference to the hot bitter springs at Machaerus where Herod sought relief from his illnesses.[62] Wormwood was an allusion to prophecies of judgement on those who turned justice to wormwood: 'O you who turn justice to wormwood, and cast down righteousness to the earth', warned Amos. 'He who made the Pleiades and Orion' would bring destruction and reduce the great house to fragments (Amos 5.7 and 6.12). The fallen ruler was a fallen star, and the death of Herod caused the third of the seven trumpet blasts marking out the years until the judgement (Rev. 8.10–11).[63] Everyone was counting and watching the stars, and visions such as these were *preserved and interpreted by Christians*. Presumably they originated in the circles into which Jesus was born.

---

[58] The extracts are from the Slavonic sections of Josephus, *War* 1.364, which do not survive in the Greek text. They are printed in the Loeb Classical Library edition of Josephus, as an appendix to Book 7 of *The Jewish War*.

[59] Josephus, *Antiquities* 16.10.

[60] Josephus, *War* 1.458.

[61] Josephus, *War* 1.559–665.

[62] Josephus, *War* 7.186.

[63] See my book *The Revelation of Jesus Christ*, Edinburgh: T&T Clark, 2000, pp. 174–5.

The visionaries knew too of a great angel who would appear in the sunrise bearing the seal of the living God to mark the faithful. Originally the faithful were from the twelve tribes of Israel – the vision must have been pre-Christian or Hebrew Christian – but it was extended to include a multitude from every nation, the wider Christian development of the original Jewish hope (Rev. 7.1–17). The seal of the living God that the angel bore (that is, wore) showed he was the great high priest preparing to mark the faithful with the Name. Since the Name was often represented by a diagonal cross, the reference was to baptism, and the angel in the sunrise was the Morning Star.

Angels were traditionally depicted as stars, especially in the Enoch tradition. The stars and their movements were mirrored on earth in the actions of people, especially kings and rulers. The LORD had asked Job if he could order the stars: 'Do you know the ordinances of the heavens? Can you establish their rule on earth?' (Job 38.33). The LORD of Hosts meant the LORD of the hosts of heaven, that is, the angel armies who appear in Revelation 19.14 with their commander, the Word of God. Enoch knew that rebel stars had distorted the calendar and thus upset the whole order of nature. The archangel Uriel had revealed to him the leaders of the stars, their tasks and their times (*1 En.* 80.1), and this passage was the conclusion of a sophisticated treatise on astronomy, also revealed to Enoch by Uriel. Fragments of this and several other texts and horoscopes have been found at Qumran (*1 En.* 72.1), which show a sophisticated knowledge of the stars. When Enoch was taken in a mystical ascent through the temple he said the ceiling was like the path of the stars, perhaps a star map. In their plan of the ideal temple the Qumran community had the gates in the eastern walls aligned as markers for the sunrise at the summer and winter solstices.[64] The ancient Jews are not often seen as astronomers, and yet the earliest Gentile writer to describe them notes this as their characteristic. Theophrastus, a Greek writing abut 300 BCE, said: 'The Jews converse with each other about the deity and at night time they make observations of the stars, gazing at them and calling on God in prayer.'[65] Those most interested in watching the stars for the sign of the king of the Jews *would have been Jews themselves,*

---

[64] See my article 'The Temple Measurements and the Solar Calendar', in *Temple Scroll Studies*, ed. G. J. Brooke, Sheffield: Sheffield Academic Press, 1989, pp. 63–6.

[65] Theophrastus, *De Pietate*, quoted in M. Stern, *Greek and Latin Authors on Jews and Judaism*, Jerusalem: Israel Academy of Sciences and Humanities, 1974, vol. 1, p. 10.

especially those in Palestine who had been suffering under Herod, or those who were living in the long exile.[66]

There was one star prophecy that everyone was pondering – about a rising star and a ruler who would dispossess Edom, the descendants of Esau. Herod was an Edomite, not a Jew.

> I see him, but not now;
> I behold him, but not near:
> a star shall go out from Jacob
> and a sceptre shall rise from Israel
> . . .
> Edom shall be dispossessed
> and Seir also, his enemies,
> while Israel acts in strength.
> (Num. 24.17–18, my translation)

The Old Greek varies here, suggesting that it was translated from a slightly different Hebrew text:

> 'I will point him out, but not now;
> I will bless him, but he is not drawing near:
> A star will arise from Jacob
> and a man shall rise up from Israel . . .'
> Edom shall be an inheritance
> And Esau[67] his enemy shall be an inheritance
> And Israel has acted in strength.

Later Jewish tradition was quite clear that the star figure was the Messiah: 'When a mighty king shall reign from the house of Jacob and there shall grow up a Messiah and mighty sceptre from Israel'.[68] The leader in the second Jewish war against Rome (132–5 CE) was given the *nom de guerre* Bar Kochbah, meaning the son of a star, and his coinage showed the messianic star, but Eusebius described him as 'a bloodthirsty bandit who, on the strength of his name . . . paraded himself as a luminary come down from heaven'.[69]

The *Testament of Judah* is a pre-Christian prophecy, probably from the mid-second century BCE, but preserved by Christians. It put into the mouth of Judah, patriarch of the royal house, a prediction of corrupt and cruel rulers, and then: 'After this there shall arise for

---

[66] See above, p. 26.
[67] In Hebrew, Seir and Esau look similar.
[68] Targum Pseudo-Jonathan Num. 24.17. Targum Onkelos is similar.
[69] Eusebius, *History* 4.6.

you a star from Jacob in peace.'[70] The *Testament of Levi*, patriarch of the priestly house, foresaw that 'the LORD will raise up a new priest . . . and his star shall rise in heaven like a king.'[71] The star prophecy was important at Qumran: it was listed in a collection of messianic texts probably written during Herod's lifetime;[72] it was quoted in the *Damascus Document*, the foundation document of the group, where the star prophecy was applied to the future interpreter of the law;[73] and in the *War Scroll* the star prophecy and its promise of triumph over enemies was the inspiration for the battle plans.[74] The star prophecy was probably 'the ambiguous oracle found in their sacred scriptures that at that time one from their country would become ruler of the world'.[75] Josephus said it predicted the rise of Vespasian,[76] but for the Christians [and their Jewish predecessors?] it would be fulfilled when the kingdom of the Messiah was established on earth, the vision of the angel with the seventh trumpet (Rev. 11.15–18). Tacitus, writing about the Jewish War against Rome from 66 to 70 CE, knew that this prophecy had shaped events: 'The ancient records of their priests contained a prediction of how at that very time the East would grow powerful and rulers coming from Judea were to acquire a universal empire.'[77]

For Christians, Jesus was the bright Morning Star (Rev. 22.16), presumably the angel who came with the sunrise to seal the faithful before the judgement, and star imagery passed into descriptions of the Christian life. Jesus promised his faithful followers that they too would become morning stars (Rev. 2.28),[78] and Peter encouraged his flock to study the prophecies 'until the day dawns and the morning star rises in your hearts' (2 Pet. 1.19). Ignatius, bishop of Antioch about 100 CE, said the birth of Jesus was made known by a great star that marked the end of the ancient empire of evil,[79] and Justin, explaining Christianity to Romans in the mid-second century, emphasized how Jesus had fulfilled prophecy, including the prophecy of

[70] *Testament of Judah* 24.
[71] *Testament of Levi* 18.2–3.
[72] *The Messianic Anthology* 4Q 175.
[73] *Damascus Document* CD VII.
[74] 1QM XI.
[75] Josephus, *War* 6.313.
[76] Josephus, *War* 3.401.
[77] Tacitus, *Histories* 5.13.
[78] 'Give him the morning star' is a Hebraism for 'appoint him as the morning star'.
[79] Ignatius, *To the Ephesians* 19.

the star.[80] Ephrem said that the star appeared because the prophets had disappeared.[81] The *Cave of Treasures* said that the magi saw the star two years before Christ was born, 'in the firmament of heaven, and the brilliancy of its appearance was brighter than that of every other star. And within it was a maiden carrying a child, and a crown was set upon his head.' This suggests that the star of Bethlehem prompted the vision of the woman clothed with the sun in Revelation 12.

The brief glimpse Matthew gives of the tension in Jerusalem when the magi arrived fits well in the situation in 7–6 BCE: murderous turmoil in the royal house over the title 'King of the Jews', an assassination plot organized by men from Arabia, fervent expectation of a star to announce the coming of the Messiah who would destroy Edom, priests calculating how many years were left before the Holy One would appear, and then magi from the east saying: 'Where is he who is *born* king of the Jews, for we have seen his star in the east and are come to worship him.' A star in the east, *en te anatole*, was a technical term. It did not mean that the observers were in the east, although the magi were 'in the east' when they saw it. It means that the star was rising in the east, making its first appearance in the dawn sky.

In 7 BCE there were extraordinary movements in the stars. Jupiter and Saturn were in a triple conjunction in the sign of Pisces, the sign for the Hebrews. A triple conjunction means that the two appeared so close together that they appeared as one, and this happened three times in 7 BCE. 'A triple conjunction is . . . an extremely rare event involving a particularly intricate set of movements of two planets. Instead of one planet making a single pass close to another, in the sky, the two bodies pass, separate, pass a second time, separate again, and then pass a third time before separating for good.' The three conjunctions are usually spread over some seven months.[82] In 7 BCE the conjunctions occurred on 29 May, on 3 October during the autumn festivals when there was a full moon and the conjunction appeared slightly east of south when seen from Jerusalem, that is, over Bethlehem, and on 4 December. In later Hebrew, Jupiter was known as *ṣedek*, righteousness, and Gentiles identified Saturn as the God of

---

[80] Justin, *Apology* 1.32. Unfortunately he attributed the prophecy to Isaiah!

[81] Ephrem, *Commentary on the Diatessaron* 2.18, see Carmel McCarthy, *Saint Ephrem's Commentary on Tatian's Diatessaron*, Oxford: Oxford University Press, 1993.

[82] See for example M. Kidger, *The Star of Bethlehem: An Astronomer's View*, Princeton, NJ: Princeton University Press, 1999.

the Jews.[83] In Virgil's fourth *Eclogue*, Saturn and the Virgin were signs of the new dispensation. This means that in Pisces, the sign of the Hebrews, Saturn met with Jupiter, power with righteousness. Herod, who had turned justice to wormwood and cast righteousness to the earth (Amos 5.7), heard that the conjunction of power and righteousness was rising in the dawn just as Wormwood was about to fall from heaven (Rev. 8.10). 'He was troubled and all Jerusalem with him.'

A good case can be made for other dates such as 5 BCE or 2 BCE,[84] but with phenomena such as this in 7 BCE – the year when an Essene prophet had predicted the end of Herod's reign – why wait for something else? If the conjunction was observed first in the early summer and then around the feast of Tabernacles it must have caused excitement. The magi from the east had seen the star at its rising, and noted the time it appeared. Herod asked them about this, so presumably he thought it indicated the time of the child's birth. Then the magi saw the star as they travelled from Jerusalem to Bethlehem, which means it was then in the south and high in the sky, as it appeared to stand over the house. This suggests the appearance at Tabernacles, and an autumn date for the visit of the magi.

The magi

The basic story is that three visitors arrived in Jerusalem asking about the newborn child because they had seen a spectacular star and believed it to be the star of the messianic prophecy. They brought three gifts: gold, frankincense and myrrh. Fertile imaginations have concluded that they must have caused a great stir, arriving with their train of camels and rich gifts, that they were mighty kings from distant lands in the east, they were the Gentiles coming to acknowledge the king of the Jews, that they fulfilled all manner of prophecies. Matthew says none of this. He cites no prophecy that was fulfilled by the magi. He does not even say there were three of them: some early interpretations said there were as many as twelve, and in early Christian paintings in Rome there are two,[85] three[86] or four.[87] Matthew says they brought three gifts and that they came 'from the

---

[83] Thus Tacitus, *Histories* 5.4, who said the Sabbath was honouring Saturn, hence our word Saturday.

[84] Kidger (n. 82 above), pp. 199–200.

[85] In the cemetery of SS Peter and Marcellinus.

[86] In the cemetery of Priscilla, third to fourth century CE.

[87] In the cemetery of St Domitilla, third century CE.

east', which for legal purposes was defined as beyond Rekem, probably Petra.[88]

The familiar picture of the magi today is largely the product of those fertile imaginations.[89] They became 'three' because three gifts are mentioned, and they became kings with names: by the sixth century, the Syriac-speaking church knew them as Hormizdah, king of Persia, Yazdegerd, king of Saba, and Perozadh, king of Sheba;[90] the Ethiopian church knew them as Hor, king of Persia, Basanater, king of Saba, and Karsudan, king of the east;[91] and the Western church knew them as Gaspar, Melchior and Balthassar, in the sixth-century mosaic in S. Apollinare Nuovo in Ravenna. They were eventually depicted wearing crowns and often with a retinue of servants. The exotic kingdoms derive from the Old Testament texts deemed to be prophecies of their coming. The gloriously restored city of Jerusalem would see her sons and daughters return, bringing the wealth of nations – camels from Midian, Ephah and Sheba with gold and frankincense, flocks from Kedar and Nebaioth as offerings for the temple altar. These people coming with gifts were exiled Jews returning, so that the holy place would be beautiful and glorious. Foreigners and kings would come – but as servants (Isa. 60.1–22). In Psalm 72, the kings of Tarshish and the isles, of Sheba and Saba bring tribute and acknowledge the Davidic king. Thus the magi came to symbolize the homage of the Gentiles.

Where they came from is not known, but the mysterious visitors were a lasting fascination, and many stories were told. Their relics were brought from Persia to Constantinople by the Emperor Zeno in 490 CE; or perhaps they had been brought from Persia to Constantinople by the Empress Helena early in the fourth century, and then transferred to Milan in the fifth, whence they were taken to Cologne in 1164 CE, two years after Frederick Barbarossa had sacked Milan. Today their three golden and jewelled coffins form a spectacular shrine behind the high altar in Cologne Cathedral, and their three crowns form the city's coat of arms.

Shortly after the relics had been installed in Cologne, however, Marco Polo saw the magi in their tombs in Persia.[92] In the city of Saveh there

---

[88] See Mishnah *Gittin* 1.2 and Josephus, *Antiquities* 4.7.
[89] A good survey in J. C. Marsh-Edwards, 'The Magi in Tradition and Art', *Irish Ecclesiastical Record* (5th series) 85 (1956), pp. 1–9.
[90] In the *Book of the Cave of Treasures*.
[91] In the *Book of Adam and Eve*.
[92] He died in 1324 CE.

were three great mausoleums with domed roofs, and inside each he saw an embalmed body. Local people said they were Beltasar, Gaspar and Melchior, three kings of the country who long ago had gone to worship a newborn prophet, and they knew that the magi had been men of different ages, old, middle-aged and young. This was widely known, and the three different ages are clearly visible in the sixth-century Ravenna mosaic, where the magi are philosophers, in the fourteenth-century mosaic in St Mark's, Venice, where they are kings, and in traditional icons of the nativity.[93] In Marco Polo's tale, each of the magi entered first on his own and saw the child as a mirror image of himself: young, middle-aged or old. When they entered together, they saw him as he really was, a baby of 13 days. This motif – the three aspects of the one LORD – appears as early as a mid-second-century Gnostic text, the *Apocryphon of John*. John had a vision of the LORD, first as a youth, then as an old man, and then as a servant, a vision with multiple forms.[94] The magi, whatever their original role, attracted to themselves a mass of ancient tradition.

Before they became kings, however, they had been Persian philosophers. Clement of Alexandria, discussing the value of Gentile philosophy around 200 CE, thought the magi were Zoroastrians from Persia who had been able 'to predict the birth of the Saviour and were guided by a star'.[95] The *Arabic Infancy Gospel* says that magi came to Jerusalem following the prediction of Zeraduscht (Zoroaster).[96] Ephrem the Syrian in the mid-fourth century knew them as Persians and even described their route down the southern branch of the old royal road of Persia. John Chrysostom in Constantinople around 400 CE also assumed they were Persians.[97] The earliest pictures of the magi show them as Persian philosophers wearing pointed Phrygian caps, for example in the paintings in the early Roman cemeteries, and in the Ravenna mosaic. When the Persians invaded Palestine in 614 CE, they destroyed the churches, but spared the church in Bethlehem because they saw there a mosaic of three men in Persian dress.

According to Marco Polo's tale, they had taken offerings of gold, frankincense and myrrh, to see what the child would accept: gold to indicate that he was a ruler, frankincense that he was divine and myrrh

---

[93] Marco Polo could have seen all of these examples.
[94] The *Apocryphon of John*, CG II.1.2.
[95] Clement, *Miscellanies* 1.15.
[96] *Arabic Infancy Gospel* 7.
[97] John Chrysostom, *On Matthew*, Homily 6.

that he was a healer.[98] The West had long had a different understanding of the gifts: as early as 200 CE, Irenaeus, who came from Asia Minor but was a bishop in southern France, said that gold indicated a king, frankincense a deity but myrrh a death.[99] Ephrem, writing in Syria in the mid-fourth century, knew both explanations of the gifts: that the myrrh represented either embalming or the work of a healer.[100] But why this choice of gifts? Attempting to trace the route of the magi by guessing where they might have been able to buy their presents is another exercise for fertile imaginations. The gifts were, as later tradition recognized, symbolic, but it is possible that Matthew would not have recognized the king, God and healer/sacrifice explanations.

Gold, frankincense and myrrh were symbolic of the temple; the temple vessels were made of pure gold, the temple incense was compounded with frankincense and was burned to invoke the presence of the LORD,[101] and myrrh was the perfumed anointing oil that imparted holiness and could not be used outside the temple (Exod. 30.29). A pre-Christian Jewish text, the *Apocalypse of Moses*, says that when Adam left Eden, he begged the angels to let him take some seeds of the perfumes of Paradise, so that he might continue to make offerings to God.[102] Adam driven from Eden represented the original priesthood driven from the temple in the time of Josiah. Taking the perfumes for his offerings was a natural part of the story, but it does not appear in post-Christian Jewish writers. Josephus, who was from a priestly family and knew stories about Adam not in the Bible, does not mention it, nor the later Midrash Rabbah,[103] nor any of the Targums. There is a related Jewish tradition that Jeremiah took the temple treasures when the Jews were being deported to Babylon, and hid them in a cave at the foot of Mount Nebo. The location of the cave was then lost, because Jeremiah prophesied: 'The place shall be unknown until God gathers his people together again and shows his

---

[98] Marco Polo, *The Travels*, Harmondsworth: Penguin, 1972, pp. 58–9.

[99] Irenaeus, *Against Heresies* 3.9.2.

[100] Ephrem, *Commentary on the Diatessaron* 2.25; see McCarthy, *Saint Ephrem's Commentary* (n. 81 above).

[101] When Solomon consecrated the temple, a huge amount of incense was burned. 'It was the sign of the presence of God . . . and of his dwelling with them in this newly built and consecrated place.' Josephus, *Antiquities* 8.4.

[102] *Apocalypse of Moses* 29.

[103] The great collection of Jewish commentaries on the various books of the Bible, compiled centuries after the New Testament was written, but preserving some ancient material.

mercy. And then the LORD will disclose these things, and the glory of the LORD and the cloud will appear' (2 Macc. 2.4–8).

Christian authors, however, knew that the lost Eden and the lost temple were part of the story of the long exile,[104] and that the gifts of the magi were also part of that story. The *Testament of Adam* is a Christian text of the mid-third century CE that incorporates earlier Jewish material. It tells how Adam was buried by his son Seth, and how his prophecies were sealed into the Cave of Treasures, along with the gold and myrrh and frankincense he had brought from Paradise. 'And the sons of the kings, the magi, will come and get them, and they will take them to the Son of God, to Bethlehem of Judea, to the cave.'[105] The story also appears in *The Book of the Cave of Treasures*,[106] which says that the cave was lower down the mountain of Paradise, and that Adam consecrated the cave as a house of prayer for his family – the temple. A longer version in *The Book of Adam and Eve*[107] tells how the three archangels were sent to Eden to bring the gifts for Adam when he had been driven from Eden: Michael brought the gold, Gabriel the incense and Raphael the myrrh. The Ethiopian church depicts the magi with wings, presumably the three angels who brought the gifts to the first Adam.

Jesus was the new Adam, the new creation, opening the way back to Eden and restoring the true temple. All these themes are in the New Testament, and so proclaiming the birth of the new Adam and the great high priest could well be the original meaning of the magi. A Hebrew version of Matthew would have had wordplay here, since 'magi from the east' is written in the same way as 'magi from ancient times'. The word *miqqedem* can mean 'from ancient times' or 'from the east'. The Garden of Eden was planted *miqqedem*, the LORD, the Holy One was *miqqedem* (Hab. 1.12), and the Lady would give birth to the great shepherd of Israel *miqqedem* (Mic. 5.3–4). The magi also came *middedem*, and so were a sign for the Hebrew Christians that the ancient ways were being restored.

---

[104] See above, p. 26.

[105] *Testament of Adam* 3.6, in OTP 1.

[106] *The Book of the Cave of Treasures* is a Syriac text, a history of the world traditionally attributed to Ephrem, who died in 373 CE. The present text is probably from the sixth century. English translation by E. A. W. Budge, London: The Religious Tract Society, 1927.

[107] *The Book of Adam and Eve* I.30, in S. C. Malan, *The Book of Adam and Eve*, London and Edinburgh: Williams & Norgate, 1882. I.31 reads: 'Kings shall bring me, in the flesh, gold as a token of my kingdom, incense as a token of my divinity and myrrh as a token of my sufferings and death.'

Of special interest is the myrrh, because the myrrh anointing oil had 'disappeared' from the holy of holies in the seventh century BCE.[108] The perfumed oil represented Wisdom (Ben Sira 24.15), whence the figurative language in the Enochic *Apocalypse of Weeks*, that Wisdom was abandoned in the time of Josiah (when the oil was hidden away), and the priesthood lost their vision (*1 En.* 93.8). The oil – known as 'the dew of resurrection' – had anointed the royal high priests after the order of Melchizedek and transformed them into sons of God. The temple link was known in the early Church and appears in an Epiphany Sermon of Pope Leo the Great. Interpreting the three gifts of the magi, he wrote: 'He offers myrrh, who believes that God's only begotten son united to himself man's true nature.'[109] The uniting of divine and human had been the mystery of the myrrh oil in the holy of holies, the 'birth' of Immanuel, and it was Pope Leo whose letter on the one person and two natures of Christ was adopted at the Council of Chalcedon in 451 CE.

Justin, a native of Palestine writing in the mid-second century, said the magi came from Arabia,[110] but his voice has been largely unheard, and the magi are invariably linked to Persia. As early as the seventeenth century, however, an English scholar of Arabic working in Oxford suggested that the magi were from Arabia. His biographer noted: 'He gives an account of the magi who were very numerous, not only in Persia and India, but in Arabia too, thinking it probable that those who were of this last country came into Judea to worship our Saviour.'[111] Exactly what Justin meant by 'Arabia', however, is not known. Herod was an Arabian but he came from Edom,[112] and Josephus said that Petra was the capital of Arabia. It was not today's Arabia.[113] After his conversion, Paul went to Arabia (Gal. 1.17), and his visit may help to identify the magi. He came back better informed about his new faith and able to explain that Christianity was rooted in something older than the law of Moses. Who instructed him? Paul

---

[108] See above, p. 27.
[109] Leo the Great, *Sermon 36 On the Epiphany*, 6, in J. P. Freeland and A. J. Conway, trans., *Sermons: St Leo the Great*, Fathers of the Church 93, Washington: Catholic University of America Press, 1996.
[110] Justin, *Trypho* 78, 102.
[111] L. Twells, *The Theological Works of the Learned Dr Pocock*, London: at the Crown and Mitre, Fleet Street, 1740, vol. 1, p. 35. He also says, p. iii, 'The Reader is further to know that the Arabic types were kindly supplied by the Society for Promoting Christian Knowledge.'
[112] See above, p. 109.
[113] Josephus, *Antiquities* 4.7.

went on to teach that Christianity antedated the Sinai covenant, and was based on righteousness through faith. Abraham was the great example, and his true heirs were righteous through faith.[114] The righteous have proved to be a significant group in the nativity story (Luke 1.17, 75; Matt. 1.19), and Abraham and his heirs were important for Zechariah and his son John (Luke 1.73; Matt. 3.9).

Jewish tradition, recorded in the fourth century CE, but presumably not invented at that time, knew that *many priests of the first temple* had settled in 'Arabia' after Josiah's temple purges in the late seventh century BCE.[115] The enigmatic oracle in Isaiah 21.13–15 was about these priests who had lived in the Forest of Lebanon, that is, Solomon's temple complex (1 Kings 7.2) and then fled to 'the thickets of Arabia'. This implies that descendants of the older priesthood were still in 'Arabia' when Paul went there, people who held the Enochic view that the second temple was impure. There were Jews from 'Arabia' in the crowd at Pentecost (Acts 2.11); perhaps there had been Jews from Arabia in 7 BCE for the feast of Tabernacles, when the star was seen. Perhaps they included some of the descendants of the older priesthood, the priests *miqqedem*, especially as *the traditional way to depict the magi in nativity icons is as three high priests.*[116]

After his time in Arabia, Paul returned to Damascus, which was the code name for Qumran – or so it would seem. The foundation document of the community described them as the men of the new covenant in the land of Damascus who had access to the fountain of living waters.[117] They are usually identified as Essenes. They were a priestly community[118] who had rejected the impurity of the second temple, the righteous who were hoping to return to Eden and be restored again to 'all the glory of Adam'.[119] The Old Greek translation of Amos, made in Alexandria towards the end of the second century BCE, has some interesting differences from the Hebrew that reflect the sectarian polemic of the time. Amos's prophecy of destruction, the shepherd taking away two legs or an ear from the mouth of a lion, was explained as the LORD taking away those who dwell in Samaria and 'those priests in Damascus' (Amos 3.12b). Now there were in Alexandria at that time a large number of Samaritans, and at a later

---

[114] This is worked out most fully in Rom. 4.
[115] Jerusalem Talmud *Ta'anit* 4.5.
[116] Indicated by a curious topknot head-dress, as on the cover of this book.
[117] CD VIII.
[118] CD IV.
[119] CD III; 1QH IV.

date, people very like the Qumran community, presumably 'those priests in Damascus'. We know about the latter – the Therapeuts – because Philo wrote about them,[120] and about Qumran because the scrolls have been found. But were there other such communities elsewhere? Josephus said that the Essenes lived 'in large numbers in every town', and had a network to support members when they travelled.[121] Were there similar settlements in 'Arabia', the home of the magi and the spiritual heirs of the ancient priesthood? Did Paul receive instruction from them about his new faith? These questions cannot be answered, but the evidence suggests they should be asked.

Philo, who died in 50 CE, gave two interesting descriptions of magi, showing how an educated Jew of his time understood the word. 'Among the Persians there is the order of the magi, who silently make research into the facts of nature to gain knowledge of the truth and through visions clearer than speech, give and receive the revelations of divine excellency.' 'Now the true magic, the scientific vision by which the facts of nature are presented in a clearer light, is felt to be a fit object of reverence and ambition, and is carefully studied not only by ordinary persons, but by kings and the greatest kings, so much so that it is said that no one [in Persia] is promoted to the throne unless he has first been admitted into the caste of the magi.'[122] Jews could also be called magi; there was a Jewish false prophet and magus on Cyprus (Acts 13.6). The question is: could other Jews who put their knowledge to better use be called magi?

The first group to consider would be the Essenes.[123] They were a conservative priestly group opposed to the current temple regime in Jerusalem, they studied prophecy and were themselves prophets, they were astronomers, and they were looking for the Messiah [or Messiahs]. They were respected by Herod and would have had easy access to him without fear of his wrath. But if they were Essenes, why did they need to ask him where the king of the Jews had been born? Herod was an Edomite and so did not know the Hebrew prophecies, but the Essenes were noted for their study of prophecy. One answer might be that they knew a different version of the Bethlehem prophecy in Micah 5.2. Instead of 'from you shall come forth *for*

[120] Philo, *On the Contemplative Life*, 64–90.
[121] Josephus, *War* 2.124–5.
[122] Philo, *Every Good Man* 74; *Special Laws* 3.100.
[123] First suggested by M. McNamara, 'Were the Magi Essenes?', *Irish Ecclesiastical Record* (5th series) 110 (1968), pp. 305–28.

me one who is to be the ruler in Israel' the Hebrew text found at Qumran has 'from you one shall *not* come forth to be the ruler in Israel', *l'* instead of *ly*.[124]

Herod told the magi to find the child and then return to say where he was. They were warned in a dream not to return to Herod and so 'they departed to their own country by another way'. Between the monastery of Mar Saba and Bethlehem there is the monastery of Dosi [St Theodosius], built on the site of an older foundation marking the cave where the magi stayed on their way home from Bethlehem. This suggests that they were going to Arabia, rather than to Persia.[125]

The flight into Egypt

When Herod realized he had been tricked by the magi, he ordered that all the baby boys in Bethlehem of two years and under should be killed. Matthew linked this to Jeremiah's prophecy: 'A voice was heard in Ramah, wailing and loud lamentation, Rachel weeping for her children; she refused to be consoled because they were no more' (Jer. 31.15). Now if Matthew had a collection of prophecies that shaped his work, it is interesting to look at the context of the original. 'The people who survived the sword found grace in the wilderness; when Israel sought for rest, the LORD appeared to him from afar. Again I will build you and you shall be built, O virgin Israel.' 'He who scattered Israel will gather him, and will keep him as a shepherd keeps his flock.' Then Rachel weeps for her lost children, and is not comforted. Her children would be brought back and return to their own country (Jer. 31.2, 3, 15–17). The promise of the new covenant follows (Jer. 31.31).

The original importance of this prophecy for an exiled group is clear: they looked for the restoration of the Virgin and her community, ruled by the LORD as their shepherd, and the promise of a new covenant. The massacre of the children was confirmation that a detail of the prophecy was being fulfilled, even though Rachel's tomb was not near Bethlehem but some way north of Jerusalem at Zelzah (1 Sam. 10.2), near Ramah, where Rachel's voice was heard by Jeremiah. People from that area, the family of Ephrath, migrated

---

[124] 4QXII[f].

[125] See E. Hoade, *Guide to the Holy Land*, Jerusalem: Franciscan Press, (1946) 1962. '5 km south of Jerusalem there is a well which the Arabs call bir qadismu because here the magi saw again the star which had guided them' (1946 edn, p. 289).

to Bethlehem, hence its name Bethlehem Ephrathah, and the original Ephrath in the Rachel story was redefined as near Bethlehem (Gen. 35.19; 48.7). 'The transplanted tradition endured, for to this day Muslims venerate the tomb of Rachel at a site just outside Bethlehem.'[126]

Joseph was warned in a dream to take Mary and the infant Jesus to Egypt, and Matthew says no more about their time in Egypt except that it fulfilled the prophecy: 'Out of Egypt have I called my son' (Hos. 11.1). Within the Coptic Church, however, a rich body of tradition developed, some attributed to a vision of Mary received by Theophilus, Patriarch of Alexandria 384–412 CE, some mentioned in other ancient sources. Churches throughout Egypt now commemorate the time when the holy family visited their land, and there is an official map showing their route. Many of the stories told about their journey derive from the Patriarch's vision, but some were known earlier. Cyril of Jerusalem, writing a generation before the Patriarch's vision, said: 'When the LORD was about to go to Egypt, to overthrow the gods of Egypt made with hands, an angel appeared to Joseph in a dream.'[127] This is a recurring theme in the stories of the holy family: the fulfilment of prophecies about Egypt. 'An oracle concerning Egypt. Behold the LORD is riding on a swift cloud and comes to Egypt; and the idols of Egypt will tremble at his presence' (Isa. 19.1). 'In that day there will be an altar to the LORD in the middle of the land of Egypt, and a pillar to the LORD at its border' (Isa. 19.19) was fulfilled when the holy family lived at Mount Qusqam.

The holy family went from Bethlehem to Gaza and then to Pelusium, before heading south-west towards what is now Cairo. There is a problem with the sources, how they relate to each other, and where various incidents were located. The *Arabic Infancy Gospel* contains several episodes from the stay in Egypt – a version of the falling idols, the miraculous tree at Matarea, the robbers[128] – and is thought to derive from a Syriac text of the fifth or sixth century. The *Gospel of Pseudo-Matthew* derives from the *Infancy Gospel of James*[129] and the *Infancy Gospel of Thomas*, but also has material not found elsewhere: Mary and Jesus being worshipped by the wild animals, the

---

[126] See R. E. Brown, *The Birth of the Messiah*, London: Geoffrey Chapman, 1993 edn, p. 205.

[127] Cyril of Jerusalem, *Catecheses* 10.10.

[128] *Arabic Infancy Gospel* 10–12, 23, 24.

[129] See next chapter.

palm tree giving its fruit. Thought to have been compiled in the eighth century, it still quotes from the old Greek text of the Bible, and so contains earlier material.

Early in their travels the holy family took shelter in a cave where there were many dragons who recognized Jesus and worshipped him. They then went quietly away, thus fulfilling the prophecy: 'Praise the LORD from the earth, you sea monsters [dragons] and all you deeps' (Ps. 148.7). Lions, panthers and other wild animals came out of the desert and walked with them, but they did not attack their pack animals nor the flock they had brought with them, thus fulfilling the prophecy: 'The wolf shall feed with the lamb . . . The lion shall eat straw like the ox' (Isa. 11.6–7 LXX). *Pseudo-Matthew* at this point quotes the Greek form of the prophecy, not the Latin form in the Vulgate.

On the third day of their journey, Mary was wearied by the heat and, when she saw a palm tree, said she would like to rest in its shade. 'And when the blessed Mary had sat down, she looked up at the top of the palm tree and saw it was full of fruits and said to Joseph: "I wish someone could fetch some of the fruits of this palm tree." ' Joseph said that the palm tree was too tall, and that their greater need was for water. Then the infant Jesus spoke to the palm tree: ' "Bend down your branches, O tree, and refresh my mother with your fruit." And immediately at this command, the palm bent its head down to the feet of the blessed Mary, and they gathered from its fruits with which they all refreshed themselves.' The palm tree remained bent, and so Jesus told it to rise again and join the trees in Paradise. Then he said to it: ' "Open beneath your roots a vein of water which is hidden in the earth, and let the waters flow so that we may quench our thirst from it." And immediately it raised itself and there began to gush out by its foot a fountain of water very clear, fresh and completely bright.'[130] No prophecy is linked to this story, but there is a reason for this, as we shall see.[131]

The holy family travelled on, wandering in the western desert and the delta region north and west of Cairo. At one point they were attacked by robbers, one of whom treated the family kindly. These two were eventually the thieves crucified with Jesus, and the good thief was the one who went to Paradise.[132] Finally the holy family turned

---

[130] *Gospel of Pseudo-Matthew* 2.
[131] See below, p. 140.
[132] *Arabic Infancy Gospel* 23.

back towards Cairo, to Matarea where there is now a miracle-working tree – 'Mary's Tree'. 'They went to that sycamore which is now called Matarea, and the LORD Jesus brought forth in Matarea a fountain in which the Lady Mary washed his shirt. And from the sweat of the LORD Jesus which he let drop there, balsam was produced in that region.'[133] Sozomen the historian[134] described a miracle-working tree in Egypt whose branches, leaves and bark cured the sick. 'It is related by the Egyptians, that when Joseph fled with Christ and Mary the Holy Mother from the wrath of Herod, they went to Hermopolis.[135] As they were entering the city, this tree bent down and worshipped Christ. I relate precisely what I have heard from many sources concerning this tree.'[136] Other sources said that Hermopolis was where the idols crumbled. When Mary and the child entered their temple, all the idols fell to the ground and shattered, showing that they were nothing, but this incident is also claimed by Tel Basta, some 60 miles north-east of Cairo. Then the holy family sailed up the Nile, stopping at many places on the way, and eventually settling at Mount Qusqam, about 200 miles south of Cairo. This is another site for the story of the two robbers. It was here that the angel appeared to Joseph and told him it was safe to take Jesus back to Palestine, 'for those who sought the child's life are dead' (Matt. 2.20).

The family went to live in Nazareth, to fulfil the prophecy: 'He shall be called a Nazarene'. There is no such prophecy in our present Old Testament, and this has long been recognized as a problem. Some ancient Hebrew manuscripts – forerunners of the Dead Sea Scrolls – were found in a cave near Jericho, and when he heard about this in 800 CE, Timothy, the Patriarch of Seleucia [now Baghdad] wrote to enquire what had been discovered. 'Books of the Old Testament and others in the Hebrew script' he was told. His letter continued: 'I asked about many passages quoted in our New Testament (as coming) from the Old Testament, but found nowhere in it, neither in copies amongst the Jews nor in those amongst Christians.' His informant said that the passages were there. Wanting further confirmation, he wrote to the Metropolitan of Damascus, asking him to investigate, and see if the newly found books contained the prophecy 'He shall be called a Nazarene', but nothing more is known of the incident.[137]

---

[133] *Arabic Infancy Gospel* 24.
[134] Writing in the first half of the fifth century.
[135] About 170 miles south of Cairo.
[136] Sozomen, *History* 5.21.
[137] G. R. Driver, *The Judaean Scrolls*, Oxford: Basil Blackwell, 1965, p. 8.

There has been much debate about the meaning of Nazarene; clearly it was wordplay and did not mean simply that Jesus would come from Nazareth, but it may have been emphasized by Matthew to counter the Jewish criticism: 'Can any good thing come out of Nazareth?' (John 1.46). The Jews were to call the Christians 'the sect of the Nazarenes' (Acts 24.5), and so the meaning of Nazarene could apply also to Jesus' followers. The first problem is how the name Nazareth was spelled in Hebrew or Aramaic in the time of Jesus. Later Hebrew spelled it *Naṣrath*, which would normally give the Greek form *Nasareth*. Matthew has Nazareth, implying a Hebrew form spelled with *z*, rather than *ṣ*. This distinction is important, because it may show what he meant by Nazarene. The name could be from the Hebrew *neṣer* meaning Branch, the messianic title derived from Isaiah 11.1: 'There shall come forth a shoot from the stump of Jesse, and a *branch* shall grow out of his roots.' This would be consistent with the later spelling *Naṣrath/Nasareth*.

Matthew, however, has the form *Nazareth*, implying that Nazarene derived from *nazir*, meaning a consecrated person, someone anointed with the holy oil. Thus 'Should I weep in the fifth month, *separating* myself as I have done these so many years?' (Zech. 7.3, AV, which is a literal translation), and meaning should *I consecrate* myself at that time. Or 'the *consecration* of the anointing oil of his God is upon him' (Lev. 21.12), referring to the high priest. It meant more than Nazirite, although that is the best-known usage, and sometimes the Hebrew word 'Nazirite' was translated into Greek as 'holy one'. Samson was a Nazirite (Judg. 13.5, 7; 16.17), but the Vatican Codex translates the word into Greek as 'a holy one' at Judges 13.7 and 16.17. 'He shall be called a Nazarene' could have been wordplay on the name Nazareth recalling the words to Mary there: 'He shall be called *a holy one*' (Luke 1.35). If Gabriel's actual words were known, rather than their Greek translation, we might have here the prophecy that Matthew had in mind. The sect of the Nazarenes would have been the holy ones, the anointed ones, which is the meaning of Christian.

5

The *Infancy Gospel of James* and translation of the text

The *Infancy Gospel of James*, also known as the *Protevangelium*, is little known in the Western churches but has been very influential in the East. The icon of the nativity and any art or literature on the life of Mary are based on it. It is the earliest written source for many beliefs about Mary, and was very popular in the early Church. The oldest text of the *Protevangelium* is a papyrus dated to the third century CE, Papyrus Bodmer V, which is the earliest known complete text of any Gospel. Its title then was 'The Birth of Mary: Revelation of James', and already there are signs of expansion. The author is unknown, as is the date and place of its composition. The earliest surviving texts are in Greek, and there are translations into many other languages of the ancient Church.

It was known in the Latin West because it was incorporated into the texts known as the *Gospel of Pseudo-Matthew* and the *Gospel of the Birth of Mary*, and it was probably the *Gospel under the name of James the Younger* rejected in the sixth century by the Gelasian Decree. The *Protevangelium* implies that Jesus' brothers and sisters mentioned in the New Testament (for example Mark 6.3) were Joseph's children by his first marriage as he was a widower when he took charge of Mary. Jerome rejected this and explained them as Jesus' cousins, a view that was accepted in the West and received approval from the Pope. This rejection of the *Protevangelium*, and the fact that most of it was incorporated into other writings, means that few early Latin versions survive.

The apocryphal infancy Gospels inspired much Christian art and poetry. 'In antiquity, in the Middle Ages and in the renaissance these writings exercised more influence on literature and art than the Bible itself.'[1] In the earliest Christian centuries too, such art as survives shows knowledge of the apocryphal stories. The earliest refer-

---

[1] O. Cullmann, in E. Hennecke, *New Testament Apocrypha*, ed. W. Schneemelcher, London: Lutterworth Press, 1963, vol. 1, p. 368.

ence to material in the *Protevangelium* is in the *Ascension of Isaiah*, perhaps from the end of the first century CE, which said that Mary was still a virgin after giving birth.[2] Clement of Alexandria, who died in 215 CE, also knew this: 'Mary was found, when examined, to be a virgin even after giving birth.'[3] These writers may not have had a *written* source; they are not proof that the *Protevangelium* existed as a book in their time. They may have known the oral traditions that were important in the early Church for several generations. Clement of Alexandria knew oral traditions about Easter, and Eusebius said of him: 'In his work *The Easter Festival*, he declares that his friends insisted on his transmitting to later generations in writing the oral traditions that had come down to him from the earliest authorities of the Church.'[4]

This may be how the *Protevangelium* material was transmitted. Oral teaching was preferred, as can be seen from Eusebius' account of Papias, bishop of Hierapolis in Asia Minor at the beginning of the second century, who collected many oral traditions and wrote them down. He emphasized that he had not heard the eyewitness generation of Christian teachers, but had heard from the second generation. 'For I did not imagine that things out of books would help me as much as the utterances of a living and abiding voice.' Eusebius added: 'He reproduces other stories communicated to him by word of mouth, together with some otherwise unknown parables and teachings of the Saviour, and other things of a more allegorical character.'[5] Irenaeus, who died about 200 CE, said the same about Polycarp, bishop of Smyrna, who died a martyr in 156 CE. 'I remember how he spoke of knowing John and the others who had seen the LORD, how they repeated their words from memory . . . To these things I listened eagerly at the time . . . not committing them to writing but learning them by heart.'[6] Oral teaching went back to Jesus himself, who, it is easy to forget, wrote nothing. He committed some things – 'higher knowledge' – to a small inner group of disciples. Eusebius says they were Peter, James and John.[7]

It would be a mistake to dismiss the stories in the *Protevangelium* as fantasy or worse. Early material outside the New Testament was

---

[2] *Ascension of Isaiah* 11.9.
[3] Clement of Alexandria, *Miscellanies* 7.16.
[4] Eusebius, *History* 6.13.
[5] Quoted in Eusebius, *History* 3.39.
[6] Eusebius, *History* 5.20.
[7] Eusebius, *History* 2.1.

compiled and preserved by people who were as Christian as Paul and Luke. The first generations had no New Testament canon, and neglect of material such as the *Protevangelium*, and failure to understand it, have impoverished understanding of the Christmas story. A nineteenth-century edition of Clement's *Miscellanies* has a note to the passage about Mary cited above, warning that this was 'a reference to a sickening and profane history of an apocryphal book'.[8] Scholars used to assume that the *Protevangelium* was just a fanciful elaboration of the stories in Matthew and Luke, but opinion is now changing. It may have drawn on the same sources as did Matthew and Luke, but it used more of them and in its own way. The two annunciations in the *Protevangelium* – first at the well, and then while Mary was spinning – may have been the original story that was summarized by Luke, just as he summarized Mark (for example, Mark 4.35–41 summarized at Luke 8.22–25). He does have two distinct parts to his account of the annunciation, but gives no setting for either of them: the angel gives the initial greeting, which the *Protevangelium* sets at the well (Luke 1.28); then the angel begins what could have been a separate address (Luke 1.30, 31, 35; Matt. 1.21), set by the *Protevangelium* while Mary is spinning. 'The stories which came to make up the *Protevangelium* and its companion gospels seem to have been a part of the life of the church during the first generations.'[9]

Irenaeus, at the end of the second century CE, was still emphasizing oral tradition, but the next generation knew a *written Gospel* that included material now found in the *Protevangelium*. Origen, writing in Palestine some time after 230 CE, mentioned that Jesus was born in a cave, a detail that appears in the *Protevangelium* but not in the New Testament.[10]

> With respect to the story of the birth of Jesus in Bethlehem, if anyone desires to have evidence in addition to the prophecy of Micah and the history recorded in the gospels by the disciples of Jesus, let him know that, just as it says in the gospel story of his birth, there is shown at Bethlehem the cave where he was born . . . And this cave is greatly talked of in surrounding places, even by enemies of the faith.[11]

---

[8] Note to *Miscellanies* 7.16 in ANF2.

[9] D. R. Cartlidge and J. K. Elliott, *Art and the Christian Apocrypha*, London: Routledge, 2001, p. 23.

[10] Luke does not actually mention a stable, only a manger. It could have been in a cave.

[11] Origen, *Against Celsus* 1.51. 'An established local tradition enabled the architects to begin work [on the original Church of the Nativity] in 326. The local people knew that at the end of the village among the trees was the cave in which was born Jesus Christ' (E. Hoade, *Guide to the Holy Land*, Jerusalem: Franciscan Press, 1946 edn, p. 308).

The 'history recorded in the gospels' cannot have been Matthew and Luke as we know them, but could have been the *Protevangelium*.

Origen also knew that Mary was called Theotokos, meaning the 'bearer of God', popularly translated as 'Mother of God'. This title was part of a huge controversy early in the fifth century, but was accepted at the Council of Ephesus in 431 CE. Socrates of Constantinople, writing shortly after these events, observed of Nestorius – who opposed using the title – that 'instead of being a man of learning, he was disgracefully illiterate'.[12] He gave examples of much earlier writers who had used the title: Eusebius, he said, had described the sacred cave adorned by the Empress Helena, where the God-bearing Virgin gave birth;[13] and Origen (in a commentary on Romans that no longer survives) gave 'an ample exposition of the sense in which the term Theotokos is used'. Nestorius, said Socrates, had objected to the title Theotokos because he did not know the 'old theologians'. The problem facing any investigation of the Christmas stories and the role of Mary is how little evidence survives from the earliest years, not only from the 'old theologians', but from the Christian communities, who may have had very little contact with the 'old theologians'. None of Origen's surviving work uses the title Theotokos, and yet, in the examples that are found in early fourth-century texts, 'in all these instances, the use of the word is incidental: it is not explained or justified and no weight is placed upon it. The implication is that by the time of the Council of Nicaea in 325, the term was already in standard use.'[14] We can only guess what else might have been in standard use. The popularity of the *Protevangelium*, even though it was never in the New Testament, and the fact that this text rather than Matthew or Luke was used for the nativity icon, suggest that popular memory and devotion – oral tradition – were important for many years in the early Church.

The Christmas story told by Matthew and Luke has only minimum detail, selecting from the human story to illustrate their theme: the birth of the Messiah *as he was expected in late second temple Palestine and recognized by the first Christians*. Prophecies were fulfilled and angels appeared, but these are the only theological markers breaking the surface of the text *that are obvious to us*. The simplest exploration of the cultural, historical, literary and above all temple context

---

[12] Socrates, *Church History* 7.32.

[13] Eusebius, *Life of Constantine* 3.44.

[14] R. M. Price, 'The Theotokos and the Council of Ephesus', in C. Maunder, ed., *The Origins of the Cult of the Virgin Mary*, London: Continuum, 2008, p. 90.

indicates, as we have seen, that much more lies just below the surface. The written text was little more than a reminder for those who knew what the story meant. Just as Jesus warned that those outside could only hear his parables as a story, so too, 'outsiders' will have missed what the Christmas story was actually saying. Each detail was there for a theological purpose, and as the Christian community moved further away from its living sources and its temple roots, especially after the second war against Rome and the expulsion of Jews from Palestine (135 CE), so more detail had to be included in the Christmas story to make sure that no part of the original understanding was lost.

In the *Protevangelium* there is emphasis on Mary's Davidic descent because Jesus was promised the throne of his father David; and on her virginity, because the new Greek translations of the Hebrew scriptures removed 'Virgin' from Isaiah's prophecy, and scandalous tales were circulating about Mary's affair with Panthera. In the mid-second century, Justin had to explain that the birth of Jesus was not like the birth of the demi-gods in Greek and Roman mythology.[15] He already knew the prophecy about the ox and the ass, and what it meant in the Christmas context, but the animals did not appear in an infancy text until *Pseudo-Matthew*, perhaps as late as the eighth century. They appeared in Christian art long before that: there is a third-century sarcophagus now in the church of St Ambrose, Milan which shows the ox and the ass at the crib,[16] and in the monastery of St Catherine on Sinai there is a seventh-century icon of the nativity in its familiar form, with the ox and the ass at the centre.

The recurring theme in the nativity stories of Matthew and Luke is their temple setting: Luke mentions the Firstborn, the manger and no room in the inn, Matthew the three gifts. Mary is the Virgin mother of the King, who was 'born' in the holy of holies. In ancient Jerusalem, his mother had been Wisdom, the Queen of Heaven, and the Qumran Isaiah scroll shows that she had been known as the Virgin, the Mother of the LORD. This is so not very different from the Mother of God. Ignatius wrote about the secrecy of Mary's virginity and childbearing,[17] reminiscent of the 'hidden' nature of the

---

[15] See above, p. 65.
[16] See Cartlidge and Elliott (n. 9 above), p. 19.
[17] Ignatius, *To the Ephesians* 19.

Lady in the temple, implicit in the Hebrew word for Virgin, *'almah*.[18]
There was nothing secret about the actual nativity; Anna told everyone (Luke 2.38). The *Protevangelium* shows symbols of Wisdom
woven into the Christmas story, and they may have been there in oral
tradition from the very beginning.

Is it possible that the Hebrew Christians who proclaimed the
fulfilment of Isaiah's Virgin prophecy, who knew the title 'Mother of
the LORD' in that prophecy and told the story of Elizabeth greeting
the mother of the LORD, never used that title for Mary? Is it possible that much later, Christians who did not use the Hebrew Old
Testament known at Qumran, suddenly decided to invent the title
'Theotokos' when their predecessors had not? Both are possible, but
it is more likely that Mary had an exalted role from the beginning,
and this was recognized. Centuries later – and nobody knows exactly
when – a beautiful hymn was composed to honour Mary. The
Akathist Hymn is in four sections: the Annunciation, the Nativity,
the Incarnation, and the Mother of God. It is a complex and beautiful piece of poetry, a masterpiece of Byzantine hymn-writing, and
is composed from the Christmas story and titles of Mary that are all
drawn from the Wisdom tradition of the temple.[19] The *Protevangelium* is the earliest written evidence for Mary clearly presented as
Wisdom, and may explain why the *Protevangelium* was so popular
and became the basis for the nativity icon.

The story

Joachim and Anna were a prosperous couple who had no children.
He was shunned by his community because of this, and his wife grieved.
One day, when she was watching a nest of sparrows in a laurel tree
and thinking that all nature was fruitful, an angel appeared to her
and said she would have a child. Anna vowed she would give the
child to the LORD, just as Hannah had offered the unborn Samuel.
Joachim was away at the time with his flocks, and he too was visited
by an angel. When he heard the news of the child, he went to the
temple with lavish offerings and saw that the golden plate on the high
priest's turban was shining, a good sign. A daughter was born. She

---

[18] See above, p. 105.
[19] See my paper 'Wisdom Imagery and the Mother of God', in *The Cult of the Mother of
God in Byzantium: Texts and Images*, ed. L. Brubaker and M. B. Cunningham,
Aldershot: Ashgate, 2009.

was named Mary and was kept in a specially consecrated room because she was promised to the LORD. When she was three years old, she was taken to the temple and left in the care of the priests, who were delighted with her.

When she was twelve and about to menstruate, the priests had to find her a husband, since she would pollute the temple with blood. All the local widowers were summoned, and Joseph was chosen to take care of Mary, the LORD's virgin. Joseph worked on buildings away from home, and so Mary was left on her own. Then she was chosen by the priests to help weave the new veil for the temple, and she collected some wool to spin. One day, when she was collecting water, she heard a voice and was frightened. She went home, resumed her spinning, and then heard the angel again, who told her she would be the mother of the holy child. Mary went to visit Elizabeth, and stayed three months. When she was six months pregnant, Joseph returned from his building work, and saw her condition. An angel spoke to him in a dream, and he was reassured, but the local scribe and priest did not believe the story. Both Mary and Joseph were sent to the temple to drink the bitter water.[20] Neither was affected. They were innocent and were allowed to go home.

Then the census was decreed, and Joseph set out for Bethlehem with Mary and his older son. About three miles from Bethlehem, Mary felt the birth was imminent, and so Joseph found a cave for her to shelter in and left his son (or sons) there while he went to find a midwife. As he walked, he had a strange vision of creation standing still: workmen were looking upwards, sheep and their shepherd were motionless. Joseph found a midwife, but she did not believe his story about a divine child. When they returned, they saw a bright light in the cave. Then Salome appeared and did not believe that a virgin could give birth and still remain a virgin. She examined Mary and found it to be true, but her hand began to burn. When she touched the child she was healed.

The wise men came with their gifts, having been to Herod and told him about the star. They found the holy family and gave their gifts, but an angel warned them to return by another route. Then Herod was angry and ordered the killing of the children. Mary hid Jesus under the straw in a manger, and Elizabeth fled with John to a cave in the hills. Herod sent to Zechariah, demanding to know where his son John had been hidden, and when he refused to say, Herod had him killed

---

[20] See above, p. 106.

in the temple. Simeon, who had welcomed the infant Jesus to the temple, took his place.

There are obscure and unusual details in the *Protevangelium*, some doubtless due to early scribal errors, but they do not necessarily imply ignorance of life in Palestine, nor of Jewish or temple custom as is sometimes asserted. Surprisingly little is known about the religion and way of life in Palestine at the end of the second temple period. The unexpected contents of the Dead Sea Scrolls are ample proof of that. Ignorance of Palestinian geography, daily life and temple custom is more likely to be on the part of later readers. That Joachim should have his offerings rejected because he had no child is possible: childless women like Elizabeth were also shunned (Luke 1.25). Joseph and Mary both drinking the bitter water is not the usual practice. The law required the unfaithful woman to drink it, but in an unusual case like this, Joseph could have been unfaithful, and so a variation of the custom is not impossible. Nor does the *Protevangelium* necessarily show ignorance of the geography of Palestine in its use of the term Judaea. The town is called Bethlehem of Judaea, and the surrounding area is simply Judaea. Thus there was a disturbance in Bethlehem of Judaea, and then Joseph prepared to go out into Judaea (*PJ* 21).

The shining of the high priest's golden plate on his turban (*PJ* 5) may not be a fanciful detail. It is not mentioned elsewhere, but the meaning is perfectly clear. The golden plate on the high priest's turban bore the Name, a sign that he was the presence of the LORD. When the LORD's presence shone on his worshipper, the LORD had been gracious and given him peace of mind. That was the promise of Aaronic blessing (Num. 6.24–26), and what Joachim was seeking in the temple. It was, however, forbidden to expound the meaning of this blessing, which could be read out but not interpreted.[21] The reason for the prohibition is not known, but it would explain why there are no other references to the shining golden plate. Josephus says that other jewels of the high priest's regalia had been used to indicate the divine presence: 'one of [the stones on his shoulders] shone out when God was present at their sacrifices', but the stones had stopped shining 200 years before his time, due to transgression of the Law.[22] Further evidence that memories of the shining vestments had faded is found in the Targum, which seems to conflate the shining stones and the

---

[21] Mishnah *Megillah* 4.10.
[22] Josephus, *Antiquities* 3.9.

shining name. Exodus 28.30 – the Urim and Thummim on the heart of Aaron – was said to mean that 'the great and holy name of God on the breastplate of the high priest' was shining.[23] As far as we know, the Name was not on the breastplate but on the turban.

It would be more fruitful to look at the incidents in the *Protevangelium* that cannot at the moment be explained, and recognize in them a measure of how little is known of the background to the Christmas story. There must have been a reason for the scene between Anna and her maid over the veil or diadem that she refused to wear (*PJ* 2). What did the nest of sparrows represent (*PJ* 3)? Why did Anna make her bedroom a sanctuary (*PJ* 6)? Why does the infant Mary walk seven steps (*PJ* 6)? What does the infant Mary in the temple indicate (*PJ* 7)? Why was she described as a temple weaver (*PJ* 10)? Why are we told the colour of the wool she was spinning – red and purple (*PJ* 10)? What do the midwives represent (*PJ* 18–20)? Why was there a light in the cave (*PJ* 19)? And why is there no mention of the shepherd who is in fact Satan in disguise, tempting Joseph not to believe the miracle? He features in the nativity icon, but not in the written texts. In the annunciation icon, Mary spins red wool when she hears the angel, but in the *Protevangelium* it is purple (*PJ* 11). The answer to all these questions may lie in the mystery of the holy of holies, and the writer of the *Protevangelium* matching the historical incidents in the nativity story to the symbolism of the ancient temple and the birth of the divine son.

Mary

Mary, as we have seen, is presented in many different ways as the lost Lady of Zion, the banished Wisdom who was the heavenly mother of the Davidic king. In the temple, Wisdom had been represented by the seven-branched lamp and the ark or throne, by the bread of the presence and the anointing oil.

The brief glimpse of her devotees in Egypt shows them burning incense and pouring out libations, and making small loaves *to represent her* (Jer. 44.19b, translating literally). This bread was set on a table in the tabernacle/temple, together with incense and wine for libations (Exod. 25.23–30; 1 Kings 7.48), and it was eaten each Sabbath by the high priests (later, by all the priests) as their most holy food (Lev. 24.5–9). 'Most holy' means that it imparted holiness.

---

[23] Targum *Pseudo-Jonathan* Exod. 28.30.

The bread was described as *'azkarah*, a commemoration or invocation offering,[24] and it was presumably in her bread that Wisdom fed herself to her devotees (Ben Sira 24.21). In other words, it was one of her sacraments. Jewish tradition remembered the bread as the most holy of all the offerings,[25] and explained: 'The House of Wisdom is the Tabernacle, and Wisdom's table is the Bread of the Presence and wine.'[26] After Wisdom had been banished from the temple, the bread on the table was not pure (*1 En.* 89.73), and Malachi said that when the bread was polluted, the LORD would not show his presence and be gracious (Mal. 1.7–9).[27] The rewards of the Aaronic blessing were not possible with polluted bread.[28]

Epiphanius, writing in the 370s about heresies, described a group of women in various places including Arabia who venerated a small loaf[29] dedicated to Mary. They draped a chair with cloth and then put the bread on it, as though enthroned. Then they ate the bread. Epiphanius, who called these women Kollyridians and linked this to the worship of the Queen of Heaven described in Jeremiah, wrote: 'If [God] does not want angels to be worshipped, how much more does he not want this for her born of Ann.'[30] Another text, from the late fifth century, suggests that this was not deemed a heresy by everyone. 'The *Six Books* apocryphon . . . directs that a liturgical ceremony almost identical to what Epiphanius ascribes to the Kollyridians should be observed in Mary's honour on three different occasions during the year.' Special bread was baked and offered with incense by the priest, saying: 'In the name of the Father, and of the Son and of the Holy Spirit, we celebrate the commemoration of my Lady Mary.'[31] The bread was then taken to people's homes, conveying 'the blessing of the blessed one'. Like the bread of the presence, it was a commemoration offering and a means of conveying holiness. Whether or not this was a heretical practice, it shows how the Wisdom tradition shaped the way Mary was celebrated.

---

[24] Targum Onkelos and Targum Neofiti Lev. 24.7 say it was the bread itself, not the incense, that was the memorial/invocation offering.

[25] Targum Onkelos Lev. 24.9.

[26] *Leviticus Rabbah* XI.9.

[27] The Hebrew and Greek texts of Mal. 1.7 have 'bread' despite some of the English translations.

[28] For detail see my book *The Great High Priest*, London: T&T Clark, 2003, pp. 246–9.

[29] *kollyris*, hence the name of the group: Kollyridians.

[30] Epiphanius, *Heresies* 79.

[31] S. Shoemaker, 'The Cult of the Virgin in the Fourth Century: A Fresh Look at Some Old and New Sources', in Maunder (n. 14 above), pp. 78–9.

Another symbol of Wisdom was a fragrant tree, the tree of life which was represented in the temple by the original menorah. It was oil pressed from this tree that became the anointing oil, Wisdom's second sacrament. In one of her poems, Wisdom describes herself as the anointing oil: 'Like choice myrrh I spread a pleasant odour' (Ben Sira 24.15). A first-century text attributed to Clement of Rome,[32] but thought to be later, has Peter explain to Clement the meaning of the title 'the Christ' and thus of the anointing oil.

> The reason for the name is this. Although indeed he was the Son of God, and the beginning of all things, He became man; Him first God anointed with oil which was taken from the wood of the tree of life: from that anointing therefore, He is called Christ.

All his followers are anointed with a similar oil, 'so that their light may shine, and being filled with the Holy Spirit, they may be endowed with immortality'. The actual origin of this text and its teaching is unknown. Its roots may lie among the Elkesaites, an early Jewish Christian group, but that in itself is not a condemnation, even though some later writers labelled them 'Gnostic'. It went on to link the oil from the tree of life and the temple oil:

> In the present life Aaron, the first high priest, was anointed with a composition of chrism, which was made after the pattern of that spiritual ointment . . . If, then, this temporal grace, compounded by men, had such efficacy, consider how potent was that ointment extracted by God from a branch of the tree of life.[33]

The myrrh oil appears in one of the high priestly Enoch texts. Nobody knows the origin of *2 Enoch*, but it has survived in Old Slavonic and preserved some glimpses of the ancient holy of holies, where the anointed one was 'born'. The parts of Psalm 110 that are now opaque once described this scene, the birth of the divine son.[34] The words that remain in the psalm seem to include 'I have begotten', 'the day of your birth', 'in the glories of the Holy One', 'from the womb/from Mary', 'Morning Star', and 'dew'. The 'Gnostic' and Enochic texts may have reconstructed as best they could from this same set of difficult words, or they may have retained a memory of what lies beneath the present damaged text of Psalm 110. 'Enoch' recounts his own 'birth' in the holy of holies. He saw the face of the

---

[32] Clement was bishop of Rome and died about 97 CE.
[33] *Clementine Recognitions* 1.45–6.
[34] See above, p. 6.

LORD and heard the song of the heavenly host. Then the archangel Michael was told to take Enoch from his earthly clothes, that is, from his mortal body, to anoint him, and dress him in the garments of the Glory of God.[35] Enoch described the oil; it shone like rays of the sun, it was perfumed like myrrh, and it was like dew. Enoch knew that he had become like one of the holy angels (*2 En.* 22).

The anointing described by the *Clementine Recognitions* and *2 Enoch* is the context for texts in the New Testament, and so from the earliest stratum of Christianity. All Christians had been anointed and marked with the Name on their foreheads, and, like Enoch, had stood before the face of the LORD: 'You have been anointed by the Holy One and you know all things . . . His anointing teaches you about everything' (1 John 2.20, 27); 'Thanks be to God, who in Christ leads us in triumph, and through us spreads the fragrance of the knowledge of him everywhere, for we are the fragrance of Christ' (2 Cor. 2.14–15); 'They shall see his face and his Name shall be on their foreheads' (Rev. 22.4). The holy child, as we shall see, was described as anointed from his birth.

Later critics of the Lady referred to her tree as an *asherah*, and there is a poem playing on the name *asherah*, happy, which says that Wisdom is the tree of life, and those who hold on to her are happy (Prov. 3.13–18). In another poem Wisdom describes herself as a river flowing forth, drenching her garden and pouring out teaching like prophecy, although in its present form the original Wisdom element has been reworked as the Law, and the poem extols the Law of Moses (Ben Sira 24.30–34). As well as baking bread, the Lady's devotees were temple weavers, 'women weaving hangings for Asherah' (2 Kings 23.7), and she was probably linked to the sun, moon and stars, and to the angels who represented them. As late as the compilation of the Mishnah in 200 CE, the Lady and her tree were forbidden: wood from the tree could not be used to bake bread, nor could it be used to make a shuttle to weave cloth, and even sitting in its shade made one unclean.[36] The *Gospel of Philip* remembered Wisdom as the mother of the angels.[37] All these symbols can be seen in John's vision, where the woman clothed with the sun was crowned with stars and standing on the moon, and an army of angels fought the dragon who tried

---

[35] These were the vestments of the high priest. Exod. 28.2: holy garments for Aaron . . . for glory and for beauty.

[36] Mishnah *'Abodah Zara* 3.8–9.

[37] *Gospel of Philip*, CG II.3.63, cf. the Lady in Ugarit as the mother of the 70 sons of El, see above, p. 104.

to destroy her son (Rev. 12.1–9). The dragon then went off to attack the rest of her children, the Christians (Rev. 12.17). In his final vision, John saw her tree restored to the holy of holies, the river of life flowing from its roots, and those with the Name on their foreheads, that is, the anointed ones, standing before the throne (Rev. 22.1–5).

The Lady had been one of the objects of Josiah's temple purge, when the temple weavers, the 'angels',[38] and the *asherah*, together with their sacred vessels, were removed (2 Kings 23.4–7). There had been earlier attempts to remove her: one of them involved a queen mother called Anna (the Greek text of 1 Kings 15.13); another prompted the call vision of Isaiah, when he saw the LORD in the holy of holies between the two creatures, and recognized his unworthiness. 'Woe is me for I kept silent.[39] I am a man of unclean lips' (Isa. 6.5). Isaiah had allowed something to pass without protest, and, in the light of what follows, this may well have been violation of the *asherah*. The punishment for the people would be a loss of understanding; they would live with the consequence of their action and keep what they had chosen. 'Hear and hear and do not understand; see see, and do not perceive', exactly how Jesus explained the role of parables, that some people would see and hear only the surface story, but not understand (Mark 4.11–12). The Enoch tradition said that when the Lady was banished, the priests lost their vision and could no longer perceive (*1 En.* 93.8). Tradition simply said that the oil had been hidden away. Isaiah asked how long that situation would last. He was warned that the land would be desolate 'until the abandoned [Lady] is great in the midst of the land' (Isa. 6.12b).[40] What follows is an opaque text about a sacred tree that has been felled yet still preserves the sacred seed within it, and there are several words that look like a corruption of *asherah*.[41] This was the tree John saw restored to the temple, with the water flowing at its roots, and this is why the incident of Mary resting in the shade of the palm tree, with the stream flowing from its roots, was significant. There is no reference in that story to prophecy being fulfilled; it was a temple image realized.

Wisdom describes herself in Proverbs 8, a poem that must be read in its temple context. The temple represented the whole creation, with the holy of holies as the invisible state beyond time and matter, and

---

[38] By changing the vowels, the word for 'holy ones' becomes 'prostitutes'.
[39] The other and older way to understand 'I am lost'.
[40] Isa. 6.12b is ambiguous, and can mean also 'the forsaken places are many in the midst of the land'.
[41] For detail see my book *The Great High Priest*, London: T&T Clark, 2003, pp. 238–43.

the great hall as the material world. In the poem, Wisdom says she was begotten and born before the visible world was made (Prov. 8.22 'begotten'; 8.24, 25 'brought forth' in the sense of birthed).[42] With a temple world view, this means that Wisdom was born in the holy of holies. This is where she reappears in John's vision, about to give birth to her son, and this is why the *Protevangelium* says that Mary had to leave the temple when she was old enough to give birth to her son (*PJ* 8). The story is told presenting Mary as Wisdom. Wisdom was beside the Creator as he made the world, and was his delight, rejoicing before him and delighting in his creation (Prov. 8.30–31). Philo, the exact contemporary of Jesus, described Wisdom as 'the first born mother of all things'.[43] The *Protevangelium* has Mary entering the temple as a three-year-old child and then 'dancing with her feet' and delighting all the house of Israel (*PJ* 7). She is the child Wisdom in the world; why else should there be an otherwise irrelevant reference to her dancing in the temple?

Now Miriam, Mary's namesake, had also become a symbolic figure. The stories of Amram's family – Miriam, Aaron and Moses – were written so as to give a thinly veiled account of power struggles in Jerusalem during the second temple period. These can be reconstructed, albeit tentatively, from references in the later Jewish commentaries on the Pentateuch. Miriam was remembered as the great Lady of Israel's history, in no way inferior to her brothers. In the desert wanderings, three good things were given to Israel because of the merits of their leaders: the pillar of cloud for Aaron, the manna for Moses and a well for Miriam.[44] Miriam was the deliverer in Israel, while Moses and Aaron were the redeemers.[45] Aaron became the high priest, Moses the king, and Miriam 'took' wisdom, 'and it was from her that Bezalel descended, from whom in turn, David who was a king'.[46] Miriam, then, represented Wisdom, the tabernacle/temple, the Davidic house, and water. Josiah's purge marked the end of Wisdom and began the increased emphasis on Moses and the Law. This is reflected in the way the Miriam, Aaron and Moses story is told in Numbers 12.[47]

---

[42] Despite what some English versions say.

[43] Philo, *Questions on Genesis* IV.97.

[44] Babylonian Talmud *Ta'anit* 9a.

[45] *Exodus Rabbah* XXVI.1.

[46] *Exodus Rabbah* XLVIII.4.

[47] See C. V. Camp, *Wise, Strange and Holy: The Strange Woman and the Making of the Bible*, Sheffield: Sheffield Academic Press, 2000, pp. 268–78.

The power struggles at the beginning of the second-temple period are clear in that chapter. Miriam and her brother Aaron, representing Wisdom and priesthood, challenged the supremacy of Moses, representing the Law, because he had married a foreign woman (Num. 12.1). In other words, there were alien elements in second-temple Judaism, while indigenous people and their traditions of priesthood and Wisdom were rejected. Miriam was smitten with leprosy, the punishment for blasphemy, and, although she was cured, she had no more part in the story. She died at the beginning of Numbers 20, and was buried in Qadesh, a name meaning 'holy place'. The story continues: 'Now there was no water for the congregation, and they assembled themselves together against Moses and against Aaron' (Num. 20.2). Miriam, the older sister, was ousted in favour of foreign women, and when she died, *there was no water*. The *Protevangelium* has Mary at the well when she first hears the angel (*PJ* 11).

The veil

When Mary was twelve years old she left the temple, and the priests found Joseph, a widower with a family, to take care of her. Then the priests decided to make a new veil for the temple – not impossible because Herod was rebuilding the temple at that time. The Mishnah says that two new veils were woven each year, but that seems excessive. The detail of manufacture is not clear either, but it seems it was made from 72 pieces of fabric each a handbreadth wide and on 24 linen warp threads. The veil was woven by 82 young girls.[48] The priests sent out for [extra] workers, searched and found seven eligible – pure virgins from the house of David. Then they remembered Mary, and she too was recruited. Thus we learn that Mary was from the house of David, something not made clear in the New Testament Gospels, and that she worked as a weaver.

The veil itself, apart from being a heavy and valuable piece of fabric, symbolized matter, the veil that hid the Glory of God from human eyes. In the temple it closed off the holy of holies, heaven, from the great hall of the temple, earth. It was woven from four different threads: a warp of natural linen, and weft of blue, red and purple wool. These were symbolic, representing the four elements from

---

[48] Mishnah *Shekalim* 8.4–5.

which the creation was made: linen was earth, blue was air, red was fire and purple was water. Josephus wrote: 'The comparison is in two cases suggested by their colour, and in that of the fine linen and the purple by their origin, as the one is produced by the earth and the other by the sea.' He described the fabric as Babylonian tapestry.[49] Philo knew the same explanation.[50] According to the specification in Exodus, which gives no reason for the veil being as it was, it had to be woven from the four threads, 'in skilled work', *ḥošeb*, which presumably was what Josephus meant by 'Babylonian tapestry'.

The special fabric of the veil was also used for the outer vestment of the high priest, with the addition of gold (Exod. 28.5–6). Since the high priest 'was' the LORD with his people, his vestment functioned as did the sanctuary curtain: to veil the Glory. When he was in the holy of holies, the high priest wore white linen like the angels in heaven (Lev. 16.4; cf. Rev. 1.13), but when he was in the material world, he was both veiled and clothed in matter. This was common knowledge in the early Church: that Jesus opened a way 'through the curtain, that is through his flesh' could be written without any explanation (Heb. 10.20). When he died, the veil of the temple was torn (Matt. 27.51; Mark 15.38; Luke 23.45). As his mother was pregnant, she was weaving a new veil for the temple.

This incident of weaving the temple veil shows how a simple story was recognized as a sign and became the vehicle for a sophisticated theology. To those whose eyes had not been opened, Mary was weaving a piece of fabric for the temple; but to those who were relating the heavenly and earthly stories – on earth as it is in heaven – the incident symbolized the process of incarnation. The high priest's vestment also symbolized putting on wisdom, or so it would seem from an early Christian Wisdom text.

> Wisdom summons you in her goodness saying, 'Come to me, all of you foolish ones, that you may receive a gift, the understanding which is good and excellent. I am giving you a high priestly garment which is woven from every (kind of) wisdom.' . . . Clothe yourself with wisdom like a robe . . . From now on, then, my son, return to your divine nature . . . Return to your first Father, God, and to Wisdom your mother from whom you came into being.[51]

---

[49] Josephus, *War* 5.212–13.
[50] Philo, *Questions on Exodus* II.85.
[51] *The Teaching of Silvanus*, CG VII.4.89–91.

The resting-place

The decree was issued for the census, and so Joseph set out with his family. One or more of his sons accompanied him and Mary as they went to Bethlehem. Three miles from Bethlehem she felt the beginning of her labour, and so Joseph helped her down from the ass and found a cave where she could rest while he went to fetch a midwife (*PJ* 17). This incident, known as the sitting, *kathisma*, of Mary, was marked initially by worship at the site, as attested by the Jerusalem Armenian Lectionary from the early years of the fifth century which mentions a feast in the memory of Mary, celebrated on 15 August. The prescribed readings are all about the birth of Jesus, and the celebration was exactly where the *Protevangelium* described the birth: at the third mile from Bethlehem. A wealthy woman named Ikelia had a church built at the site in the mid-fifth century, with a monastery attached. A contemporary text, however, calls it the Old Kathisma church, implying there was another more recently built.

The older church with its monastery was uncovered by archaeologists in the 1950s, midway between Jerusalem and Bethlehem. A second church was uncovered in the 1990s, an octagonal building near a cistern known as the *bir al-Qadismu*, the well of the magi. It seems that the original Greek *kathisma*, sitting, had passed into Arabic as *qadismu*, meaning holy, and the site had been linked to the magi. This holy site had a great rock in the centre of the church, and a water source nearby. A great rock with a spring nearby was mentioned by the Piacenza Pilgrim, writing in the 560s, who said it had been in the road,[52] and was where Mary stopped – but on her journey to Egypt. This means that by the end of the sixth century, traditions about the two resting places – on the way to Bethlehem and on the way to Egypt when Mary rested under a palm tree – had coalesced. Part of a renewed mosaic floor was uncovered in the south-east of the octagonal church, which seems to confirm the fusion of the two stories: it depicts a large palm tree set between two smaller ones, all three laden with fruit.[53] This may account for a detail in the Muslim story of the nativity, that Mary gave birth under a palm tree:

---

[52] It had been cut and taken away to be an altar.

[53] R. Avner, 'The Recovery of the Kathisma Church and its Influence on Octagonal Buildings', in *One Land, Many Cultures*, ed. G. Bottini and others, Jerusalem: Franciscan Printing Press, 2003, pp. 173–86; S. Shoemaker, *Ancient Traditions of the Virgin Mary's Dormition and Assumption*, Oxford: Oxford University Press, 2002, pp. 78–98.

In the early seventh century, probably after the Muslim takeover of the area, [the church] was restored, and one of its new mosaic floors shows a palm tree remarkably similar to one of the mosaic trees on the wall of the dome of the rock. Further, the Dome of the Rock's inscription gives particular importance to Mary, in its statement about Christianity, and the palm tree under which she rested is part of the Muslim message.[54]

The cave

Joseph found a cave and brought Mary to it. He left his son[s] with her and went to look for a midwife. At this point the text changes and becomes Joseph's own account of his experience.[55] Everything stopped moving. The writer is trying to communicate the idea that time stood still, and that the timeless entered time. Sheep and goats were motionless. Workmen looked up to the sky but did not move. All these details – the shepherd with his stick raised, the young goats drinking at the stream – can appear in the nativity icon. Then everything resumed its natural course, and Joseph found a midwife.

The cave is presented as the holy of holies. A cloud overshadowed it, and as the cloud withdrew, there was a bright light. As the light diminished, the child was seen, who then began to suckle and so showed he was fully human. In the *Ascension of Isaiah*, the infant by his suckling deceived the hostile heavenly powers: 'He sucked the breast, as was customary, that he might not be recognized.'[56] James has transferred the ritual birth in the holy of holies to the cave, exactly as Luke did in the manger scene. The two writers expressed this in different ways, showing that birth in the holy of holies was in the tradition they received, but each illustrated it in his own way. James describes first a bright cloud – reminiscent of the cloud of the Glory that settled on Sinai (Exod. 24.15–17); the cloud and the Glory that consecrated the new tabernacle (Exod. 40.34); and the cloud that came to consecrate Solomon's new temple: 'A cloud filled the house of the LORD, so that the priests could not stand to minister because of the cloud; for the Glory of the LORD filled the house of the LORD' (1 Kings. 8.10–11). There was a cloud at the transfiguration; Matthew described it as a bright cloud, from which a voice proclaimed: 'This

---

[54] O. Grabar, *The Dome of the Rock*, Cambridge, MA: Harvard University Press, 2006, p. 105.

[55] This section is not in Papyrus Bodmer V.

[56] *Ascension of Isaiah* 11.17.

is my beloved Son' (Matt. 17.5). John described the incarnation as 'beholding the Glory'; he was thinking in the same way. James chose to depict this graphically, perhaps for the generation that was in danger of losing touch with the imagery.

Closest of all is Ezekiel's description of the Glory leaving the temple. He was describing the end of the second temple, when the chariot throne of the Lord, with all its fiery creatures and lightning, was moving out from the holy of holies: 'The Glory of the Lord went forth from the threshold of the house' (Ezek. 10.18). Ezekiel saw the Glory coming to Babylon, and described what he saw: 'a great cloud with brightness round about it' (Ezek. 1.4). In the midst of the living creatures that formed the throne, he saw 'burning coals of fire, like torches moving to and fro' (Ezek. 1.13); and at the centre, above the creatures and the fiery torches, he saw: 'the likeness as it were of a human form . . . the appearance of the likeness of the Glory of the Lord' (Ezek. 1.26, 28). Ezekiel saw this Glory departing, but he also saw it return. The angel revealed to him the correct measurements of the true temple, and all that that implied,[57] and then he saw the Glory of the Lord coming back from the east: 'the Glory of the Lord filled the temple' (Ezek. 43.5). Doubtless the original was a sunrise vision, just as John had described the angel in the sunrise with the great seal (Rev. 7.2), but it was also one of the great hopes from the sixth century BCE, being fulfilled in the birth of Jesus. The Glory had returned. Prophetic voices in the sixth century BCE had warned that the light would never rise on the rebuilt city because of its sins – priests and people alike (for example, Isa. 58.1–9), but when the Glory of the Lord did rise again on his people, kings would be drawn to its brightness (Isa. 60.11–12). Ezekiel's description of the chariot and of the Glory of the Lord in human form, had, by 200 CE, become forbidden reading for Jews: 'They may not use the chapter of the chariot as a reading from the prophets'; and Ezekiel 16, the chapter that calls Jerusalem the harlot, was also forbidden.[58] The two prohibitions could have been related to Christian claims: that it was Jerusalem and not Mary that was the true harlot – as the book of Revelation makes clear – and that the Glory of the Lord had been seen in human form.

Detail accumulated around the description of the cave. In the *Arabic Infancy Gospel* the cave is a place of worship: perhaps it evoked the holy of holies or perhaps it was a memory of the church of the nativ-

---

[57] See above, p. 3.
[58] Mishnah *Megillah* 4.10.

ity. The old woman who was to help Mary's delivery came with Joseph to the cave: 'And behold it was filled with lights more beautiful than the gleaming of lamps and candles, and more splendid than the light of the sun. The child, wrapped in swaddling clothes, was sucking the breast of the lady Mary.'[59] When the shepherds came, 'The cave was at that time made like a temple of the upper world, since both heavenly and earthly voices glorified and magnified God on account of the birth of Christ.' The comparable scene in the old temple liturgy was the people who had walked in darkness and seen a great light, and the angel voices in the holy of holies at the birth of the Son: 'Unto us a child is born, unto us a son is given' (Isa. 9.6–7).

An even fuller version of the scene appeared in a mediaeval Latin infancy Gospel known as Arundel 404,[60] which derived ultimately from the *Protevangelium*. The narrator was the midwife, who described time standing still, as in the *Protevangelium*. Mary looked up into heaven and she became 'like a vine', the imagery of the tree that was used by Ezekiel in his lament for the exiled queen (Ezek. 19.10–14).[61] Then the light came forth, and Mary worshipped the child she had borne. The child himself was shining brightly and brought an aura of peace:

> In that hour when he was born, the voice of many beings proclaimed in unison 'Amen'. And that light which was born was multiplied and it obscured the light of the sun itself by its shining rays. The cave was filled with the bright light and with a most sweet smell. The light was born just as dew descends from heaven to the earth. For its perfume is fragrant beyond all the smell of ointments.[62]

The light gradually diminished, and the child was seen. When the midwife held the child, she said he was perfect, 'His whole body was shining, just as the dew of the Most High God. He was light to carry, radiant to see.' This recalls, in considerable detail, the 'birth' of the divine child in the holy of holies: bright light, perfume, and dew. How such detail survived the centuries is unknown, but the correspondence is too great for coincidence. Here, in what seems to be an elaborately exaggerated apocryphal account of the nativity, is the ancient holy of holies.

---

[59] *Arabic Infancy Gospel* 3.
[60] The designation of the manuscript in the British Library.
[61] Some scholars have tried to emend this to make more 'sense' but the meaning is clear.
[62] Text quoted from J. K. Elliott, *The Apocryphal New Testament*, Oxford: Clarendon Press, 1993, p. 110.

The earliest reference to this miraculous birth of the child is found in the *Ascension of Isaiah*, where the pregnant Mary is at home and one day suddenly sees a small child. Joseph does not see it. Mary's womb is found to be in its virgin state after the child has come. Joseph asked why Mary was astonished, and then his eyes were opened and he too saw the LORD. They heard a voice say: 'Do not tell anyone of this vision.' People were amazed that the child had been born with no pain and no midwife, but their eyes were not opened and they did not 'see' who he was.[63] All these apparently naive attempts to describe the birth of Jesus were setting it in a more than earthly context. The physical details, emphasizing that the baby suckled, that Joseph at first saw nothing unusual, alert us to the other level on which the story must be read. This was a meeting of heaven and earth, indicated in the *Protevangelium* with that glimpse of eternity entering time, and time standing still for an instant.

The midwife came out of the cave and met Salome, who refused to believe the story of the virgin birth. She examined Mary, found that the story was true, and then discovered that her hand was burning. When she picked up the child, she was healed. The virgin state of Mary after the birth was deep-rooted in the mythology of the region. The Lady of Ugarit, more than one thousand years earlier, had been a Virgin goddess but also the mother of seventy sons. There was the enigmatic Eve, daughter of Wisdom in the undateable Gnostic text *On the Origin of the World*, who healed herself, and who resembled the Mother and Bride in Revelation.[64] Of immediate relevance, however, is the opinion of Philo, the exact contemporary of those who first told the Christmas story, and himself an educated Jew. He was discussing Sarah and the birth of Isaac, having already said that Isaac was a divine child: 'Sarah conceived at the time when God visited her in her solitude (Gen. 21.1)'.[65] He understood the biblical phrase 'it had ceased to be with Sarah after the manner of women' (Gen. 18.11, meaning she had reached the menopause) to mean she was no longer a woman but had become virgin again. What Philo is doing in this extraordinary passage is relating a biblical story in terms of something he already believes. The Old Testament characters have to fit his framework, and it is the framework that is important for any exploration of the Christmas story. Philo says that what has been

---

[63] *Ascension of Isaiah* 11.8–15. Cf. Isa. 66.7–9, where Lady Zion gives birth without pain.
[64] CG II.5.114, see above, p. 103.
[65] Philo, *Cherubim* 46.

touched by God is restored again and made new. The mother who
bears a divine child is therefore left in her virgin state after the birth.

> God is the husband of Wisdom . . . for it is meet that God should hold
> converse with the truly virgin nature, that which is undefiled . . . But
> it is the opposite with us. For the union of human beings turns vir-
> gins into women, but when God begins to consort with the soul, he
> makes what before was a woman into a virgin again . . . Thus he will
> not talk with Sarah till she has ceased from all that is after the man-
> ner of women, and is ranked once more as a pure virgin.[66]

In another passage he describes the high priest who has been born
of heavenly parents and anointed; the imagery is exactly that of the
Arundel mediaeval gospel.

> The high priest is not a man but a divine Logos . . . his father being
> God who is likewise Father of all, and his mother Wisdom through
> whom [fem.] the universe came into existence. Moreover, his head has
> been anointed with oil, and by this I mean that his ruling faculty is
> illumined with a brilliant light, in such wise that he is deemed wor-
> thy to put on the garments.[67]

The story continues in the *Protevangelium* with Joseph going out to
see what had caused a disturbance, and finding that the wise men
had arrived. They had seen Herod and told him about the star, and
then had followed it until it stood over the cave. They gave their gifts,
and then went home by another route. Herod realized he had been
tricked and sent out his men to kill the children. Mary hid Jesus under
the straw of the manger, Elizabeth fled to the hills with John and found
refuge in a cave that appeared miraculously. When John's father
Zechariah was accused of hiding his son, he was killed in the temple
by Herod's soldiers. This is said to be confusion with the murder of
another Zechariah, the son of Jehoiada, high priest in the reign of
Joash (2 Chron. 24.22).[68] Knowing Herod's record, it is not impossible that Zechariah was yet another priest that he killed. Jesus spoke
of the murder of Zechariah son of Barachiah (Matt. 23.35), but the
Old Testament prophet of that name died peacefully at a great age,
according to the story current in Jesus' time.[69] The Zechariah murdered by Joash was the son of Jehoiada not of Berachiah, but we

---

[66] Philo, *Cherubim* 50.
[67] Philo, *On Flight* 108–10.
[68] Joash died in about 800 BCE.
[69] *The Lives of the Prophets* in OTP 2.

do not know the name of John the Baptist's grandfather. Zechariah son of Berachiah, murdered between the sanctuary and the altar, could well have been a reference to the murder described in the *Protevangelium*.

The temple building itself recoiled in horror at the deed: the panels wailed and split (*PJ* 24). The temple coming alive in this way is found also in the Dead Sea Scrolls; in the *Songs of the Sabbath Sacrifice*, the walls and the furnishings of the temple join in the liturgy, 'the doors and the gates proclaim the glory of the king'.[70] The story, and the way it is told, all fit into what little is known of first-century Palestine.

There has been relatively little study of the *Protevangelium*. It is all too easy to dismiss the text as 'a sickening and profane history' in an apocryphal book, but closer study shows how close it is in spirit to the earliest understanding of the Christmas story. Its influence has been enormous, even on those who were not aware of its existence.

---

[70] *The Songs of the Sabbath Sacrifice* 4Q 405.23.

The *Infancy Gospel of James* [71]

1. It is written in the histories of the twelve tribes of Israel that there was a man named Joachim who was very rich. He offered his gifts to the temple twice over, saying: 'The whole people shall have the gift from my prosperity, but the LORD shall have the one for my forgiveness, that I may be forgiven.' When the great day of the LORD approached, and the people of Israel offered their gifts, Reuben stood opposite him and said: 'It is not lawful for you to offer your gifts first, for you have fathered no children in Israel.' Joachim grieved, and went to the records of the twelve tribes, to see if he was the only one who had fathered no children. When he searched, he found that all the righteous had fathered children. He remembered the patriarch Abraham and how, at last, God gave him a son, Isaac. Joachim was distressed, avoided his wife's company, and went off into the desert where he pitched his tent and fasted for forty days and nights. He said to himself: 'I will not go down for food or drink until the LORD my God has visited me. Prayer shall be my food and drink.'

2. Anna his wife lamented and wailed for two reasons. She said: 'I am lamenting because I am a widow, and because I have no child.' When the great day of the LORD approached, Judith [72] her maid said to her, 'How long will you humble your soul? The great day of the LORD has come and it is not lawful to mourn. Take this veil, [73] which the mistress of my work [74] gave me, but it is not lawful for me to wear it, for I am a servant and it looks like a royal garment.' Anna said: 'Go away. I will not do this. The LORD has humbled me very much. Perhaps someone cunning gave it to you, and you have come to make me as much a sinner as you are.' Judith said, 'How could I make things worse than they are, seeing that the LORD had closed your womb [75] and given you no child for Israel?' Anna was very distressed and mourned greatly, because all the tribes of Israel reproached her. Then she said to herself: 'What shall I do? I will pray with tears to

---

[71] This translation does not deal with issues arising from the various texts. For a critical edition, see E. de Strycker, *La Forme plus ancienne du Protévangile de Jacques*, Brussels: Société de Bollandistes, 1961.

[72] The maid's name varies in different texts.

[73] This word has many meanings. It could be a diadem, something wrapped round the head, or even a veil.

[74] A literal translation. The meaning is not known.

[75] The versions vary here. Another version of her words is: 'What shall I bring on you for not listening to what I say?'

the LORD my God, to visit me.' Then she changed out of her mourning clothes, put on her bridal garments and adorned her head. At about the ninth hour she went to walk in the garden. She saw a laurel tree, sat down under it, and prayed to the LORD. 'O God of our fathers, bless me and hear my prayer, as you blessed the womb of Sarah and gave her a son, Isaac.

3. Looking up to heaven, she saw a nest of sparrows in the laurel tree, and she wept quietly, saying to herself:

> I am wretched. Whoever brought me into the world? What womb gave birth to me just to be cursed by the people of Israel and reproached and mocked so that I cannot go to the temple of the LORD?
> Who is as wretched as I am? I am not like the birds of the heaven, for even they have young before you, O LORD.
> Who is as wretched as I am? I am not like the beasts of the earth, for even they have young before you, O LORD.
> Who is as wretched as I am? I am not like these waters, for they bring forth before you, O LORD.
> Who is as wretched as I am? I am not like the earth that brings forth fruits in their season and blesses you, O LORD.

4. Then an angel of the LORD appeared to her and said, 'Anna, Anna, the LORD has heard your prayer, and you will conceive and have a child, and your offspring shall be known throughout the world.' Anna said: 'As the LORD my God lives, whether I have a male child or a female, I will offer it as a gift to the LORD my God, and it shall serve him all its life.' Then two messengers came to her and said: 'Your husband Joachim is coming home with the flocks.' An angel of the LORD came down to him and said: 'Joachim, Joachim, the LORD God has heard your prayer. Go down, for Anna your wife has conceived a child.' Joachim went down and called to his shepherds: 'Bring me ten lambs without blemish or spot for the LORD my God, and twelve tender calves for the priests and for the assembly of elders, and a hundred kids for the whole people.' Joachim went [home] with his flocks, and Anna stood at the gate and saw him coming. She ran and hugged his neck and said: 'Now I know that the LORD God has blessed me, for the widow is no longer a widow, and the woman who had no child will conceive.' Joachim rested for a day at home.

5. The next day he took his offerings, saying to himself: 'If the LORD accepts me, the [gold] plate [on the high priest's turban] will show

me.' As Joachim offered his gifts, he looked at the high priest's gold plate as he went to the LORD's altar, and he saw he was not a sinner. Joachim said: 'Now I know that the LORD has been gracious to me and forgiven my sins.' He went home from the temple of the LORD knowing that all was well. After her nine months, Anna had her baby, and she said to the midwife: 'What is it?' She said: 'A girl.' Anna said, 'My soul is magnified this day' and then she lay down, and when the time came, she purified herself and began to feed the baby. She called her Mary.

6. The child grew stronger by the day, and when she was six months old, her mother put her on the ground to see if she could stand. She walked seven steps, and then returned to her mother, who picked her up and said: 'As the LORD my God lives, you shall not walk on the ground again until I take you to the temple of the LORD.' Then she turned her bedroom into a holy place, and allowed nothing impure or unclean into it. Then she called for young Hebrew girls who carried the baby around. When she was one year old, Joachim gave a great feast and invited the priests and scribes, the assembly of elders and all the people of Israel. Joachim brought the child to the priests, and they blessed her: 'O God of our fathers, bless this child, and give her a name that will be famed for ever, among all generations'. All the people said 'Amen.' Then he brought her to the high priests, and they blessed her: 'O God of the high heavens, look on this child, and bless her with the greatest of all blessings.'[76] Then her mother picked her up, took her to the holy place in her bedroom and fed her. Anna sang to the LORD God:

> I will sing a hymn to the LORD my God, because he has come to me
> and taken away the reproaches of my enemies.
> He has given me a fruit of his righteousness, unique and precious
> before him.
> Who will go and tell the sons of Reuben that Anna is feeding her baby?
> Listen, listen you twelve tribes of Israel, Anna is feeding her baby.

She put the child down to sleep in the holy place of her bedroom, and went out to look after the guests. When the feast was over, they went back home rejoicing and glorifying the God of Israel.

7. The months passed, and the child was two years old. Joachim said: 'Let us take her to the temple of the LORD, to fulfil our promise, in

---

[76] Literally, 'bless her with the final blessing that has none after it'.

case the LORD does not accept our gift.' But Anna said: 'Let us wait until she is three, so that she does not miss her father and mother.' Joachim agreed. When the child was three, Joachim said: 'Call for the pure Hebrew girls, and let each of them take a lighted lamp so that the child does not turn around and be distracted away from the temple of the LORD.' This they did until they came to the temple of the LORD. The priest received the child, kissed her and blessed her and said: 'The LORD has made your name great among all generations, and in the last days the LORD will reveal through you the redemption of the people of Israel.' He made her sit on the third step of the altar, and the LORD put grace on her and she danced with her feet and all the house of Israel loved her.

8. Her parents were amazed as they went down from the temple, praising the LORD God because the child had not turned away [from entering the temple]. Mary was in the temple of the LORD, brought up like a dove and fed by an angel. When she was twelve years old, the priests conferred and said: 'Mary has grown to be twelve years old in the temple of the LORD. What shall we do so that she does not pollute the temple of the LORD [with menstrual blood]?' They said to the high priest, 'You stand at the altar of the LORD. Go in and pray about her. Whatever the LORD reveals to you, we will do.' The high priest took the vestment with the twelve bells and went into the Holy of Holies, and prayed about her. An angel of the LORD appeared to him and said: 'Zacharias, Zacharias, go out and call together all the widowers, and let every man bring a rod with him. The LORD will give a sign to the one who is to have her as his wife.' The heralds went all through the country around Judaea, the trumpet of the LORD sounded, and all the men came [to hear].

9. Joseph put down his adze and ran to meet them. They assembled and went to the high priest, taking their rods. The high priest took all their rods and went into the temple to pray. When he had finished his prayer, he took the rods out again and gave them back to the men, but there was no sign. Joseph received his rod last, and a dove came from it and flew onto Joseph's head. The priest said to Joseph, 'You have been chosen to take the LORD's virgin and keep her for yourself.' Joseph refused, saying: 'I have sons and I am an old man. She is only a girl, and the people of Israel will laugh at me.' The priest said to Joseph: 'Fear the LORD your God, and remember what God did to Dathan, Abiram and Korah, how the earth opened up and

swallowed them because they disobeyed. Be careful Joseph, that this does not happen to your house too.' Joseph was afraid, and took [Mary] and kept her for himself. He said to her: 'I have received you from the temple of the LORD. I will leave you in my house while I go away to work on my buildings, and then I will come back. The LORD will watch over you.'

10. The priests held a council and said: 'Let us make a new veil for the temple of the LORD.' And the priest said: 'Summon to me the pure virgins of the tribe of David.' The officers departed, searched and found seven. Then the priests remembered that the child Mary was of the tribe of David and pure before God. The officers went and brought her. They brought them all into the temple of the LORD, and the priest said: 'Cast lots for me, which shall weave the gold, and the undefiled, the fine linen, the silk, the hyacinth coloured, the scarlet and the true purple.' The lots for the true purple and the scarlet fell to Mary, and she took them home. It was at this time that Zacharias became dumb, and Samuel took his place until he could speak. Mary took the scarlet and began to spin.

11. She took her pitcher and went to fill it with water. There was a voice saying: 'Hail, thou that art highly favoured, the LORD is with thee. Blessed art thou among women.' She looked around to the right and left, to see where the voice was coming from. Trembling, she went home and put the pitcher down. Then she took up the purple, sat down on her seat,[77] and drew out the thread. Then an angel of the LORD stood before her saying: 'Fear not Mary, for thou hast found grace before the LORD of all things, and thou shalt conceive of his word.' When she heard this, she questioned with herself and then said: 'Shall I conceive from the living God, and bring forth in the same way as all women?' The angel said: 'No, Mary, for a power of the LORD shall overshadow you, and so the holy one to be born from you shall be called the Son of the Highest. You will give him the name Jesus, for he shall save his people from their sins.' Mary said; 'Behold, the servant of the LORD is before him; let it happen as you have said.'

12. She worked the purple and scarlet and brought them to the priest, who blessed her and said: 'Mary, the LORD God has made your name great, and you will be blessed among all the generations of the earth.'

---

[77] The word is *thronos*, which can be a throne, or a special chair of office.

Mary rejoiced, and went to Elizabeth, one of her family. She knocked at the door, and when Elizabeth heard it, she put down the scarlet wool, ran to the door and opened it. When she saw Mary, she blessed her and said: 'How has this happened to me, that the mother of my LORD should come to me? The child within me leaped and blessed you.' Mary forgot the mysteries that the archangel Gabriel had told her; she looked up to heaven and said: 'Who am I, LORD, that all the generations of the earth are blessing me?' She stayed three months with Elizabeth, and day by day her womb swelled. Mary was afraid, and went home and hid herself from the people of Israel. She was sixteen when these mysteries happened to her.

13. When she was six months pregnant, Joseph came home from his building work, went into the house and saw that she was pregnant. He beat his face and threw himself onto the ground, on sackcloth, and wept bitterly, saying: 'How can I turn to the LORD my God? What shall I pray for, for this young woman? I received her as a virgin from the temple of the LORD my God, and I have not kept her safe. Who has trapped me like this? Who has done this wicked thing in my house and made the virgin unclean? Is not this the story of Adam repeating itself? When he was giving thanks to God at the time for prayer, the serpent came and found Eve and deceived her. It has happened to me too.' Joseph stood up from the sackcloth and called Mary. He said to her: 'You who were cared for by God, why have you done this? Have you forgotten the LORD your God? Why have you humiliated yourself, you who were fed in the holy of holies, and received food from the hand of an angel?' Mary wept bitterly and said: 'I am pure, I have not been with a man.' Joseph said: 'So how have you become pregnant?' She said: 'I do not know how this has happened to me.'

14. Joseph was very frightened and left her alone. He wondered what he should do with her. He said: 'If I hide what she has done wrong, I shall be resisting the law of the LORD; but if I show her to the people of Israel, I am afraid that this might be an angel child, and I shall be handing an innocent woman over to judgement and death. What should I do? I will let her go away quietly.' Then night fell, and an angel of the LORD appeared to him in a dream, saying: 'Do not worry about this young woman, for the child within her is from the Holy Spirit, and she will have a son whom you must name Jesus, for he will save his people from their sins.' Joseph rose from

his sleep, and glorified the God of Israel who had so favoured her. Then Joseph watched over her.

15. Annas the scribe then came to him and said: 'Why did you not appear in the assembly?' Joseph replied: 'I was tired from my journey and so rested the first day.' When Annas turned round, he saw that Mary was pregnant. He went quickly to the priest and said: 'Joseph, for whom you vouched, has committed a great sin.' The priest said: 'In what way?' Annas said: 'He has had relations with the virgin whom he received from the temple of the LORD. He has married her secretly, and not said anything to the people of Israel.' The priest answered: 'Has Joseph really done this?' Annas said: 'Send officers and you will see that the virgin is heavily pregnant.' The officers went and found that she was pregnant, and so brought her and Joseph to the priest for judgement. The priest said: 'Mary, why have you done this? Why have you fallen so low and forgotten the LORD your God, you who were raised in the holy of holies and fed by the hand of an angel? You, who heard the [temple] hymns and danced – why have you done this?' Mary wept bitterly, saying: 'As the LORD my God lives, I am pure and have not been with a man.' The priest then said to Joseph: 'Why have you done this?' Joseph said: 'As the LORD my God lives, I am innocent in this matter.' The priest said: 'Do not speak falsely. Only tell the truth. You have married her secretly and not told the people of Israel. You have not bowed your head under the mighty hand, that your children should be blessed.' Joseph said nothing.

16. The priest said: 'Bring back the virgin whom you received from the temple of the LORD.' Joseph was deeply distressed. The priest said: 'I will give you the water of the LORD's judgement to drink and that will reveal your sin.' The priest took some of [the bitter water], made Joseph drink it, and then sent him away into the hill country. He returned, and the water had not affected him. He also made Mary drink the [bitter water], and sent her into the hill country. She too returned with no [sign of the curse]. All the people were amazed because there was no sign that they had sinned. The priest then said: 'If the LORD God has not revealed your sin, I do not condemn you.' He let them go. Joseph took Mary and went to his house rejoicing, glorifying the God of Israel.

17. A decree was sent out from Augustus the king that all that were in Bethlehem of Judaea should be registered. Joseph said: 'I will

register my sons, but this young woman, what shall I do with her? How shall I register her? As my wife? But I am ashamed to do that. As my daughter? But all the people of Israel know that she is not my daughter. On this day of the LORD, He shall do as he wills.' He saddled the she-ass and set Mary on it. His son led it, and Joseph followed behind [or: His son Samuel followed behind]. As they drew near [to Bethlehem] when it was about three miles away, Joseph turned round and saw the sad expression on Mary's face. He said to himself, 'Perhaps the baby is giving her pain.' When he looked again, he saw that she was laughing. He said: 'Mary, what is wrong. One moment I see you are laughing and the next you are sad.' Mary said to Joseph: 'It is because I can see two peoples: one is weeping and lamenting, and the other is rejoicing and triumphant.' About half way, Mary said to him: 'Take me down from the ass, because the baby is pressing to be born.' He took her down from the ass and said: 'Where shall I take you for privacy, for this is a desert place.'

18. He found a cave there and brought her to it. He put his sons there [to watch] and then set out to look for a Hebrew midwife in the country round Bethlehem.

> As I, Joseph, was walking, I did not walk. I looked up into the air in amazement. I looked up to the highest spot in the heavens, and saw it was still, and the birds of the air were not moving. When I looked to the earth I saw a dish set there, and workmen reclining with their hands in the dish. The ones that had been chewing were not chewing, the ones that were taking food [to their mouths] stopped moving. All their faces were looking upwards. There were some sheep being driven, and they stood still. The shepherd about to strike them with his staff remained with his hand in the air. There were kids about to drink from the stream, and they did not drink. And then, suddenly, everything began to move again.[78]

19. Then there was a woman, coming down from the hill country, and she said to me: 'Where are you going?' I said: 'I am looking for a midwife from the Hebrew people.' She answered: 'Are you a man of Israel?' I said I was. She said: 'And who is the woman giving birth in the cave?' I said: 'The woman who is betrothed to me.' She said to me: 'Is she not your wife?' I said: 'It is Mary, who was brought up in

---

[78] This section where Joseph speaks is not found in Papyrus Bodmer V.

the temple of the LORD; she became my wife by lot, but she is not my wife. She has a child from the Holy Spirit.'

Then the midwife said to him: 'Is this the truth?' Joseph said: 'Come here and see.' The midwife went with him.

They stood by the cave, and there was a bright cloud [or: a dark cloud] overshadowing it. The midwife said: 'My soul is magnified this day, because I have seen marvellous things. Salvation has been born for Israel.' Immediately the cloud withdrew from the cave, and a light appeared there [or: there shone forth a great light], so great that we could not look at it. Gradually the light withdrew [or: diminished], until the young child appeared who went and took the breast of its mother Mary. The midwife cried out: 'What a great day this is for me, for I have seen this new thing happening.' The midwife came out of the cave, and Salome met her. She said to her: 'Salome, Salome, I have just seen something I have never seen before. A virgin has given birth to a child, which is against nature.' Salome said: 'As the LORD my God lives, until I have tested and proved she is a virgin, I will not believe that a virgin has given birth.'

20. The midwife went in and said to Mary: 'Prepare yourself, for there is a fair bit of trouble about you.' Salome examined her and cried out: 'Oh my sin and my unbelief, because I put the living God to the test and now my hand is burning.'[79] An angel of the LORD appeared and said to her: 'Salome, Salome, the LORD has heard you. Put your hand near the young child and pick him up, and you will have healing and joy.' Salome went near the child and picked him up saying: 'I worship him, for a great king has been born in Israel.' And immediately, Salome was healed, and she came out of the cave restored. And there was a voice that said: 'Salome, Salome, do not speak about the marvellous things you have seen, until the child goes to Jerusalem.' [The oldest version[80] has: Speak about the marvellous things you have seen before the child goes to Jerusalem.]

21. Joseph prepared to go out into Judaea, and there was a great disturbance in Bethlehem of Judaea. Wise men had come saying:

---

[79] Some versions have here: She fell on her knees before the LORD and said: 'O God of my fathers, remember that I am descended from Abraham, Isaac and Jacob. Do not shame me in front of the people of Israel, but restore me to the poor, for you know LORD that I performed my cures in your name, and did receive my hire of thee.'

[80] Papyrus Bodmer V, thought to be third century CE.

'Where is he that is born King of the Jews, for we have seen his star in the east and have come to worship him.' When Herod heard it he was troubled and sent officers to the wise men. He sent for the high priests and questioned them: 'What has been written about the Messiah and where he is to be born?' They say to him: 'In Bethlehem of Judaea, for so it is written.' He let them go. He questioned the wise men: 'What sign did you see for the great king that has been born?' The wise men said: 'We saw a very great star among the others, out-shining them so that they dimmed and could not be seen. That is how we knew a king had been born in Israel, and we have come to worship him.' Herod said: 'Go and search for him, and if you find him, tell me so that I may come and worship him.' The wise men went out, and the star they had seen in the east went before them until they went into the cave. It stood over the head of the cave. The wise men saw the young child with Mary his mother, and they brought gifts out of their packs: gold and frankincense and myrrh. Warned by the angel that they should not go into Judaea, they went home by another route.

22. When Herod realized he had been tricked by the wise men, he was very angry and sent out murderers, saying: 'Kill the children who are two years old and younger.' When Mary heard that the children were being killed, she was afraid. She took the young child, wrapped him in swaddling clothes and hid him in an ox manger. When Elizabeth heard they were looking for John, she went up into the hills and looked for a place to hide him, but there was nowhere. Elizabeth groaned loudly: 'O mountain of God, take in a mother with a child.' Immediately the mountain split and took her in. There was a light shining constantly, for an angel of the LORD was with them, keeping watch.

23. Herod searched for John. He sent officers to Zacharias saying: 'Where have you hidden your son?' He answered: 'I am a servant of God and am continually attending to the temple of the LORD. I do not know where my son is.' The officers went away and told Herod. He was angry and said: 'His son is to be king over Israel.' He sent again to [Zacharias] saying: 'Tell the truth. Where is your son? For you know that I have the power to shed your blood.' The officers went and reported all this to [Zacharias]. He said: 'I am a martyr of God if you shed my blood. The LORD will receive my spirit if you shed innocent blood in the forecourt of the temple of the LORD.'

Zacharias was murdered at dawn, and the people of Israel did not know that he had been killed.

24. When the priests went into the temple at the time for the greeting, Zacharias did not come to bless them as he usually did. The priests stood waiting for him to greet them with the prayer, and to glorify the Most High God. When he still did not come, they were afraid, and one of them was bold and went in. He saw congealed blood by the altar, and a voice said: 'Zacharias has been killed, and his blood will not be wiped away until someone comes to avenge him.' When he heard those words, he was afraid and went out to tell the [other] priests. They took courage, went in, and saw what had happened. The panels of the temple wailed and they split from top to bottom. They did not find his body, but his blood had turned to stone. They were afraid, and went out and told all the people that Zacharias had been killed. When all the tribes of the people heard about it, they mourned and lamented for him for three days, and nights. After the three days, the priests conferred together about who should succeed him. The lot fell on Symeon, the man who had been told by the Holy Spirit that he would not die until he had seen the Messiah in the flesh.

25. I, James, wrote this history in Jerusalem. When there were riots following the death of Herod, I went into the desert until Jerusalem was quiet again. I was glorifying the LORD God who gave me the gift and the wisdom to write this account. Grace shall be with those who fear our LORD Jesus Christ, to whom be glory for ever and ever. Amen.

Peace to the one who writes and to the one who reads.

6

The Qur'an and translation of selected passages

A part of the Christmas story appears in two places in the Qur'an, and there are allusions to it elsewhere. In Surah 3, *Imran*, there is the story of the birth of Mary and how she was put into the care of Zakariyya and fed by God. Then there is the story of Zakariyya's hearing the angels and the promise of his son John, and then the annunciation to Mary. In Surah 19, *Maryam*, the story of Mary resumes. She withdrew from her family to a place in the east, and then the angel appeared before her in human form to announce the birth of a holy son. When the birth was near, Mary was under a palm tree in a desert place; God provided a stream of water for her, and when she shook the tree, the dates fell for her to eat. Then she brought her baby to her family, who were disconcerted at the child, but the child himself spoke to them and told them who he was. For Christian readers, some of this is very familiar.

Arabia has often been mentioned in this exploration of the Christmas story: the ousted priests from the first temple settled there, presumably taking with them the ways of their lost temple, and this may lie behind a story told in the earliest biography of Muhammad. Just before he appeared, four men set out to seek the true religion of their father Abraham, which they believed their people had corrupted. 'They went their several ways in the lands, seeking the Ḥanifiya, the religion of Abraham.' One of them met a Christian monk who told him that nobody was left who could guide him to the religion of Abraham, but a new prophet would soon appear.[1] The emphasis in the biblical Christmas stories – in the Magnificat, in the Benedictus and in the teaching of John the Baptist – is very similar: restoring the children of Abraham (Matt. 3.9; Luke 3.8).

---

[1] *The Life of Muhammad*, a translation of Ibn Ishaq's *Life of the Prophet*, with introduction and notes by A. Guillaume, (1955) repr. Lahore etc.: Oxford University Press, Pakistan, 1967, pp. 98–103.

The earliest reference to the magi outside the New Testament, as we have seen, says they came from Arabia. There were Jews from Arabia in Jerusalem at Pentecost when the disciples received the gift of the Spirit. Paul, after his conversion, went to 'Arabia' and there learned more about his new faith – that it was based on the faith of Abraham and not on the Law of Moses. There were Christian and Jewish communities established in Arabia before the rise of Islam; Epiphanius said there were women in Arabia who venerated Mary and offered her loaves. There is also the story that Muhammad found an icon of Mary and Jesus in the Ka'aba when he ordered it to be cleansed. 'Apart from the icon of the Virgin Mary and the child Jesus and a painting of an old man said to be Abraham, the walls inside [the Ka'aba] had been covered with pictures of pagan deities. Placing his hand protectively over the icons, the Prophet told ''Uthman to see that all the other paintings, except that of Abraham, were effaced.'[2]

The story in the Qur'an of the birth of Mary is similar to the story in the *Protevangelium*, but some names are different. Mary's mother is not named, and her father is not Joachim but Imran, like that of her namesake in the Old Testament, Amram the father of Miriam, Aaron and Moses (1 Chron. 6.3). Mary is also called the sister of Aaron (19.28). As in the *Protevangelium*, Mary's mother dedicates her unborn child to God, and is surprised to have a baby girl who is just as acceptable to God (3.37). The child is given into the care of Zakariyya – no priest is named in the *Protevangelium* – and she is mysteriously fed by God. In the *Protevangelium* she is fed by an angel. The lots were cast with arrows to find which man should take care of her (3.44), as in the *Protevangelium* where the rods were brought to the temple to determine who should care for Mary.

The story of the birth of John the Baptist is found in the Qur'an (3.39–41 and 19.2–15), but with some difference from Luke's account. His father is Zakariyya, as in Luke's account, but his mother is not named. John, Yahya, is a name not previously given to one of God's chosen (19.7), rather than not previously given to anyone in his family. John's conception was a miracle, because his parents were old (3.40; 19.9). His father was dumb for three days and nights (3.41; 19.10), rather than dumb until his son was born and named. John

---

[2] M. Lings, *Muhammad: His Life based on the Earliest Sources*, Cambridge: Islamic Text Society, 1991, p. 302. A note on this page says that later tradition held that all the pictures had been removed.

was born, and God commanded him to take hold of the Book, and he gave him wisdom and purity. He was a good son, kind to his parents, and so peace was upon him (19.12–15).

The story of the annunciation to Mary is found in 3.42–51 and 19.16–22. The angels spoke to Mary (3.42) [in 19.17 it is one angel in the form of a man] and told her she would have a Word from God, who would be Christ Jesus (3.45), a holy son (19.19). In both accounts Mary asked how this would be possible, and was told the child would be a direct creation from God, decreed by him (3.47; 19.21).

Mary gave birth to Jesus in a desert place under a palm tree which shed its dates for her to eat. A stream appeared from under the tree so that Mary could refresh herself (19.22–26). The palm tree setting for the nativity is reminiscent of the palm tree resting-place for Mary that was originally on the way to Egypt but then transferred in popular piety to the resting-place near Bethlehem. The palm tree mosaic found in the octagonal church there is 'remarkably similar to one of the mosaic trees on the wall of the dome of the rock',[3] which is also an octagonal building. There has been speculation about their relationship.[4]

Then Mary took the child back to her family, and the child spoke: 'I am indeed a servant of Allah, he hath given me revelation and made me a prophet, and hath made me blessed wheresover I be and hath enjoined on me prayer and charity as long as I live' (19.30–31). The infant Jesus also spoke from his cradle in the *Arabic Infancy Gospel*: 'I am Jesus the Son of God, the Word whom thou has brought forth, as the angel Gabriel announced to thee; and my Father has sent me for the salvation of the world.'[5] Mary is greatly honoured in the Qur'an, but the high status accorded to Mary in the early centuries of the Church is shown by the Qur'an's equally strong condemnation of worshipping her. 'And behold! Allah will say: "O Jesus the son of Mary! Didst thou say unto men 'Worship me and my mother as gods in derogation of Allah'?" He will say: "Glory to thee! Never could I say what I had no right to say." ' (5.116).

---

[3] O. Grabar, *The Dome of the Rock*, Cambridge, MA: Harvard University Press, 2006, p. 105.

[4] R. Avner, 'The Recovery of the Kathisma Church and its Influence on Octagonal Buildings', in *One Land, Many Cultures*, ed. G. Bottini and others, Jerusalem: Franciscan Printing Press, 2003, pp. 173–86.

[5] *Arabic Infancy Gospel*, 1.

The Christmas story in the Qur'an is told in a brief and enigmatic way, with few details. Joseph is not mentioned, nor Elizabeth, neither Bethlehem nor Jerusalem nor Nazareth. There is nothing to date the story, no mention of Herod and the census. There is nothing to connect the birth of Jesus to the Davidic house and to the fulfilment of Old Testament prophecy. There are no shepherds and no magi. The story had become timeless and without context. What is important is the meaning of the birth of Jesus, and the impossibility that God should have a son.

The Qur'an emphasizes the miraculous nature of Jesus' birth from the Virgin Mary: it was a direct creation from God. The emphasis is that his birth was because God commanded it: 'He says "Be" and it is' (3.47); 'It is a matter so decreed' (19.21), 'It is not fitting (to the majesty of Allah) that he should beget a son. Glory be to him! When he determines a matter, He only says to it "Be" and it is' (19.35). This is language reminiscent of the meaning of the Name in Jewish sources. The Palestinian Targums to Exodus 3.14 expand and so explain the Name revealed to Moses at the burning bush: 'He who said to the world from the beginning, "Be there", and it was there, and is to say to it "Be there" and it will be there'. For the Qur'an, Jesus was a miraculous creation, but no more than a creation. Early Christian writers used the language of new creation when they compared Adam and Jesus: the one formed from the Virgin earth, the other from the Virgin Mary, but this was always to describe the incarnation of the eternally begotten Son.

For Christians, the only way to express Jesus' uniqueness was to use the language of family relationships, and so 'begotten not made', describing the birth in eternity, became part of the Nicene creed. 'Begotten' is most commonly expressed as being Son of God, and here the Qur'an is emphatic that this cannot be. Jesus is Son of Mary – that title is often used of him to recognize the Virgin birth, but the teaching of the Qur'an, *even though it tells the story of the Virgin birth of Jesus, is very different from the Christian understanding of the same story. A miraculous creation is not the same as the incarnation of the eternally begotten Son of God.* The Qur'an says Jesus was a servant of God, a messenger from God and a Sign – Christians would agree with all of these – but he was never Son of God. 'For Allah is One God: Glory be to Him: (Far exalted is He) above having a son (4.171). 'It is not fitting to Allah that he should beget a son' (19.35).

'Begetting' is the difficult word. The earliest biblical reference to a divine Son made it clear that it was not to be confused with the human process; when Nathan gave the LORD's promise to David about his heir, he said: 'I will be his father, he shall be my son' (2 Sam. 7.14). Solomon was the physical son of David, but as king he would also be the divine Son. It was never the human process of begetting a son. Son of God was a temple term, indicating the one who had been anointed and 'born' in the holy of holies. As with all temple tradition and ritual, the Christians understood this as foreshadowing what was realized in Jesus. An explanatory note to 'It is not befitting to the Glory of Allah that he should beget a son' (19.35) says: 'Begetting a son is a physical act depending on the needs of men's animal nature . . . It is derogatory (to Allah) to attribute such an act to Him.'[6] Christians would agree with that too, and have been emphasizing the theological and mystical meaning of begetting from the very beginning.

Misunderstanding of the manner of the incarnation, and emphasizing that Son of God referred to the eternal generation of the Son, was apparent in the early years of the Church. The *Gospel of Philip* cannot be dated, but was probably early because it was still reasoning within a Semitic framework where 'spirit' is a feminine noun: 'Some said Mary conceived by the Holy Spirit. They are in error. They do not know what they are saying. When did a woman ever conceive by a woman?'[7] The process of incarnation did not involve conception in the physical sense of that word. In the mid-second century, Justin was aware of mistaken ideas circulating in the Roman world, understandable in a culture that had stories of gods and their human mistresses. 'But lest some . . . should charge us with the very things we have been laying to the charge of the poets who say that Jupiter went in to women through lust, let us try to explain the words: "the Virgin shall conceive and bear a son". It means that a virgin should conceive without intercourse.'[8] Despite this danger of misunderstanding, the Apostles' Creed, in use in Rome shortly after the time of Justin, described the process of incarnation as '*conceived* by the Holy Spirit'.[9]

Early in the fourth century, Lactantius, just before the Nicene Creed was formulated, set out clearly where the problems of misunderstanding lay:

---

[6] Note on p. 855 of Abdullah Yusuf Ali's translation and commentary on The Holy Quran.

[7] *Gospel of Philip*, CG II.3.55.

[8] Justin, *Apology* 1.33.

[9] *qui conceptus est de Spiritu Sancto*.

For though he was the Son of God from the beginning, he was born again a second time according to the flesh: and this twofold birth of his has introduced great terror into the minds of men, and overspread with darkness even those who shared the mysteries of true religion . . . He who hears the Son of God mentioned ought not to conceive in his mind so great impiety as to think that God begot him by marriage and union with a woman, which none does but an animal possessed of a body and subject to death. But with whom could God unite himself, since He is alone? Or since His power was so great that He accomplished whatever he wished assuredly he did not require co-operation of another for procreation.[10]

The Nicene Creed described the incarnation as from the Holy Spirit and the Virgin Mary, although exactly how these words are to be rendered in English is an ongoing debate. The Book of Common Prayer has: 'was incarnate by the Holy Ghost of the Virgin Mary and was made man'. The new *Common Worship* has 'was incarnate from the Holy Spirit and the Virgin Mary', an exact rendering of the Greek,[11] and in other parts of the Church the discussion continues.

The great debates in the Church about the process of the incarnation, and exactly what words could be used to express the inexpressible, occupied many minds for many years, and produced much division and bitterness. The Qur'an comments: 'But the sects differ among themselves' (19.37), and sums up the Virgin birth by saying: 'This is part of the tidings of the things unseen, which we reveal by inspiration' (3.44). The story of the birth has a mystic not a literal meaning,[12] *but this is also true of the title 'Son of God'*, and one wonders what popular misconceptions inspired the strong Qur'anic condemnation of the title, and the choice of those particular verses about Allah having no son for the Dome of the Rock, believed by many to be the very site of the temple where the mystical title 'Son of God' originated.

---

[10] Lactantius, *Divine Institutes* 4.8, in *Ante-Nicene Fathers*, vol. 7.
[11] *sarkothenta ek Pneumatos Hagiou kai Marias tes Parthenou.*
[12] Note on p. 153 of Abdullah Yusuf Ali's translation and commentary on The Holy Quran.

Extracts from the Abdullah Yusuf Ali Translation of The Holy Quran

Surah 3. Al 'Imran

35. Behold, Imran's wife
    Said: 'O my Lord! I do
    Dedicate to Thee
    What is in my womb
    For thy special service.
    So accept this of me:
    For Thou hearest
    And knowest all things.'

36. When she was delivered
    She said: 'O my Lord!
    Behold! I am delivered
    Of a female child!'
    And Allah knew best
    What she brought forth –
    'And nowise is the male
    Like the female.
    I have named her Mary
    And I commend her
    And her offspring
    To Thy protection
    From Satan the rejected.'

37. Right graciously
    Did her Lord accept her.
    He made her grow
    In purity and beauty.
    To the care of Zakariyya
    Was she assigned
    Every time that he entered
    (Her) chamber to see her
    he found her supplied
    With sustenance. He said:
    'O Mary! Whence (comes) this
    To you?' She said:
    'From Allah: for Allah
    Provides sustenance
    To whom he pleases
    Without measure.'

38. There did Zakariyya
    Pray to his Lord, saying:
    'O my Lord! Grant unto me

From Thee progeny
That is pure. For Thou
Art he that heareth prayer!'

39. While he was standing
In prayer in the chamber,
The angels called unto him:
'Allah doth give thee
Glad tidings of Yahya,
Witnessing the truth
Of a word from Allah, and (be
Besides) noble, chaste,
And a Prophet –
Of the (goodly) company
of the righteous.'

40. He said, 'O my Lord!
How shall I have a son
Seeing I am very old
And my wife is barren?'
'Thus' was the answer
'Doth Allah accomplish
What he willeth.'

41. He said: 'O my Lord!
Give me a sign!'
'Thy sign' was the answer,
'Shall be that thou
Shalt speak to no man
For three days
But with signals
Then celebrate
The praises of thy Lord
Again and again
And glorify Him
In the evening
And in the morning.'

42. Behold! The angels said:
'O Mary! Allah hath chosen thee
And purified thee – chosen thee
Above women of all nations.

43. 'O Mary! Worship
Thy Lord devoutly:
Prostrate thyself,
And bow down (in prayer)
With those who bow down.'

44. This is part of the tidings

Of the things unseen,
Which we reveal to thee
(O Messenger!) by inspiration:
Thou wast not with them
When they cast lots
With arrows, as to which
Of them should be charged
With the care of Mary:
Nor was thou with them
When they disputed (the point).

45. Behold! The angels said:
'O Mary! Allah giveth thee
Glad tidings of a Word
From Him: his name
Will be Christ Jesus,
The son of Mary, held in honour
In this world and the Hereafter
And of (the company of) those
Nearest to Allah;

46. 'He shall speak to the people
In childhood and in maturity.
And he shall be (of the company)
Of the righteous.'

47. She said: 'O my Lord
How shall I have a son
When no man has touched me?'
He said: 'Even so:
Allah createth
What he willeth:
When he has decreed
A Plan, He but saith
To it, "Be," and it is!

48. 'And Allah will teach him
The Book and Wisdom
The Law and the Gospel,

49. 'And (appoint him)
A messenger to the Children
Of Israel, (with this message):
"I have come to you,
With a Sign from your Lord,
In that I make for you
Out of clay, as it were,
The figure of a bird
And breathe into it,

And it becomes a bird
By Allah's leave:
And I heal those
Born blind, and the lepers
And I quicken the dead,
By Allah's leave;
And I declare to you
What ye eat, and what ye store
In your houses. Surely
Therein is a Sign for you
If ye did believe;

50. ' "(I have come to you)
To attest the Law
Which was before me.
And to make lawful
To you part of what was
(before) forbidden to you;
I have come to you
With a Sign from your Lord.
So fear Allah,
And obey me.

51. ' "It is Allah
Who is my Lord
and your Lord
Then worship Him.
This is a Way
That is straight." '

Surah 19. Maryam

16. Relate in the Book
(The story of) Mary
When she withdrew
From her family
To a place in the East.

17. She placed a screen
(to screen herself) from them;
Then We sent to her
Our angel, and he appeared
Before her as a man
In all respects.

18. She said: 'I seek refuge
From thee to (Allah)
Most Gracious. Come not near
If thou dost fear Allah.'

19. He said: 'Nay, I am only
    A messenger from thy Lord
    (To announce) to thee
    The gift of a holy son.'

20. She said: 'How shall I
    Have a son seeing that
    No man has touched me
    And I am not unchaste?'

21. He said. 'So (it will be):
    Thy Lord saith, "That is
    easy for Me: and (We
    Wish) to appoint him
    As a Sign unto men
    And a Mercy from Us"
    It is a matter (so) decreed.'

22. So she conceived him,
    And she retired with him
    To a remote place.

23. And the pains of childbirth
    Drove her to the trunk
    Of a palm tree:
    She cried (in her anguish)
    'Ah, would that I had
    died before this! Would that
    I had been a thing
    Forgotten and out of sight!'

24. But (a voice) cried to her
    From beneath (the palm tree):
    'Grieve not! for thy Lord
    Hath provided a rivulet
    Beneath thee:

25. 'And shake towards thyself
    The trunk of the palm tree:
    It will let fall
    Fresh ripe dates upon thee.

26. 'So eat and drink
    And cool (thine) eye.
    And if thou dost see
    Any human, say, "I have
    Vowed a fast to (Allah)
    Most Gracious, and this day
    Will I enter into no talk
    With any human being." '

27. At length she brought

The (babe) to her people,
Carrying him (in her arms).
They said: 'O Mary
Truly an amazing thing
Hast thou brought!

28. 'O sister of Aaron!
Thy father was not
A man of evil, nor thy
Mother a woman unchaste!'

29. But she pointed to the babe.
They said: 'How can we
Talk to one who is
A child in the cradle?'

30. He said: 'I am indeed
A servant of Allah.
He hath given me
Revelation and made me
a prophet;

31. 'And he hath made me
Blessed wheresoever I be,
And hath enjoined on me
Prayer and Charity as long
as I live;

32. '(He) hath made me kind
to my mother, and not
Overbearing or miserable;

33. 'So peace is on me
The day I was born
The day that I die
And the day that I shall be raised up
To life (again).'

34. Such (was) Jesus the son
Of Mary: (It is) a statement of truth, about which
They (vainly) dispute.

35. It is not fitting
To (the majesty of) Allah
That he should beget
A son. Glory be to Him!
When he determines
a matter, He only says
To it 'Be' and it is.

36. Verily, Allah is my Lord
And your Lord. Him
Therefore serve ye: This is

A Way that is straight.

37. But the sects differ
Among themselves: and woe
To the Unbelievers because
Of the (coming) Judgement
Of a momentous Day!

Surah 66. At Taḥrim

12. And Mary the daughter
Of Imran, who guarded
Her chastity; and We
Breathed into (her body)
Of our Spirit, and she
Testified to the truth
Of the words of her Lord
And of His Revelations.
And was one of the
Devout (servants).

Primary sources

Abbreviations and English translations that are not given in the footnotes.

The Old Testament Pseudepigrapha, vols 1 and 2, ed. J. H. Charlesworth, London: Darton, Longman & Todd, 1983, 1985, contain:
OTP1:
Assumption of Moses [under its other title *The Testament of Moses*]; *2 Baruch*; *1 Enoch*; *2 Enoch*; *Testaments of the Twelve Patriarchs*; *Testament of Adam*; *Sibylline Oracles*.
OTP2:
Life of Adam and Eve, and its Greek version, the *Apocalypse of Moses*; *Ascension of Isaiah*; *Book of Jubilees*.

The Complete Dead Sea Scrolls in English, by G. Vermes, London: Penguin, 1997, has all the non-biblical Qumran texts used in this book.
The Dead Sea Scrolls Bible, by M. Abegg, P. Flint and E. Ulrich, Edinburgh: T&T Clark, has most of the Qumran biblical texts cited.
Photos of the Isaiah Scroll are in *The Dead Sea Scrolls of St Mark's Monastery*, by M. Burrows, J. C. Trever and W. H. Brownlee, New Haven, Conn.: American Schools of Oriental Research, 1950.

The Loeb Classical Library, Cambridge, Mass.: Harvard University Press.
The Works of Philo of Alexandria, 12 vols, tr. F. H. Colson, G. H. Whittaker and R. Marcus, 1929–63.
The Works of Josephus, 13 vols, tr. H. St J. Thackeray and R. Marcus, 1927 ongoing.
Basil of Caesarea, 4 vols, tr. R. J. Defarri, (1926) 1950.
Eusebius, *Church History*, 2 vols, tr. K. Lake and J. E. L. Oulton, 1926, 1932.

Mishnah, tr. H. Danby, Oxford: Oxford University Press, (1933) 1989.
Tosefta, ed. J. Neusner, New York: Ktav, 1979 ongoing.
Jerusalem Talmud, in *The Talmud of the Land of Israel*, tr. J. Neusner, Chicago and London: University of Chicago Press, 1989 ongoing.
Babylonian Talmud, tr. I. Epstein, London: Soncino, (1935–52) 1961.
Targums are in the Aramaic Bible series, Edinburgh: T&T Clark, 1987 ongoing.
Genesis Rabbah, tr. H. Freedman, 2 vols; *Exodus Rabbah* tr. S. M. Lehrman; *Leviticus Rabbah*, tr. J. Israelstam and J. J. Slotki; *Numbers Rabbah*, tr. J. J. Slotki; all published London: Soncino Press, (1939) 1961.
Zohar, tr. H. Sperling and M. Simon, 5 vols, London: Soncino Press, 1984.

The Ante-Nicene Fathers [ANF], Grand Rapids, Mich.: Eerdmans, various dates, are the American version of *The Ante-Nicene Christian Library*, but volume contents do not correspond.

Primary sources

ANF 1 Justin, *Apology* and *Trypho*, Ignatius' *Letters*, and Irenaeus, *Against Heresies*.
ANF 2 Clement of Alexandria, *Miscellanies* and *Instructor*.
ANF 3 Tertullian, *Against Marcion* and *Apology*.
ANF 7 *The Apostolic Constitutions*.
ANF 8 *Arabic Infancy Gospel* [available online], *Clementine Homilies*, and *Clementine Recognitions*.

Nicene and Post-Nicene Fathers, repr., Grand Rapids, Mich.: Eerdmans, 1969 ongoing.
I.12 John Chrysostom, *Homilies on Matthew*.
II.2 Socrates, *Church History* and Sozomen, *Church History*.
II.9 John of Damascus, *On the Orthodox Faith*.

The Fathers of the Church [FC], Washington: Catholic University of America Press.
FC 2 Cyril of Jerusalem, *Catecheses*, tr. L. P. McCauley, 1968.
FC 49 Lactantius, *The Divine Institutes*, tr. M. F. McDonald, 1964.
FC 80 Origen, *Commentary on John*, books 1–10, tr. R. E. Heine, 1989.
FC 93 Leo the Great, *Sermons*, tr. J. P. Freeland and A. J. Conway, 1996.
FC 94 Origen, *Homilies on Luke*, tr. J. T. Lienhard, 1994.
FC 97 Origen, *Homilies on Jeremiah*, tr. J. C. Smith, 1998.

The Coptic Gnostic Library texts [CG] used in this book are in *The Nag Hammadi Library in English*, ed. J. M. Robinson, Leiden: Brill, 1977.

The Book of the Cave of Treasures, tr. E. A. Wallis Budge, London: Religious Tract Society, 1927 [available online].
Augustine, *Sermons for Christmas and Epiphany*, tr. T. C. Lawler, Westminster, Md.: Newman Press, 1952.
Epiphanius, *Heresies*, tr. as *Panarion Book 1*, by F. Williams, Leiden: Brill, 1987.
Eusebius, *Life of Constantine*, tr. A. Cameron and S. G. Hall, Oxford: Oxford University Press, 1999.
Irenaeus, *Proof of the Apostolic Preaching*, tr. J. A. Robinson, London: SPCK, 1920.
Origen, *Against Celsus*, tr. H. Chadwick, Cambridge: Cambridge University Press, 1953.

Index of primary sources

Index of primary sources

Index of persons, places and subjects

Aaronic blessing 70–2, 92, 135
  explanation forbidden 135
Abraham 98, 121, 162
Adam 35–7, 64, 98, 103
  driven from Eden 118
  and gifts of magi 118
  as high priest 39
  second 38
adulteress 106, 134
Akathistos Hymn 133
'almah 100–2, 105, 133
Amram 163
angel with the seal 111
angels 2, 90
  humans as 12–13, 40
  as shepherds 24, 79
  singing 81, 89
  as stars 111
  as warriors 27
Anna, mother of Mary 133
Anna the prophetess 83–6
annunciation 48, 54, 162, 164
  two 130, 134
anointing 9, 25, 35, 127, 139–40
  myrrh oil 120, 136–8
  oil restored 27
Aquila 101
Arabia 109, 114, 121–2, 137,
  162–3
  Jews in 121
Arabic Infancy Gospel 117, 124, 146,
  164
Arius 11
Armenian Lectionary 144
ascent to heaven 5, 45
Asherah 85, 104, 139–40
ass 64, 76, 132
astronomy 111
  Jews and 111
Atonement, Day of 32–4, 54, 62, 71,
  87

baptism
  of Christians 50
  of Jesus 41, 50–1
Bar Kochbah 112
Bathsheba 99
Beatitudes 55
'begotten' 9, 50, 141, 165
Benedictus 28, 70–1
Bethlehem 74, 78, 164
  massacre of children 109, 123
Bezae, Codex 50–1, 59, 106
bir al-Qadismu 144
births
  eternal 11, 166
  as resurrection 6
  ritual 31, 43, 49–50, 67, 77, 132,
    136, 138, 145
  two xii, 11, 32, 60
bitter water 134–5
Bride 43, 103

calendar 24, 54, 109
  and temple 111
cave 80, 130, 134, 144–5
  as holy of holies 145, 146
Cave of Treasures, Book of the 38–9,
  119
census 74, 134, 165
  date of 74–5
  as prophecy 75
Chalcedon, Council of 120
cherubic hymn 90
cherubim 64, 77
Church of the Resurrection xii
cloud, bright 29, 33, 52, 134, 145
Coptic tradition 108, 124–5
covenant
  with Abraham 70, 72
  bonds of 92
  everlasting 38
  renewed 25, 81, 123